Sliding Billy Hamilton

Sliding Billy Hamilton

The Life and Times of Baseball's First Great Leadoff Hitter

Roy Kerr

McFarland & Company, Inc., Publishers
Jefferson, North Carolina, and London

LIBRARY OF CONGRESS CATALOGUING-IN-PUBLICATION DATA

Kerr, Roy, 1947–
   Sliding Billy Hamilton : the life and times of baseball's first great leadoff hitter / Roy Kerr.
      p.   cm.
   Includes bibliographical references and index.

   ISBN 978-0-7864-4639-1
   softcover : 50# alkaline paper ∞

   1. Hamilton, Sliding Billy, 1866–1940. 2. Baseball players — United States — Biography. I. Title.
GV865.H243A3   2010
796.357092 — dc22   2009042934
[B]

British Library cataloguing data are available

©2010 Roy Kerr. All rights reserved

No part of this book may be reproduced or transmitted in any form or by any means, electronic or mechanical, including photocopying or recording, or by any information storage and retrieval system, without permission in writing from the publisher.

On the cover: Kansas City Cowboy Billy Hamilton, 1889 (courtesy Howard "Skip" Reynolds); inset ©2010 Wood River Gallery

Manufactured in the United States of America

McFarland & Company, Inc., Publishers
  Box 611, Jefferson, North Carolina 28640
    www.mcfarlandpub.com

For my home team:
Annie and Ed

Acknowledgments

Many people helped make this book possible. Bill Jenkinson, baseball historian, mentor, and cheerleader, provided support and encouragement throughout the project. Ed Borsoi, Leon Lyday, Skip Reynolds, Terry Ingano, Pete Meyer, and Gordie Howell all provided feedback on text and context. Nora Galbraith at the Florida Southern College Library helped me track down microfilm, and director Randall MacDonald generously allowed me to use the inter-library loan service. Jim Hastings of the Clinton, Massachusetts, School District cleared the way for my review of school records. Maureen O'Rourke of the New Jersey Historical Society and Catherine Medich of the New Jersey State Archives went out of their way to assist me in the search for Billy Hamilton's origins.

Skip and Kathy Reynolds opened their home to me and shared their Hamilton photos, documents and mementos. Hamilton and Gail Starr shared rare family photos. Joan Richards of the Lancaster, Massachusetts, Historical Commission and Massachusetts sportswriter Paul Della Valle got me started on my research journey. Pastor Cindy Kohlmann of the Clinton Presbyterian Church allowed me to review church membership files from the Hamilton era. Terry Ingano of the Clinton Historical Society provided photos, records and encouragement. Marc Iacobucci at the Clinton City Hall gave up a lunch hour to track down real estate records for a man who had walked in off the street with no appointment. The Clinton Library staff led me to a marvelous find in their building. The National Baseball Hall of Fame Library staff at Cooperstown patiently complied with all my requests.

I am particularly grateful to Phyllis Reynolds, my personal link to Billy and Rebecca Hamilton, for her willingness to share her remembrances of those days so many years ago.

Finally, I express my sincere gratitude to David Nemec, dean of nineteenth century baseball studies, and Charlie Bevis, historian of the New England League. Their pioneering efforts made this book possible.

Table of Contents

Acknowledgments	vi
Preface	1
Introduction: Billy Who?	3
1. Billy Baseball	15
2. Early Innings	38
3. Cowboys and Ponies	60
4. Boston Billy	103
5. Home to Clinton	142
6. Late Innings	168
7. In the Country of Baseball	184
Appendix A: The Hamilton Legacy	189
Appendix B: Hamilton's All-Time Records	191
Notes	193
Bibliography	201
Index	205

Preface

I became aware of Billy Hamilton's existence while conducting research for an unrelated project a few years ago. It was a discovery that left me with more questions than answers.

Despite Hamilton's status as a member of the Hall of Fame and the fact that many records he set more than a century ago still stand, few specifics about his life emerged from the scattered, frequently contradictory references to him that I found in books, in articles and online. There appeared to be no consensus in these documents, even with regard to such basic details as whether he threw left-handed or right-handed, which minor league teams he played for prior to becoming a major leaguer, or where and how he spent his adolescence and his retirement.

The journey I undertook to address these and other issues resulted in much more than a definitive resolution of specific inconsistencies. A complete review of box scores, game accounts, and sports journal commentary of the era, for example, added context and substance to Hamilton's published playing record, and in the process unearthed several previously unreported records that he either established or equaled. Simple statistical accounts of his hitting, stealing, and base running abilities acquired greater significance when viewed within the historical and cultural context of his day-in-day-out playing performance.

On the personal side, new research discoveries began to add a depth and dimension to the portrait provided by the meager information previously available. Myth was replaced with fact, with truth often proving to be more interesting and laudatory than legend. Slowly, the name in the record book became a man of flesh and blood. And what a man he was — teenage cotton-mill worker, baseball player, manager, scout, club owner, loving father and husband, security officer, real estate investor, industrial administrator. One of many unexpected discoveries regarding Hamilton's previously undocumented personal life was that his spirit of sporting competition transcended the baseball field. Before, during, and after his major league career, he regularly and actively participated in numerous other professional and amateur sports, many of which subsequently disappeared down the dusty corridors of history.

As the pieces in the Billy Hamilton puzzle fell into place, it became clear that his personal odyssey resembled that of many other working-class men during the late–Victorian age, a period of great change and transition, both in major league baseball and U.S. history. In the end, Hamilton's remarkable personal story became emblematic of an era.

On the baseball diamond or on the field of life, the historical Billy Hamilton proved to be a man for all seasons.

Introduction: Billy Who?

> "Concerning the grand playing of that little base ball fiend, Hamilton, a book might be written."
> —*Philadelphia Inquirer,* June 6, 1890

Until a few years ago, I had never heard of Billy Hamilton. At the time, I was writing *The Loving of the Game,* a memoir commemorating a baseball tour that my then-twelve-year-old son and I had taken, during which we had crossed the country in whirlwind fashion, attending five games in different cities over a ten-day period. During the writing phase of the project, I conceived of the idea of including in each chapter a brief biography of an old-time player who had performed for the teams whose ballparks we were visiting. I had a particular interest in highlighting players who were adept at the "inside" game, men who could bunt, steal, sacrifice, and execute the hit-and-run. These were usually not great, powerful sluggers, but less imposing physical specimens who, through hustle, guile, or sheer will, managed to raise their natural playing abilities to a major league level.

I felt that I had done a respectable job in selecting such players until I came to the Philadelphia Phillies, an ironic turn of events given that in my youth they were my hometown team. My personal memories of them dated from the mid-1950s, and the only players I could recall prior to that era were Chuck Klein and Ed Delahanty, imposing power hitters and members of the Hall of Fame, and obviously cut from a different bolt of cloth than my other selections. The subsequent research that led me to "Sliding" Billy Hamilton, however, left me with the strong conviction that in comparison to other stars of his era, the 1890s, his career, records and personal biography largely had been overlooked. Thereafter, in conversations with friends and fellow baseball enthusiasts, I began, only half-jokingly, to refer to Hamilton as "the greatest ballplayer you've never heard of."

Since the conclusion of Billy Hamilton's major league career in 1901, his name and accomplishments have emerged briefly from baseball oblivion on three occasions: once in the months leading up to his 1961 nomination by the twelve members of the Old-Timers Committee to the Hall of Fame, and twice when other players were approaching the all-time stolen base record — Lou Brock in 1979 and Rickey Henderson in 1990. As Henderson was closing in on the record, a *San Francisco Chronicle* reporter, referring to Hamilton as a "nineteenth-century ghost," cited comments by then–Hall of Fame librarian Tom Heitz: "He's kind of a shadowy figure ... we know there was a lot of Ty Cobb about him. He was the kind of guy that the home fans always loved, but wasn't appreciated on the road."[1] The announcement of his election to the Baseball Hall of Fame provided *The Sporting News*[2] with the opportunity to assign Hamilton two new nicknames — the "Fast Flyhawk" and the "Speedster from Grandpop's Day"— and to confirm that he was "known affectionately to his fans of the 1890s as "Sliding Billy." Overall, however, the "shadowy" image of a player relegated to baseball history's background instead of its foreground persisted in their reports.

More recently, Hamilton's status as a nineteenth century baseball "ghost" was confirmed by contemporary baseball historian Bill James: "Hamilton was completely invisible in the literature of the sport up to 1960. He left no legend behind him, no stories, no anecdotes.... Even now in books about nineteenth century baseball, he is often not mentioned at all, and is never presented as a fully formed character."[3] While agreeing with James's assessment of Hamilton's essential invisibility in baseball history, I prefer to believe his assertion that Hamilton left behind no legend or stories or anecdotes was made not as a statement of fact, but rather as a challenge to someone like me to take up the cause and reintroduce a multi-dimensional Billy Hamilton to the annals of baseball and to the many fans who had never heard of him. This volume is the result of my efforts.

Glancing at just a few of Sliding Billy's accomplishments, it seems incomprehensible that a player of such talent could be forgotten: first all-time in runs scored in a season (196 in 129 games), and first in the history of the sport in career runs scored per game; third all-time in stolen bases, and third all-time in on-base percentage, behind Ted Williams and Babe Ruth; tied with Williams for sixth place all-time in batting average, and one of only two players in baseball history to steal seven bases in a game.

Understandably, there has been some quibbling among baseball historians regarding Hamilton's stolen base record given the fact, as we shall see, that during part of his career steals were sometimes recorded differently. Nevertheless, this aspect of his accomplishments, given his total performance statistics, could not alone account for his relative invisibility today. Neither could the simple passage of time be the deciding factor, since many contemporaries with similar or equal records, such as Cap Anson and Ed Delahanty, are still remembered and indeed revered by serious students of the game.

I suggest that Hamilton's "invisibility" in baseball lore stems not from any aspect of his playing record. Rather, it derives at least partially from the fact that the "stories, anecdotes, and legends" that he did *indeed* leave behind simply would not have been considered newsworthy by most sportswriters of his era, who tended to focus more on the adventures of the game's showmen and scalawags in their columns. In this sense, much like his Boston manager, Frank Selee, who waited nearly a hundred years to be elected to the Hall of Fame, Hamilton "simply lacked the flash for which baseball in the Gay Nineties was remembered."[4]

While all players of the era certainly "were not uncouth ruffians fit only for playing ball,"[5] written reports of the day were replete with accounts of "saloon brawls, hotel and sleeping car disturbances, occasional assaults on women and even thefts,"[6] attributed to ballplayers when off the playing field. The showman-scalawag *par excellence* and media superstar of the era was a second-generation Irish American whose remarkable baseball skills were compromised, and ultimately destroyed, by rampant alcoholism. Tall, dark and handsome, with sparkling eyes and a fashionable handlebar moustache, Michael Joseph "King" Kelly of the Chicago White Stockings was the consummate utility man, playing all nine positions in his career. He twice led the league in hitting, and possessed a base-stealing prowess so formidable that it became the subject of a popular song, "Slide, Kelly Slide!" A born self-promoter, he was a vaudeville entertainer in the off-season, and the first ballplayer to publish an autobiography. Nevertheless, Mike smoked, gambled away his paychecks, and drank heavily, both while in uniform and out. He was a "sporting idol whose lifestyle centered on the theater, race tracks, and late-hour clubs of the major league cities. As a result, Kelly could not hold onto, or save his earnings."[7] When playing the outfield, "King Kel" regularly exchanged pleasant banter or insults with the "cranks" (as fans were known in the era), depending on the circumstances, and on occasion would burst into song. As a hitter, he took frequent advantage of the single umpire system then in effect by cutting corners on the base paths when the lone arbiter was following a play in the other direction. Once he scored from second base by skipping third base and running directly from second to home. A frequent tactic was cutting behind the pitcher's box (it wasn't yet referred to as the pitcher's mound) when running from first to third, disregarding second base entirely. Regarding Mike's creative stretching of the rules, it "was often said at the turn of the century that ninety per cent of the baseball rulebook had been written specifically to thwart trick plays dreamed up by King Kelly."[8]

Despite Kelly's league-leading hitting statistics in 1886, Cap Anson, the legendary player-manager of the White Stockings, was exasperated by the star's drunken on-field antics, and traded him to Boston for the then-astronomical figure of $10,000. By 1894, alcohol and a raucous lifestyle had taken its toll on the "King," robbing him of his skills, ruining his constitution, and ending his baseball career. In November of that year

> he booked an appearance in Boston and traveled up the coast by boat. On the way he took ill and a cold worsened into pneumonia. Upon arrival, he was rushed to a hospital, but as the stretcher bearers entered the doorway one of them stumbled and Kelly fell to the floor. Legend has it the once great ballplayer looked up with a smile and whispered in a hoarse voice: "This is me last slide."[9]

A few days later, three weeks shy of his thirty-seventh birthday, Kelly died, leaving his wife and infant child destitute.

Atrocious off-the-diamond behavior by ballplayers found a parallel in some players' on-field performance. The 1895 *Spalding's Official Base Ball Guide*, a major baseball publication of the era, both defined and decried a new style of play in the game:

Introduction 7

There was but one drawback to the creditable success of the entire championship campaigns of 1894, and that was the unwonted degree of "hoodlumism" which disgraced the season in the professional arena, and this, we regret to say, was painfully conspicuous among the players of the National League.... Much of the "hoodlumism," — a technical term applicable to the use of blackguard language; low cunning tricks unworthy of manly players; brutal assaults on umpire and players; that nuisance of our ballfields, "kicking" [vociferous, usually profane haranguing or physical abuse of umpires] and the dishonorable methods comprised in the term "dirty ball playing" — indulged in 1894 was largely due to the advocacy of the method of the so-called "aggressive policy," which countenanced rowdy ball playing as part and parcel of the work in winning games.[10]

The quintessential "rowdy" style of team play was favored by the "the bad boys of Baltimore," the Orioles, and in particular by their fiery infielder, John "Mugsy" McGraw. Pugnacious, arrogant and abrasive, McGraw, nicknamed "Little Napoleon," allegedly "ate gunpowder for breakfast and washed it down with warm blood."[11] A dozen years before the Ty Cobb era, he regularly sharpened his spikes "with murderous intent,"[12] and, on one occasion, in a single inning managed to spike two players.[13] McGraw commonly employed such "dirty ball" practices as "diving into the first baseman after he had caught the ball, throwing masks in front of runners at home plate, catching a base runner by his clothes, interfering with base runners, and blocking the view of opposing catchers."[14] He and his cohorts spared no one from such tactics, including the umpire, as affirmed by one from their ranks, John Heydler: "I've seen umpires bathe their feet by the hour after McGraw and others spiked them through their shoes."[15]

Billy Hamilton's on- and off-the-field comportment offers a contrast to that of players like Kelly and McGraw. His aggressive, daring running and hitting style exhibited none of the "hoodlum" tactics that tended to make headlines. Off the field, he was a religious family man who abstained from alcohol. Notoriously thrifty, he saved money and invested in real estate. This frugal nature elicited ridicule from one of his famous teammates. The ill-fated Ed Delahanty allegedly chided Hamilton frequently about his "closeness in money matters." Billy ignored the taunts, affirming, "I have everything I want.... I don't see why I should throw away my earnings to prove I am a good fellow." Delahanty, however, "always had a quick retort and laughs at Hamilton's responses."[16] Big Ed, an enormously talented hitter who ranks fourth all-time in batting average, "had a penchant for glitter and fame ... and enjoyed being a popular host at the best clubs and hotels.... Ed was always the congenial celebrity, entertaining in the hotel bar."[17] On the evening of July 2, 1903, after having been thrown off a train in New York State due to drunken, abusive behavior, he tumbled off a trestle bridge over the Niagara River and drowned. His body went over the falls and was found days later, horribly mutilated by the ordeal. He was thirty-six years old. Like King Kelly, he left behind an infant daughter and a penniless wife.

Billy Hamilton's life took a different direction. "Unlike many players of his era, Billy had invested his earnings wisely and owned a considerable amount of property. It enabled him and his wife Rebecca to live comfortably at their home ... until his death."[18] Whenever Hamilton played at the South End Grounds in Boston during his years with the Phillies and later with the Beaneaters, he would quickly change from his uniform to street clothes after the game and head for Back Bay Station, where he would board a train for his hometown, Clinton. After arriving and eating dinner with wife Rebecca — and in later years with his daughters — he would walk the few blocks from his home to the corner of Church and High streets. There, at an hour when many of his teammates were socializing in saloons back in Boston, Hamilton "would calmly relate to a dozen or so local fans (all of whom were hero worshippers) the highlights of that day's game in which he played."[19] Unlike many of his more famous contemporaries, "Billy was never fined or verbally scolded by his managers during his career. He did not smoke or drink, and was not a nightclubber. In fact, he usually went to bed at about 9 o'clock."[20]

Could the life of a "straight arrow" player, an abstemious family man, be of any interest to today's baseball fan? Perhaps so. Perhaps such a life, deemed "old-fashioned" in Hamilton's day as it would be in ours, has acquired a certain resonance in the post-steroid era of the game, when fans, disheartened by deceit and scandal, may be looking for different heroes, different models of conduct. Sliding Billy was no "goody two shoes." He played an aggressive, daring style of baseball in a rough, hardscrabble era of the game. His critics accused him of being a "record player," more interested in his own statistics than his team's success. However, in most of his life choices, he opted for a road less-traveled — a road, consequently, less noted by the press.

Hamilton's on-field accomplishments can best be understood

within the context of the changes in the game that took place during his major league career. Pitching and hitting rules, equipment, uniforms, playing fields — all underwent dizzying transformations in this era. Many regulation changes brought an abrupt end to the careers of some players who did not possess Hamilton's ability to adapt. Chapter 1, "Billy Baseball," places Hamilton within the baseball context of his era, and details how and why the game changed from the beginning to the end of his career, citing examples, when possible, from his career. Such changes "ended half a century of experimentation and delineated the basic structure of the game on the field as it has existed down to the present day."[21] When his career ended, modern baseball began. He therefore can be viewed as one of the key "bridge" players between the early professional game's relative unknowns, such as George Wright, Al Spalding, and Deacon White, and players such as Christy Mathewson, Nap Lajoie, and Honus Wagner of the succeeding generation, men whose names and exploits modern fans still recall.

Although he was born in Newark, New Jersey, and spent the first year of his life there, Billy Hamilton's pre- and post-major league years are intimately connected to central Massachusetts and, in particular, to the town of Clinton, a few miles northeast of Worcester. In the last decades of the nineteenth century, eighty percent of U.S. cotton textile output came from the New England region. Thanks to the entrepreneurial efforts of Horatio and Erastus Bigelow and other inventor-investors who set up mills in Clinton, the town, like others in New England, experienced an economic boom that transformed it into a busy manufacturing site. Billy Hamilton's family was one of many that settled there during this period. In Clinton and its environs, he met, courted, and married his wife, Rebecca Carr, raised four daughters, participated through middle age in numerous non-baseball regional sports, developed business interests, and informally coached and encouraged many aspiring young ballplayers.

Chapter 2, "Early Innings," traces his early life through the signing of his first major league contract, placing special emphasis on his Clinton years. In much the same way that Hamilton the ballplayer is a product of his era in the game, Hamilton the man is a product of his adopted hometown, Clinton, which boasts a rich history in baseball and other regional sports. Hamilton is also a product of a broader cultural framework, since the first half of his life corresponds almost exactly to the late–Victorian age in U.S. history. Until recently, this period has been much maligned by historians, who have viewed it primarily as an epoch of greed, prudery and prejudice. Revisionist historian Gertrude Himmelfarb, however, asserts that considered from the perspective of *its own time period*, "Victorian society was the least exploitative, the least repressive, the least tyrannical society in the world."[22] Furthermore, the age's virtues, such as family values, self-discipline, responsibility, temperance and respectability, "are modest, mundane virtues dependent upon no special breeding or status, or wisdom, or grace, or money. They are, we might say, democratic virtues."[23] They are distinctly Hamiltonian virtues also, finding an echo in many aspects of his life.

With regard to Hamilton's personal biography, I have relied on information that has been generously provided by his surviving grandchildren and great grandchildren, on data from U.S., New Jersey and Massachusetts vital records, local historical societies, schools and churches. Part of the labor in restoring a multi-dimensional aspect to his persona has involved the correction of numerous errors that have crept into the literature about his life and career, such as the date and year of his birth, his date of death, whether he threw right-handed or left-handed, where he spent his childhood years, and where and how he spent his final years.

In 1871, five years after Billy Hamilton's birth, the first professional baseball league was formed. During the ensuing thirty years, the number of leagues would increase to three, decrease to two, again increase to three, and finally, in 1901, his last major league season, settle definitively on two leagues, the National and the American, thus establishing the essential organizational structure that still exists in the game today. For his entire big league career, as he was busy waging war on opposing pitchers and defenses, the owners, players and other assorted interest groups were waging war against each other for the control of professional baseball. Chapter 3, "Cowboys and Ponies" (contemporary nicknames for the Kansas City and Philadelphia teams, respectively), reviews that struggle within the context of Hamilton's own career, from his year-and-a-half stint with the Cowboys of the American Association, derisively termed by some the "Beer and Whiskey League," to his six years of service with the National League Philadelphia Phillies. In the City of Brotherly Love, Billy played under the tutelage of legendary manager Harry Wright, formed part of the most prolific offensive outfield that ever played the game, nearly died from typhoid fever, and returned the following year to post "unheard of statistics"[24] in his greatest single season in the game.

In November 1895, Billy Hamilton was involved in one of the most controversial, and ultimately, one of the most lopsided trades in baseball history. After having averaged .366 with 66 stolen bases and 142 runs scored for six years in Philadelphia, he was traded to the Boston Nationals for slick-fielding third baseman Billy Nash, who had averaged .278 during the same six-year period. Chapter 4, "Boston Billy," reviews the details of the trade, chronicles Hamilton's six-year sojourn with the Beaneaters, conjectures on his rationale for leaving the major leagues when he was still a sought-after player, and presents a summary and analysis of his major league record.

Back in Clinton in 1902, with his major league career concluded and his financial future stable due to his prudent investments, Hamilton could have rested on his laurels. That was not the Hamilton way. Before hanging up his spikes, he would spend another fifteen years in the game, initially as a player-manager in the New England League, then as a scout for his former Boston team, and finally as a non-playing manager for other New England League, Eastern League, and Tri-State clubs. He could still play the game. As a player-manager for the Lynn team in 1910, at the age of 44, he banged out 125 hits in 109 games, stole 23 bases, and hit for a .332 average. Chapter 5, "Home to Clinton," documents this rich but less well-known era in Hamilton's baseball life, one that coincided with a time period that New England League historian Charlie Bevis classifies as the heyday of the league.[25] In addition to dealing with Billy's continuing baseball career, Chapter 5 also provides heretofore unknown details about his active involvement in other regional sports of the era at which he excelled, including roller skating, professional roller polo, harness racing, sleigh racing and horse breeding.

In the last part of his life, Hamilton moved a few miles south to Worcester and took yet another career path, working eighteen years for a large leather manufacturing company there and for a time managing its ball team. Chapter 6, "Late Innings," discusses this final phase in his life, notes his passing from the scene at age 74, details the revival of interest in his career in the late 1950s that led to his induction to the Hall of Fame in 1961, and concludes with a final assessment of Hamilton the ballplayer and Hamilton the man. The brief Chapter 7, "In the Country of Baseball," reviews the post-baseball years of several of Sliding Billy's former teammates and opponents, and concludes by reaffirming Hamilton's status as a legendary individual player whose life and times offer the modern fan a unique glimpse of the era that links the pioneer days of professional baseball with today.

Far from being a "shadowy figure" or a "nineteenth-century ghost," Billy Hamilton led an active, engaged life during an important transitional period, both in professional baseball and U.S. history.

"The future is always fresh and exciting, and it has a pull on us that times past simply can never muster. Yet it may well be that our greatest wealth as human beings can be 'discovered' by simply looking behind us."

—David Baldacci, from Author's Note to *Wish You Well*

1

Billy Baseball

> *Baseball ... the very symbol, the outward and visible expression of the drive, and push, and rush, and struggle of the raging, tearing, booming nineteenth century.*
> — Mark Twain, 1889

William Robert "Sliding Billy" Hamilton, a 1961 inductee to the Hall of Fame, played fourteen years of major league baseball, with the Kansas City Cowboys (1888–89), the Philadelphia Phillies (1890–95), and the Boston Beaneaters (1896–1901). Born ten months after president Abraham Lincoln was assassinated, he appeared in his last major league game more than two years before Orville and Wilbur Wright made their first successful airplane flight at Kitty Hawk, North Carolina, in 1903.

By any standard, that was a very long time ago. Imagine a world with no television or radio, no personal telephones or computers. Imagine a world without automobiles, airplanes, fax machines, or fast-food restaurants. Think of a time before household electricity or motion pictures, a world before Stalin, Mao, Hitler, or Bin Laden. From our perspective, Billy's playing-era culture may appear so distinct and distant from our modern reality as to be virtually unrecognizable. How then do we begin to comprehend his world?

We can start with the game that he knew and played so well.

If, magically, we were to be transported back in time to his era, and if we were fortunate to arrive on a game day at the Huntingdon Grounds in Philadelphia, or at the South End Grounds in Boston, where Billy roamed the outfield for so many years, our first glimpse of the surroundings would be reassuring, for it would convince us that "the dimensions and the shape of the baseball diamond have changed little over the past 150 years."[1] As players take the field and the game begins, however, gradually we would become aware that the events witnessed and the equipment utilized, while curiously familiar, do not correspond exactly to their counterparts in our own era. To discover how "base ball" (the two words would not become joined into one until the twentieth century) evolved into the sport that we know today, we need to take a step back in time.

The delightfully engaging myth of baseball's "immaculate conception," that is, the notion that the game did not exist until it was conceived in the mind of Abner Doubleday in 1839, has long ago been disproven by historical research, which has, in turn, revealed the game has enjoyed a much more complex and diverting historical evolution. Children's ball and stick games were commonplace in Europe long before our revolt against Britain. By the 1830s a great variety of them, with colorful nicknames such as wicket, rounders, town ball, and round-town, were being played enthusiastically by children in America's northeastern towns and cities. Most versions employed a square playing field with four bases, and the action involved a batter striking a pitched ball and circling the bases until being "soaked," or struck by the ball, which had been retrieved and thrown by one of the fielders. Such children's games were gradually adapted for adults, who played them after work, as much as a manner of socializing and male bonding as for the physical exercise they could afford. One of the earliest known references to such efforts is a challenge by ballplayers from the town of Hamden, New York, issued to all comers in July of 1825:

> The undersigned, all residents of the new town of Hamden, with the exception of Asa C. Howland, who has recently moved into Delhi, challenge an equal number [nine] of persons in any town in the County of Delaware, to meet them at any time at the house of *Edward B. Chase*, in said town, to play the game of BASS-BALL [sic], for the sum of one dollar each per game. If no town can be found that will produce the required number, they will have no objection to play against any selection that can be made from the several towns in the country.[2]

Other than town affiliation, the most common unifying principle in the creation of such ball teams was occupation: "Early baseball clubs in the New York City area, for example, included those made up of policemen, barkeepers, milkmen, schoolteachers, and physicians."[3] At this point in the game's development, winning the contest was a happy coincidence, but in no way as significant as the opportunity to enhance camaraderie and friendship. Adult amateur baseball clubs blossomed in every Eastern city prior to the Civil War. The bewildering variety of rules and regulations in such bat-and-ball matches began to be standardized in September 1845, when the New York Knickerbocker club developed, adopted, and published a set of rules for what by then had become known as "base ball." The Knickerbocker rules eliminated the practice of "soaking," and mandated the use of a round bat and harder ball. They established three strikes as an out, three outs as a hand or (half) inning, and set the length of the match at nine innings. By the Civil War's end, the "regulation game," as it came to be known, was fast becoming the standard format just about everywhere it was being played. The first documented game played under these rules occurred on October 6, 1845.

As baseball's popularity increased, so did the players' skills, and these factors moved the sport inexorably from the amateur to the professional level. The first fully professional team to achieve a national reputation, the Cincinnati Red Stockings, was formed in 1869, three years after Billy Hamilton's birth. On St. Patrick's Day 1871, representatives from ten professional clubs met in New York and established the National Association of Professional Base Ball Players, or the "National Association." Each team agreed to play a best-of-five series with the other clubs, and thus, the first professional baseball league was formed. Poor attendance, wildly varying skill levels among teams and players, gambling, "hippodroming" (fixing or throwing games), and a complete lack of central organization led to the early demise of this first attempt to develop a player-controlled professional baseball league. In 1876, a second organization, the National League of Professional Baseball Clubs, or the "National League," was inaugurated. This "owners" league eliminated players from any position of authority and developed a seventy-game schedule of regular competition between teams in eight cities: Cincinnati, Chicago, Hartford, St. Louis, Boston, Louisville, New York, and Philadelphia. During the ensuing quarter-century, the league owners' attempts to monopolize the professional circuit were challenged by upstart professional organizations including the Union Association (1884); the American Association (1882–91), in which Billy Hamilton played for two years; and the Players' League (1890), which, as its name implies, was yet another attempt by the participants of the game to control their own professional destinies. In 1901, the year of Billy Hamilton's retirement from the National League but not, as we shall see, from professional competition, the American League, thereafter forever burdened with the nickname "junior circuit", was finally accepted in principle by the "senior circuit", or National League, creating the basic, bi-partite organizational structure of the major leagues that survives today. Billy Hamilton's biographical timeline from birth to his retirement from the major leagues at age thirty-five parallels almost exactly professional baseball's timeline from birth, through adolescence, to maturity.

Baseball's fundamental components — playing fields, equipment, and uniforms — underwent correspondent metamorphoses from the early amateur years to the beginning of the twentieth century. Early amateur team playing fields, for example, were just that: any available open space or field. As eastern industrial cities grew, undeveloped urban real estate became scarce. The New York Knickerbockers, notwithstanding the popularity of their innovative set of game regulations, were forced to move locations frequently until settling at a site in Hoboken, New Jersey, which had been christened with the wonderfully hyperbolic name "Elysian Fields."[4] The owner of the Elysian Fields, the enterprising Commodore John Cox Stephens, also owned the ferry line from Barclay Street in downtown New York to the Hoboken site. Stephens was happy to promote the Elysian Fields as a tourist attraction in order to sell his thirteen-cent round-trip ferry fares.[5] The idea of charging a fee for game attendance gradually gained favor among amateur teams, and in 1862, promoter William Commeyer built the country's first enclosed field, the Union Grounds, on the site of a failed ice-skating rink in Brooklyn.[6]

Billy Hamilton's major league career ended before the era of the modern stadiums. He beat out bunts and chased down fly balls in enclosed wooden ballparks whose locations were determined by "access to cheap rapid transit, the cost of rent, and the social character of the neighborhood."[7] At their most basic, such sites consisted of rows of uncovered wooden-plank seating, the "bleaching boards," located in foul territory along the first and third base lines, and a two-story covered "grand stand" behind home plate. Although completely enclosed, the actual real estate of many sites like New York's Polo Grounds extended far beyond normal outfield distances. In such cases, the farthest official reaches of the baseball playing field within the grounds were determined not by walls or fences, but by cordoning off the outfield "in play" areas with rope. During important games in parks with this type configuration, the "cranks" and "cranklets" (as male and female fans were then called) not only occupied the bleachers and the grandstands, but also were able to observe the action while standing behind the outfield ropes or relaxing in the comfort of their horse-drawn carriages. These fans' proximity to the outfielders frequently distracted the players, especially those from the opposing teams, and their presence caused understandable havoc when a ball in play escaped the grasp of the outfielder and entered the gallery.

Even when fences were present, the unkempt condition or haphazard configuration of early parks led to some unusual circumstances, both planned and accidental. The Baltimore club, for example, was famous for hiding spare baseballs in the overgrown outfield grass, substituting one of them when the ball in play got beyond the outfielders.[8] Billy Hamilton was not exempt from poor field conditions, a fact that sometimes produced hilarious results.

> The old ballpark, where the Boston Beaneaters played in the 1890s, was built alongside a railroad track and tended to collect trash. In the space of three years, there were three incidents of balls in play being lodged in old tin cans. One baseball rolled up to and under the fence by the railroad track. Billy Hamilton, retrieving the ball, discovered it was stuck in a tin can. He tried to shake it lose [sic] but it would not budge, so he threw the can to the shortstop, who tagged out the runner with the canned baseball.[9]

Billy occasionally benefited from the irregularities of such fields and the general lack of ground rules for playing on them. On May 14, 1893, for example, at the Phillies' home park at Broad and Huntingdon streets, Billy had a grand day against the Washington Senators, hitting two of his forty career home runs, both of them line-drive shots over the right field fence. But in the eighth inning

> with Reilly on third and two out, Hamilton hit to Sullivan [Washington's shortstop], who threw wildly to first. The ball went through the right field gate screen. Maguire [the Senators first baseman] jumped over the fence for it, but one of the peanut vendors underneath the grandstand, whose sympathy was, of course, for the Phillies, kept Maguire from finding the ball. The

peanut man got "slugged" but that did not prevent two runs from coming in, and the crowd was happy.[10]

A more serious downside of the wooden ballparks was their susceptibility to catching fire. The league experienced more than twenty fires in the 1890s, and in 1894 alone one-third of all parks were damaged in this fashion. On Sunday, August 5, 1894, Chicago's park caught fire during the seventh inning of a game. The next day, during a morning team practice in Philadelphia, Phillies players noticed a fire at the Huntingdon Grounds. In less than twenty-four hours, fires had completely destroyed both of these ballparks. The most catastrophic conflagration of the year took place in Boston in May, when several boys set fire to some trash under the grandstand during the third inning of a Boston-Baltimore matchup. The fire engulfed the park, as well as a nearby schoolhouse and fire station and continued to blaze for hours. A total of 164 wooden dwellings and thirteen brick buildings were consumed, leaving approximately 1,000 families homeless.[11] Such firetraps would gradually give way to magnificent new parks made of safer, longer-lasting materials in the early twentieth century.

In 1911, a decade after his retirement from the major leagues, Hamilton, then a scout for his former Boston team, represented owner W. Hepburn Russell when the team played a series in Pittsburgh. The Pirates' new venue, Forbes Field, the first steel-and-concrete park in the National League, featured ramps to move fans quickly to their seats, elevators to the third-deck luxury boxes, and clubhouses for umpires and visiting teams.[12] Clubhouse facilities for visiting players were a novelty for Billy. In his era, opposing teams dressed at their hotels and were transported to and from the park in open horse-drawn wagons. On many occasions while arriving or departing, hostile home fans pelted the opposition with fruit, vegetables, or rocks as they traversed the route, sometimes with serious consequences for both sides.

> After an important victory in Detroit one year, the White Stockings were returning to their hotel when an angry mob ... began pelting them with stones. [Player-manager] Anson ordered his men to stay put and keep their heads down, but the words were no sooner out of his mouth that a quid of tobacco hit him square in the face. That was more than King Kelly or Tommy Burns could take. They sprang from their carriage and waded into the crowd, swinging their fists. The police arrived to break up the melee, but not before Burns suffered a broken wrist and several toughs in the mob had their heads cracked and their noses bloodied.[13]

Clubhouse facilities for visiting teams would not become mandatory until 1907.[14]

Sporting Life recorded the reaction of Sliding Billy, the wooden-ballpark journeyman, to the wonders of Forbes Field:

> W. Hepburn Russell ducked Pittsburg this trip, but sent as his Representative, Billy Hamilton, old timer, whose presence was perhaps more agreeable to the Pittsburg officials. William watched the the gates with the keenness of a magnate. This was the first time he had been on Forbes Field. He was speechless with its magnitude.[15]

The major league's last wooden ballpark, the South Side Grounds, was built in Chicago by Charles Comiskey for his new American League team, the White Stockings, in 1900.[16]

With the exception of a handful of amateur exhibition games that were played under lights between 1880 and 1897, all nineteenth century ballgames were played during daylight hours. Thomas Edison's development of the incandescent light bulb in 1879, and his subsequent marketing of a delivery system for electricity, paved the way for the first experiment with night baseball in Massachusetts, in 1880: "Looking for publicity Northern Electric [Light Company] invited the employees of the Jordan Marsh and R. H. White department stores to play baseball under its lights on September 2, 1880, at Natasket Beach."[17] Eight similar experiments, made in Indiana, Washington state, California, Delaware, and Texas, failed to popularize the concept of a game under lights. Players found the lights either too bright or too dim, and light stands placed in such awkward locations as behind the pitching box (it wasn't as yet designated as the pitching "mound") did little to advance the cause. Billy Hamilton was approaching his seventieth birthday by the time the major leagues experienced its first game under lights, in Cincinnati, on May 24, 1935.

Professional baseball was not played under the lights in Sliding Billy's time largely due to a lack of appropriate technology. Sunday baseball also was a rarity, but in this case, it was due to religious objections. The National League, bowing to the popular Sabbatarian movement, which believed Sunday to be a day solely for religious functions, proscribed Sunday games in 1878. The league reaffirmed its determination in this regard in 1880, when it expelled the Cincinnati club for violating the regulation. The Sunday prohibition conflicted with the views of most Catholic and Lutheran immigrants, who followed the

"Continental" view of Sunday as a day of rest and recreation, and with Jewish immigrants, whose Sabbath occurred on Saturday. Strong demand for Sunday baseball by these advocates of a secular Sabbath became one of the driving motivations behind the founding of the American Association in 1882. When the National League and the American Association merged in 1892, each team was granted the right to determine individually if it wanted to schedule Sunday home games. By the 1890s, nearly all the western cities had authorized Sunday ball except Detroit and Cleveland, which finally came on board in 1910 and 1911, respectively. Eastern teams, whose "blue laws" often dated from Colonial times, were much slower in changing their traditions. Billy Hamilton spent most of his major league career playing for two of the last major league venues to legalize Sunday baseball. Boston did so in 1928, and Philadelphia followed suit the next year. Pittsburgh, the final holdout, finally accepted the practice in 1934.[18]

In the early years, the game's central object, the baseball, tended to be of haphazard construction and design. Although its basic dimensions have remained the same since 1872,[19] "the practical difficulty of making and preserving a functional baseball ensured wide variation."[20] The manufacture of baseballs, which began in Brooklyn in 1855,[21] helped to standardize their weight and size. Well into the 1870s, however, "clubs around the country inevitably played with baseballs that varied in every particular."[22] This situation was exacerbated by an unwillingness to issue a new ball when the original was lost or in bad condition. "A ball a game was the norm, and if batted out of the park, the game's continuance awaited the pleasure of some anonymous 'urchin.' If he chose to return it, he was given free admission; if not, the house reluctantly put a new one in play."[23]

An 1896 rule change allegedly required "a club to keep a dozen balls on hand, and ordered an umpire to introduce a new ball whenever an old one was soiled, blackened, or scratched."[24] In an interview conducted nearly three decades after his retirement, Billy Hamilton confirmed that this requirement rarely was followed: "Another thing that I believe worked against the hitters of my day was that a ball had to be kept in play until the yarn showed through the cover or stitching."[25] Billy also described how the great hitters of his era would have responded to the "lively" ball in use in the twentieth century:

> What batting stars of my day wouldn't do to the lively ball ... think of such sluggers of that era as Larry Lajoie, Hugh Duffy, Fred Tenney, Kitty Bransfield, Ed Delehanty [sic], Jess Burkett, Jimmy Collins, Fred Clark and Pop Anson getting a crack at the present type of ball. They slammed the ball so hard that it was almost impossible to make a play on them and they were hitting the so-called dead ball.[26]

The bats that Billy and his contemporaries used for "slamming the ball" differed markedly from their modern equivalents. Amateur players of the 1840s and 1850s either whittled or carved their own bats, or commissioned their fabrication by carpenters from slabs of a variety of hardwoods. Before bat-making became a serious business, necessity often became the mother of invention. In an October 1865 game, for example, the Philadelphia Athletics, having broken all their bats in a high-scoring slugging contest, used a shovel handle as a substitute to finish their game.[27] Some of the most successful early professional hitters gripped their bats in what today would be considered a highly unorthodox fashion. Cap Anson of the Chicago White Stockings and later Ty Cobb of the Detroit Tigers, each of whom registered a batting average above .300 for more than twenty consecutive seasons, left a gap of several inches between their hands on the neck of the bat when at the plate. More radically designed bats also enjoyed a heyday. From 1885 to 1893, for example, bats with one flat side, used to facilitate bunting, were permitted. The flat-sided bat's resemblance to a cricket paddle is not serendipitous, for it was invented by Harry Wright, former professional cricket and baseball player and manager of the 1869 Cincinnati Reds Stockings. By the late 1880s, mass-produced bats like A.G. Spalding & Brothers "Wagon Tongue" models, "made of the finest straight grained, well-seasoned, second growth Ash ... seasoned at least two years,"[28] had become the norm among professionals and amateurs. Eventually, star players had their bats made to their precise personal specifications. Louisville's Pete "the Gladiator" Browning is reputedly responsible for the trademarked name a famous bat of this variety:

> A two-time batting champion when playing for his hometown Louisville in the American Association, he always insisted his bats be made to his particular specifications. One year a Louisville man named John Hillerich made him a bat that Browning called his "Louisville Slugger." Soon, other ballplayers began ordering bats from Hillerich, enabling him to open the bat-making firm of Hillerich and Bradsby.[29]

Regardless of their manufacturer, nineteenth-century bats were significantly heavier than their modern counter parts, thicker in the handle, tapered much less from barrel to handle, and were finished off with a minimal knob-end. In Hamilton's era, however, not even the strongest competitor would have been able to vent his frustration by laying a bat on a thigh and snapping it in half, as such modern sluggers as Bo Jackson occasionally have done.

Sliding Billy's earliest extant major league photos consist of a series of posed studio shots that later were used in the Old Judge Tobacco photocard series. By creating these mementos, more than 2,000 of which are known to exist, Goodwin and Company of New York, Old Judge brand's manufacturer, took advantage of an enormously popular cultural craze of America's Victorian period — the photo postcard. Simple postcards that advertised businesses and vacation spots were introduced in the United States in the mid–1870s. Soon the government authorized their use for regular mail. In 1910 alone, nearly 100 million were posted across the country.[30] Photocards, photos developed and printed as postcards, were the next step in the postcard's evolution, and in the case of baseball, served as the forerunner of the modern baseball card. These early versions, however, were not packaged with a slab of pink chewing gum or hygienically sealed in plastic wrappers, but rather were paired with plug chewing tobacco or a few ounces of loose tobacco.

Billy Hamilton as a Boston Beaneater, 1897 (courtesy Transcendental Graphics).

Billy Hamilton's Old Judge photos capture him in several batting and fielding postures (see page 64). For the observant modern viewer, the most striking aspect of the fielding poses is the fact that Billy is portrayed as fielding a ball barehanded. No, he did not forget to bring his glove to the photo shoot. Like all players of his era, he began his baseball career as a barehanded defender. In 1911, Al Spalding, Chicago and Boston's star pitcher from the mid–1860s to the mid–1870s, later owner of the Chicago White Stockings, and a successful sporting goods entrepreneur, narrated the story of his introduction to the baseball glove:

> The first glove I ever saw on the hand of a ballplayer in a game was worn by Charles C. Waite, in Boston, in 1875. He had come from New Haven and was playing at first base. The glove worn by him was of flesh color, with a large, round opening in the back. Now, I had for a good while felt the need of some sort of hand protection for myself.... For several years I had pitched in every game played by the Boston team, and had developed severe bruises on the inside of my left hand. When it was recalled that every ball pitched had to be returned, and that every swift one coming my way, from infielders, outfielders, or hot from the bat, must be stopped, some idea may be gained of the punishment received.... It was not until 1877 that I overcame my scruples against joining the "kid glove aristocracy" by donning a glove ... when I did at last decide to do so, I did not select a flesh-colored glove, but got a black one, and cut out as much of the back as possible to let the air in.[31]

Early gloves progressed from Charles Waite's dress glove to two other models: a fingerless style similar to modern day handball or weight-lifting gloves that was form fitting and padded around the knuckles; and a split-fingered workman glove style. These Spartan versions gradually evolved into other styles. The first resembled an oversized oven mitt, with no separate slots for fingers; the second variety was a more heavily padded version of the split-fingered work glove. After overhand pitching motions were approved in 1884, catchers out of necessity soon adopted the playing glove. Deacon White, who switched from catching to third base mid-way through his eighteen-year pro career, claimed to have been the first professional catcher to play with a glove, long before the overhand pitching motion was approved: "Toward the end of his life, White told a writer that he had used a padded glove as early as 1872, when all other catchers were bare-handed."[32] In 1890, Earle "Harry" Decker, who caught for Pittsburgh that year, patented the "Dexter Safety Mitt," which was little more than a glove stitched to the back of a pillow-like pad that covered the hand. While catcher's masks and chest protectors followed, the catcher's use of leg protection would have to wait until 1907, when New York's Roger Bresnahan strapped on the first pair of shin guards on Opening Day against the Phillies.[33] A few enterprising ballplayers of the 1870s, such as Al Spalding and Al Reach, capitalized after they retired on the trend of using fielding gloves by forming sporting goods companies that manufactured gloves for both professionals and amateurs. In 1896, *Sporting Life* reported that when Billy Hamilton finally decided to add a fielding glove to his personal equipment, he took a different approach.

> Billy Hamilton plays ball with a glove of his own make. It is about half the size of those worn by the general run of players and is nicely padded. The thumb is not separate from the body of the glove, but is tacked on with some stitches. Delahanty, Lange, and two or three other fielders have gloves like it.[34]

When did the majority of players begin using gloves? A hint can been seen by an ardent protest that the editors of *Sporting Life* offered in July 1894: "The abuse is rapidly growing ... pretty soon all fielders will use the unsightly mitts and next we may expect nets brought into use."[35] The last position player to field gloveless, Jerry Denny of Louisville, retired in 1894.

Early amateur teams of the pre–New York Knickerbocker era used their fields' existing rocks or tree stumps as bases. If the playing field were clear, wooden stakes were employed. An 1857 National Association of Baseball Players rule required bases to be white-painted canvas bags filled with sand or sawdust.[36] In 1861, an observer of an early game played in Saint Louis referred to the bases as "square bags of sand with leather straps around them by which they were buckled into iron rings fastened to wooden stakes that were driven about two feet into the ground."[37] Nearly a hundred and fifty years later, little has changed in this regard. Modern "sacks" are fifteen-inch squares filled with a lightweight material and anchored to the ground.

The first home plates actually *were* dish or plate-like objects used for that purpose. In 1869, the plate became a twelve-inch square of marble or stone, with points of the square facing the pitcher and catcher, respectively. By the mid–1880s, both the American Association and the National League required that the square be made of rubber in order to prevent injury. Before Billy Hamilton's last year as a Boston player, the modern 17-inch, five-sided home plate was adopted.

A baseball uniform's basic function of visually distinguishing the players from the spectators invests with it a lasting and particular significance. For the pioneering Knickerbockers of the 1840s, a gentleman's baseball uniform consisted of long blue trousers, a white shirt, a string or ribbon tie, and a straw hat. The cumbersome pants were soon exchanged by most teams for more practical cricket-style knickers. There followed a brief period of wild experimentation in baseball shirts, during which silk tops of varying colors and stripes, each specific to a particular fielding position, were employed. These in turn gave way to the more practical wool or wool/cotton blend flannel shirt and knickers, a combination that Billy Hamilton models on his Old Judge tobacco card. Shirt-backs were blank; the introduction of player numbers would not appear for another forty years. Most shirts were slip-ons with buttons or lace ties at the neck. The handy and practical zipper was nowhere to be found on these uniforms. The earliest prototype zipper did not debut until the World's Columbian Fair in Chicago in 1893, and was not patented and put into production until almost a quarter-century later.[38]

Billy Hamilton wore collared shirts during his entire big league career. The New York Giants premiered the first collarless baseball shirts in 1906, an innovation conceived by none other than their irascible curmudgeon manager, John McGraw.[39] Close inspection of Billy's Old Judge photos further reveals that his pants, of similar material as his shirt, were quilted at the knees and the hips in order to provide extra protection for base stealers while at the same time preventing wear and tear as the season progressed. Although traditionally teams wore white for home games and gray while on the road, some clubs preferred darker colors, including black, not only for their visual impact, but to hide dirt and stains. Stripes, checks, pin-striping, patterns, and colored piping were the source of frequent experimentation. Solid color socks often served as the origin of a team's temporary or permanent nicknames, such as the Chicago White Stockings or the Saint Louis Brown Stockings. "High topper" football-style spiked shoes would remain the norm in baseball footwear into the twentieth century. Player-managers in the Hamilton era wore uniforms, but bench managers preferred formal street attire, consisting of three-piece suits, stove hats, derbies, or bowlers, spats, and gloves. (See accompanying photos of Harry Wright and Frank Selee of the 1892 Phillies and 1900 Boston Beaneaters, respectively.) An anachronistic echo of this sartorial predilection was carried

Philadelphia Phillies, 1892, featuring five future Hall of Famers: Billy Hamilton, seated, first right, Ed Delahanty, seated, second left; manager Harry Wright, in formal attire; Sam Thompson and Roger Connor, standing to the left and right, respectively, of Harry Wright (courtesy National Baseball Hall of Fame Library, Cooperstown, New York).

over into the mid–twentieth century in the person of Connie Mack, who continued to manage the Philadelphia Athletics in street clothes until his retirement in 1950.

The baseball cap, like the uniform, would undergo numerous permutations as it evolved into its current form. The Knickerbocker straw hat promptly gave way to more practical styles, among them the hard pillbox style, which Billy Hamilton sports in his 1889 Kansas City photos, and the soft jockey cap, which as its name implies was patterned after those worn on the racing circuit and sported a large crown and long bill. The pillbox style cap was reintroduced in 1976 to celebrate the centennial of the National League. The modern Pittsburgh Pirates admired this style so much that it remained their cap style from 1976 to 1986, and in the minds of some, will be a style forever associated with Pittsburgh Hall of Famer Willie Stargell. The jockey-style cap with a short bill became the norm through the 1930s, and its modern form, with longer bill, remains the standard today.

1900 Boston Nationals. Future Hall of Famers include Hugh Duffy, top row, second from the right; Billy Hamilton, bottom row, second from left, followed by Kid Nichols and manager Frank Selee. Jimmy Collins sits first on the right, front row (courtesy Boston Public Library, McGreevey Collection).

Article Two of the New York Knickerbockers' original 1845 rules state that "when assembled for exercise, the President, or in his absence, the Vice President, shall appoint an Umpire, who shall keep the game in a book provided for that purpose, and note all violations of the By-Laws and rules during the time of exercise."[40] In the early amateur phase of the game's development, most umpires were "distinguished members of the community with no special knowledge of the game or rules."[41] Since at the time there were still few judgment calls required, owing to the fact that there were no balls or strikes, "the umpire's primary role was to make sure players did not breach the club rules by acting in an ungentlemanly fashion."[42] By the late 1860s, however, a thorough familiarity with the rules was required for the job, and it was stipulated that no discourtesy toward the arbiter would be permitted. In 1879, the National League appointed a staff of twenty umpires from which clubs could chose for their contests.[43] The upstart American Association became the first league to hire a permanent staff of four umpires in 1882, require that their selections wear blue flannel jackets, and take an oath of impartiality.[44] The National League soon followed suit. Until 1898, only one umpire per game was assigned by the National League.

As the role of the umpire evolved from that of a distinguished observer to the central authority figure in the game, he became the "heavy of the baseball drama, the villain of the piece and the object of antagonism and abuse from the fans and players both."[45] In the "rowdy" baseball era during which Billy played, such abuse was often physical as well as verbal. Players angered at a call spat tobacco in the umpire's face or stomped on his shoes with their spikes. When crowds of fans got involved in the "kicking," as umpire harassment was designated in the time period, the situation could sometimes become life-threatening: "Umpires were cursed, bombarded with beer bottles and rotten eggs, and subjected to beatings."[46] In one such incident at the Polo Grounds in 1884, a crowd of 2,000 attacked an umpire, and "the police had all they could do to save him as they beat off the crowd with their clubs."[47] In St. Louis during the same year, a former player-turned-umpire was severely beaten by a mob before the police could intervene.[48] In Philadelphia, umpire Billy McClean was assaulted by enraged home team fans when he called a game on account of darkness.[49]

While the league allegedly sided with the umpires, some owners, if not openly encouraging the practice of umpire baiting, did little to restrict it.[50] Indeed, club owners and league presidents at times went on the field to dispute decisions or entered the umpire's dressing room to complain about a call.[51] Even the most distinguished and respected arbiters, such as John Gaffney, did not escape abuse.

> In 1884 Umpire Gaffney suffered a cut eye in a fight with John Ward [New York's pitcher/infielder]. Since Ward apologized and took Gaffney to a surgeon, he received only a fine and a brief suspension, but this incident prompted the league to invoke $200 fines for future offences. Yet the reluctance of the club owner to "throw the book" at a player was evidenced a year later, when a player's apology excused him for having struck Umpire Dick Pierce.[52]

Despite such constant, occasionally life-threatening abuse, some umpires persisted. The most innovative and well respected of the era was John H. "Honest John" Gaffney. Born in Worcester, Massachusetts, in 1860, he turned to umpiring in 1880 when his promising playing career as a third baseman ended due to an arm injury. His fame as an Ivy League arbiter attracted the attention of the National League, which hired him in 1884. He left umpiring briefly for an unsuccessful stint as a major league manager (Washington, 1886–87), and then jumped to the American Association in 1888, where he earned a record-setting $2,500 a year plus expenses. His innovations were many. He revolutionized the single-umpire system by moving from behind the catcher to behind the pitcher when runners were on base. He was the first umpire to wear spiked shoes for better traction, and the first to base a fair/foul call on a ball hit over the fence on the point the ball sailed over rather than the place it landed.[53]

Gaffney's Worcester origins and his service in the American Association during Billy Hamilton's years with the Kansas City Cowboys played a crucial role in Sliding Billy's baseball future. In this era, formalized recruiting of new players was in its infancy. There were no paid scouts, and initially, no "minor" league affiliates controlled by major league teams. Promising players were discovered during barnstorming trips or by word-of-mouth, or through ads placed by clubs and players in weeklies such as the *Sporting News* or *Sporting Life*. Given this state of affairs, any recommendation of a player by someone as respected as Umpire Gaffney would merit serious attention by a major league team looking for prospects. In 1897, *Sporting News* revealed how Billy Hamilton, then a star for Boston, had managed years earlier to make it to the majors.

> It was Gaffney, the umpire, that introduced Billy Hamilton to fast company. Gaffney was then [1888] an umpire in the American Association. He told a number of managers about Hamilton, who is a resident of Gaffney's home, Worcester, Massachusetts. It was not until he told Kansas City about him that Billy secured a place.[54]

Although the *Sporting News* was off by about fifteen miles in regard to Billy's hometown, Hamilton was in fact playing for Gaffney's hometown team, Worcester of the New England League, when purchased by the Kansas City Cowboys of the American Association on July 31, 1888.

Baseball slang in the Hamilton era served as a rich, expressive second language for its initiates. Among themselves, players developed and used their own terminology:

To kick was to complain. To throw down was to pull the double cross, while to trot on the square was to play it straight. To guy a fellow player was to kid him, which the funsmiths on the team did. To roast was to criticize. Eyes were called lamps, and hats were known as lids. A rookie was a yannigan, unless he happened to make an ass of himself, in which case he became a donkey. At the other end of the spectrum, when a player no longer was effective, he became a back number and resided in Hasbeen Valley.[55]

The game's growing impact on the national consciousness, coupled with a greater general interest in the sporting world, exercised a commensurate effect on the press. From 1878 to 1898, space assigned to sport in daily papers increased sevenfold. "Day in and day out, baseball got the lion's share of this increasing sports coverage. Its news value was more apparent to editors, particularly with the advent of the colorful American Association."[56]

In 1874, Henry Chadwick, often referred to as the dean of American baseball writers, published a book of baseball slang terms to help British writers cover contests played in that country during baseball's first international tour that took place that year. The volume's entries, which include the terms "pop ups," "fungoes," "double plays," "grounders," "assists," and "balks," all were coined by early sports journalists during the post–Civil War transition of baseball from an amateur to a professional endeavor.[57]

The most creative slang terms coined by the players were reserved for the nicknames that they applied to each other. While we do have our Big Papi, Pudge, and A-Rod today, as well as our Scooter (Rizzuto), Blue Moon (Odom), and Hammerin' Hank (Aaron) of the recent past, the nickname predilection was much more prevalent, creative, and colorful in the era of King Kelly, Mugsy McGraw, and Sliding Billy Hamilton. In addition to his "Sliding Billy" moniker, Hamilton was also known as "Good Eye Bill" because of his "seeming uncanny judgment of balls."[57] During his two seasons with Kansas City, Billy played with third baseman "Jumbo" Davis, right fielder "Monk" Cline and substitute "Fatty" Briody. In addition to sharing outfield duties with "Big Sam" Thompson and "Only Del" Delahanty in Philadelphia, Hamilton encountered pitchers "Phenomenal" Smith," "Kid" Gleason, "Kid" Carsey and "Nixey" Callahan. Playing with the "Beaneaters" (a term that baseball historian Cait Murphy affirms is the "worst team nickname in history") of Boston, Sliding Billy hobnobbed with the likes of "Cozy" Dolan, "Piano Legs" Hickman, "Stub" Smith, "Boileryard" Clark, and Hall of Famer "Kid" Nichols. Some of the more memorable nicknames applied to other players of the era include "Egyptian" Healy, "Chicken" Wolf, and "Icebox" Chamberlain, all of Louisville; "Cowboy" Jones and "Cupid" Childs from Cleveland; "Oyster" Burns from Baltimore; "Icicle" Reeder of Cincinnati; and the inimitable "Buttercup" Dickerson, who played for Troy.[58]

Players, fans, and sportswriters all had a hand in the creation of many of the colorful nicknames teams employed in the nineteenth century. As befitting an age of change and transition, teams in the era frequently changed monikers. Boston's National League team was originally called the Red Caps; then, in the Hamilton era, they became the Beaneaters. In the first decades of the twentieth century, they were known first as the Doves, and later as the Rustlers. New York supported the Highlanders before they became the Yankees, and the Phillies were first cheered as the Quakers. The Giants were the Gothams and the Cubs were the Orphans, while Cleveland fielded the Spiders, and Louisville the Colonels. Brooklyn, like the Boston team, never seemed to be able to make up its mind. Among its team titles were the Superbas, the Robins, and the Bridegrooms. In contrast to this musical-chairs attitude toward team nicknames in the nineteenth century, only a few teams in recent memory, such as the Houston Colt 45s, now the Astros, and the former Tampa Bay Devil Rays, now merely the Rays, have officially changed their nicknames.

Baseball's development into the "National Pastime" is intimately connected with the correspondent development of rail transportation in the last quarter of the nineteenth century. By the 1890s, four transcontinental lines crisscrossed the country, and the railroad had become the largest industry in the United States.[59]

Using interstate train routes, the Excelsiors of Brooklyn were able to undertake a thousand-mile playing tour in 1860. After the Civil War, teams from Brooklyn and Philadelphia embarked on similar excursions, at times venturing beyond their home state borders. These pioneering efforts, all made possible due to the railroad's rapid and spectacular development, did much to publicize and spread enthusiasm for the game of baseball.[60] In 1867 the Nationals of Washington, D.C., became the first eastern team to tour west of the Allegheny Mountains. During their 3,000-mile trek, they made stops in cities such as Cincinnati, Louisville, Saint Louis, and Chicago. A few years later, all these urban centers would field professional teams, either in the National League or the American Association.

The pioneering railroad tours of the early amateurs set an example for the first professional teams. In 1869, the Cincinnati Red Stockings, after seven early-season victories against local and regional teams, began their first eastern tour, playing opponents in New York, Philadelphia, and finally, Washington, D.C., where they were greeted by President Grant. Later in the season they toured the far West, taking on all comers from Ohio to California, and ending the campaign with a record of fifty-seven wins and one tie.[61] When the National League was formed a few years later, part of its eventual success and longevity was due to the fact that it was able to develop and implement professional baseball's first uniform playing schedule. This accomplishment was predicated on the availability of safe, reliable, moderately priced travel to all the venues in the league.

When the eastern or western clubs of the 1890s went on the road, the trip to their opponents' home cities could last as long as a month. Getting there was not always an enjoyable task. It would be another dozen years, for example, before the fastest available train, the American Limited, could make the trip from New York to Chicago in a span of twenty hours. Sleeper trains thus became a ballplayer's home-away-from-home for long stretches of the season. Conditions on early sleeper trains were primitive. As late as 1888, poor European immigrants to the Midwest made the journey from the East Coast in economy class "zulu" railroad cars that consisted of "double berths made of wooden slats astride a narrow aisle. Travelers padded the slats with their own blankets and clothing. The zulu cars contained a cooking stove on which the passengers prepared their food en route."[62]

Fortunately, all but the most financially troubled baseball teams of the Hamilton era employed more comfortable Pullman coach or sleeper cars on their extended road trips. Developed by furniture maker George Pullman, these popular trains, which were constructed entirely of wood until 1908, featured upper berths that were hinged to the side of the car and supported by two jointed arms. Although the cars were luxuriously decorated and appointed, some considered the Pullman sleepers "shoddy and uncomfortable."[63] By 1892, Pullman, who leased his cars rather than sell them, had 2,239 in operation. Until the late

1880s none offered bathing facilities. Even traveling in comparative Pullman luxury, the prospect of spending 15–20 hours in a wooden rail car traveling across the Midwest in the mid-summer heat must have tested the mettle of the hardiest team member.

Since the only means of communication between a ballplayer and his family during these long absences was by letter or telegram, some families occasionally made the effort to join their player on the road when possible. In a personal correspondence from 1959, Billy Hamilton's daughter, Ruth, provides a brief but telling glimpse of the sort of travel adventure such an undertaking could be.

> We didn't split rails as Abe Lincoln did, but we sure rode the old rails.... We traveled the hard way in those days, blazing the "trail" for the present popular leagues. Poor railroad accommodations, terrible hotels or rooming houses according to what we could afford and get; Mother [Rebecca Hamilton] even told me about going from Worcester, Mass. by boat-train-horse car-etc. to Kansas City when Dad played there ... as Dad was having a "batting slump" without her there.[64]

Other than the aforementioned evolutionary, and at times revolutionary, changes that professional baseball's playing fields and equipment underwent in the nineteenth century, most official rule changes primarily affected either the pitcher or the hitter. National League pitchers were required to throw underhanded during the first six years of the organization's existence (1876–1882). Sidearm pitching was allowed in 1883, and the following year, all restrictions with regard to pitching motion were removed. By a similar evolutionary process, the distance between the pitcher and home plate gradually was increased. During the National Association's professional era, in the mid–1870s, pitchers were able to throw underhand from anywhere within a 6 foot-by-6 foot "pitcher's box," whose front line was 45 feet away from home plate. In 1881, the distance between the front line of the box and home plate was increased to 50 feet. In 1887, although the front line distance from home remained 50 feet, the back line was set at 55 feet 6 inches from home, and the pitcher was required to keep one foot on the back line until delivering the ball, at which point he could take one step forward. Finally, in 1893, the "pitcher's box" was replaced by a simple slab of white rubber, 60 feet 6 inches from home plate, from which the pitcher could take one step when delivering the ball. This distance has remained a baseball constant for one hundred and fifteen years.

For the first five years of his fourteen-year major league career, therefore, Billy Hamilton was facing fireballers like Amos "the Hoosier Thunderbolt" Rusie and Denton "Cy[clone]" Young from a distance of 55 feet 6 inches. After taking their allowed step while delivering the ball, their ninety-mile-per-hour-plus fastballs were being released about 50 feet from the waiting Sliding Billy.

The number of balls required for a walk, or strikes for a strike-out, also varied greatly in the nineteenth century. In 1876 it took nine balls to gain first base on a walk, but by 1884 that number had been reduced to the present-day four. The number of strikes required for an out was reduced from four to today's three in 1888. In 1895, bunting a ball foul with two strikes was declared an out, and in 1901, foul balls began being counted as strikes.

By the end of Sliding Billy's major league career, a long process of transformation, evolution, and change in the rules and playing conditions of major league baseball largely had come to an end. Baseball had entered the modern era.

The thirty-five-year period between the end of the Civil War and the dawn of the twentieth century was an era of remarkable economic and social change in the United States. America underwent a second industrial revolution. New factories dotted the landscape in the Northeast, and cities grew exponentially as a combination of formerly rural citizens and European immigrants sought new opportunities in urban settings. With the 1858 completion of the transatlantic cable, the telegraph provided high-speed communication across continents. Alexander Graham Bell's first telegraphic transmission of human speech took place in 1876; by 1900 Americans owned 1.3 million telephones.[65] Edison's phonographic cylinders, first tested in 1887, developed into "nickel-in-the-slot" machines in soda fountains and saloons by the 1890s — thus were born the first jukeboxes. George Eastman's snapshot photographic camera went on sale for $1.00 in 1900. In the 1880s, Edison's invention of the kinetograph and kinetoscope successfully reproduced objects in motion, and the first commercially exhibited "living pictures" premiered in New York in 1896.

Trains and electric streetcars facilitated urban and interurban transport. Trolley company owners developed amusement parks and ballparks along their routes in order to increase ridership on their lines. In 1898, for example, construction costs for the Brooklyn baseball team's new ballpark were shared by two streetcar companies that had routes passing a block from the field. In 1884, the Brooklyn team adopted the nickname "Trolley Dodgers" (later shortened to "Dodgers") "in tribute to their fans, who had to avoid speeding cars in the maze of trolley lines crisscrossing the city."[66]

Mechanization of manufacturing processes resulted in mass production of consumer goods. As food, clothing, housing, and transportation became more affordable, the burgeoning urban middle class found itself with more time for leisure activities including vaudeville, burlesque, amusement parks, and sports. Participatory sports took on new forms. Croquet, archery, and lawn tennis were played at the homes of the elite, while roller skating and bicycling became the middle class fads of the 1880s and 1890s. Professionalization, however, changed the dynamic of sport in the era by putting "skilled players on the field and unpracticed spectators in the stands."[67] The age of spectator sports had arrived. Baseball, formerly a child's game, was at the right place at the right time. By the end of the nineteenth century, it had indisputably become the "National Pastime."

To this encapsulated summary of the era, another template, that of Victorian values, must be added. Victorian culture was primarily middle class in origin, and took shape as a product of the Industrial Revolution. However, to the extent possible, "working class people were brought into the ambience of Victorian culture."[68] Internalization of Victorian cultural values, therefore, could provide social mobility for a member of the working class. Preeminent among such values was the importance of the family and the home. Others included Christian ethics, hard work, competitiveness, self-discipline, frugality, sobriety, responsibility, and propriety.[69]

Billy Hamilton's story is similar to that of thousands of other sons and daughters of nineteenth century working-class immigrants to the United States. He was born in the urban Northeast and imbued with the Victorian values of dedication to family, hard work, frugality, temperance, and a fierce commitment to competition. When combined with his talent for playing the National Pastime, such characteristics enabled him to achieve a remarkable level of personal and professional success. His personal odyssey can be understood and appreciated, therefore, not only as the story of a man, but as the story of his era and of the game that he loved to play.

2

Early Innings

> "No other player in the land gets to first base as often as Hamilton."
>
> —*Sporting News*, June 4, 1898

Founded in 1666 by Congregationalist dissidents from New Haven Colony, Newark, New Jersey, was blessed with an advantageous geographical location that would assure it a significant role in the future economic development of the northeastern United States. Located on the west bank of the Passaic River, just eight miles from Manhattan Island and in proximity of a deep-water port, the city blossomed into a major manufacturing site in the latter part of the eighteenth century. Its growing industrial importance was enhanced in 1821 by the completion of the Morris Canal, an engineering marvel of its day, which enabled coal mined in Pennsylvania's Lehigh Valley to be transported by barge across northern New Jersey to what would become the state's largest industrial center. By the beginning of the Civil War, seventy-five percent of Newark's population worked in manufacturing, primarily in the leather and brewing industries. Many of the city's earliest immigrants were Ulster Presbyterians from Northern Ireland, and some of them fought with Washington against the British. They were followed to Newark by Catholics from southern Ireland, who were fleeing their country's potato famine.[1]

While some newcomers to the city made it their permanent home, others, including Thomas Edison, used it as a stopping-off point before moving on. This was also the case of Samuel and Mary Hamilton of Ireland, whose first child, William Robert, was born in Newark in 1866.

Although all previous historical references to Billy Hamilton's birth, including those at Cooperstown, refer to his birth date as February 16 of that year, he actually made his entrance a day earlier. Individual birth certificates were not issued in New Jersey until 1878, but Newark archival records confirm that on February 15, 1866, a son was born to "Mrs. Hamilton."

Census and other archival records of the Hamilton family reveal a long-standing ambivalence with regard to their perception of their actual ethnic origin and homeland. While Ireland is most often cited, Scotland and "Ireland English" also appear. Today, Billy Hamilton's living relatives remember him as classifying himself proudly as Scottish. This ambivalence strongly suggests that Billy's family were "Ulster-Scots," descendants of the original Scottish immigrants to Northern Ireland in the early seventeenth century.[2] The presence of large numbers of Ulster-Scots in Newark in the nineteenth century may have been a motivating factor in Samuel and Mary Hamilton's decision to select the city as their first stop in the United States.

By the time of Billy's birth, however, the locus of major manufacturing growth in the United States had shifted to New England, and in particular, to Massachusetts. Sometime between February 1866 and the birth of Billy's sister, Mary Jane, in October of 1868, the Hamilton family left Newark and resettled in the small town of Clinton, in rural Massachusetts, about a dozen miles north of Worcester. Clinton, named in honor of New York statesman Dewitt Clinton, was a relative latecomer to the textile industry that formed the foundation of New England's economy in the nineteenth century. Cotton yarn had been produced by machine in the region since the 1790s. The introduction of the power loom by Francis Cabot Lowell in 1813 mechanized the process of turning the yarn into cloth. Prior to the Civil War, the coal-fueled, steam-powered mill replaced its predecessor, the water-powered mill, resulting in an enormous increase in productivity. By the time the Hamiltons relocated to Clinton, eighty percent of the country's cotton textile output came from New England.[3]

What Francis Cabot Lowell did for the town that would eventually bear his name, Erastus and Horatio Bigelow did for Clinton. Erastus invented the carpet power loom, the coach lace loom (braided trim for coach interiors), the wire cloth loom (making window screens available for the first time), and the gingham loom, all in the 1840s.

His brother Horatio built factories for the production of these goods in a section of the rural Worcester County farming community of Lancaster, known as Clintonville. In 1850, this area was incorporated as the town of Clinton.[4] Horatio Bigelow's subsequent generosity to the city was particularly noteworthy: "The school department, fire department, library, local banks, and many churches in town all got their start thanks to Horatio Bigelow.[5] The 1870 U.S. census of Clinton's inhabitants lists the Hamilton family as residents, with Samuel's occupation noted by the phrase "Works in Gingham Mill." The gingham mill mentioned, part of Bigelow's enormous Lancaster Mills, still stands today on Green Street in Clinton.

Sitting amid the thickly wooded, gently rolling hills of eastern Worcester County, Clinton today projects an aura of quaint, small-town charm. The Nashua River, earlier the power source of Clinton's mills, pursues its meandering northeasterly course through town as it did a hundred years ago. Remnants of the past, the long-abandoned textile mills, sit like disconsolate dinosaurs alongside the town's filling stations and donut shops. Many of the two-story brick buildings constructed in Billy Hamilton's day continue to stand watch on High Street, and the tree-shaded areas near City Hall and the Clinton Commons evoke the small-town nostalgia of a bygone era.

Somewhere along the winding corridors of baseball history, a legend developed that Billy Hamilton attended Newark High School, and while there, ran a 10¾-second one-hundred-yard dash. While in most cases such legends tend to be more engaging than the facts, in Billy's case, the opposite is true. The 1880 U.S. census lists Hamilton, age fourteen, as a cotton mill worker in Clinton. In 1875, the average yearly wage of a mill worker was about $400. Poverty-line annual income for a family of four to six was $585. This meant that "other members of a household, including children, needed to work just so the family could get by minimally."[6] Massachusetts law of the time allowed children of fourteen who could read and write to terminate their schooling and turn to millwork. Beginning in 1874, the standard work week for mill employees was "reduced" from sixty-six to sixty hours, spread over six days. Workers typically spent 11–12 hours on the job during weekdays, with half-days on Saturdays. Sliding Billy's journey from the cotton mill to the Baseball Hall of Fame is one that few could imagine, and one that even fewer could realize.

2. Early Innings

Although Billy Hamilton's native state of New Jersey hosted the first documented game of baseball (October 6, 1845, at the Elysian Fields in Hoboken[7]), his adopted state of Massachusetts has a rich and storied tradition of the game. Originally, it even had its own version of the sport, the "Massachusetts Game," one that was contemporaneous with the "New York Game" of the Knickerbockers. An old-timer from Stockton recalled it in this fashion:

> We used to play what was called the Massachusetts game. That was where we had a square instead of a diamond, and ran four bases. We had a small ball and a small bat, and a ball could be thrown at a base runner, and if it hit him before he got to the base he was out.[8]

While the earliest New England teams, the 1854 Boston Olympics and the 1855 Elm Trees, played under these rules, a newly formed club in 1857, the Tri-Mountains, decided they would only play under the New York (Knickerbocker) rules, which they had learned from New York watch-case maker Edward G. Saltzman, who had moved to the area and taught them the alternative game. A second front on the battle of game rules was opened on the high school level in 1861, when John A. Lowell persuaded two Boston-area private schools to switch to the New York rules. His suggestion was enhanced by an offer to provide free equipment for those teams that would make the switch, and to present a trophy in the form of a silver baseball to the champion New England high school club that played under these rules.[9] Given this history, it is no surprise that the first intercollegiate baseball game using New York rules was played between Harvard and Yale in 1863, in Worcester, just down the road from where Billy Hamilton's parents would eventually settle in Massachusetts.[10]

The Bay State was among the earliest to host professional teams. When the first professional league, the National Association, came into being in 1871, Boston was one of the nine cities that fielded a team. Its star pitcher, A. G. Spalding, would go on to become a manager, a team owner, and a sporting goods magnate. Its player-manager, outfielder Harry Wright, would manage for another two decades, in the National Association and later in the National League. Nineteen years after his managing debut with the National Association Bostons, Wright, then pilot of the National League Phillies and always on the lookout for new talent, would spend $3,000 to purchase the contract of a speedy outfielder from the Kansas City Cowboys, who in 1889 hit .301 and stole 111 bases for his team. That speedster was Billy Hamilton. The New England Association, a regional professional baseball organization that was the forerunner of today's New England League, also fielded five teams in Hamilton's region during the late 1870s, in the mill towns of Lowell, Fall River, Manchester, and Providence, and in the shoe-making center of Lynn. By the time Billy reached his mid-teens, however, professional baseball was even more prevalent in New England, and for a few years, was as close as a dozen miles away in Worcester, which fielded a National League team in 1880 and 1881. Boston and Providence did likewise from 1880 to 1885, and a second Boston team played in the short-lived Union Association in 1884.

It is unclear how much a working-class lad toiling in a Clinton cotton mill would have known about the exploits of the early Boston professional teams of the National Association and the National League or their contemporaries in the New England Association. In all probability, given the fact that there was no television, no radio, and at the time, still very limited newspaper coverage of sports, the young Hamilton knew very little about them. Since all games were played in the afternoon and none were played on Sunday, even if Billy could have attended, it would have been unlikely for him to have spent one-quarter of a day's wages for admission. There were, however, other options closer to home for the future Sliding Billy.

Organized baseball began in Clinton proper a year before Hamilton was born — the inaugural season of the town's "We'll Try Base Ball Club" was in 1865. In the late 1870s Clinton fielded its own professional team, which included future Hall of Fame pitcher Tim Keefe, from Cambridge. Keefe, then a third baseman, played two years for Clinton, and in 1880, signed his first National League contract with Troy. As a pitcher, he went on to win 342 games in 14 seasons, finishing up with the Philadelphia Phillies in 1893, where one of his teammates was a stocky outfielder with blazing speed and who as a lad of twelve had most probably watched the great pitcher perform in Clinton. That outfielder was Billy Hamilton.

With such a rich quantity and quality of baseball being played in and around his hometown, it is no surprise that the game attracted the interest of the young Billy Hamilton. He honed his baseball skills on empty lots, in open fields, on the Clinton Commons, now known as Central Park, and, whenever possible, on one of the regulation fields in town. One of those fields today enjoys a national historic reputation. Fuller Field, located on the north end of High Street, Clinton's main thoroughfare, has been hosting ballgames since before 1878, and was recognized in 2007 as the oldest continuous-use baseball diamond. Fuller Field's principal competition in this regard came from Labatt Park in London, Ontario, which opened in 1877. Labatt's claim, however, is tainted by the fact that its ball field's configuration changed several times since its inception. The layout of the Fuller Field diamond is exactly the same as it was 130 years ago. Perhaps as important for baseball aficionados as the Guinness certification is the acceptance of the authenticity of the Fuller Field claim by the Society for American Baseball Research, whose representative stated:

> It is clear that baseball has been played on this location at Fuller Field since 1878 without fail. It is also clear that the core diamond itself has not substantially changed its location within the playing area since that time. And it is clear that other fields across the nation and in Canada have later dates of origin, changes in the core diamond, or an unfortunate demise due to the natural march of time and development.[11]

At 5'6", Billy Hamilton was small even for his era, but his 165-pound body was packed into a burly, compact frame. Barrel-chested, with bulging forearms and powerful calves and thighs, he was described most frequently by the sportswriters in Philadelphia and Boston as "stocky," "thickly-built," "stubby," or even "stout." Notwithstanding his body type, he was, without question, the fastest "sprinter" (as runners were then called) of his time. A left-handed "slap" hitter and a masterful bunter, Billy is frequently mischaracterized both in print and online as having been a right-handed thrower. This inaccuracy ultimately was corrected by one who must be considered an irrefutable source: Billy's daughter. In April 1978, Clifford Kachline, then historian of the Baseball Hall of Fame, wrote to Billy's only surviving daughter, Dorothy [Hamilton] Starr, with the following query:

> Did Billy throw righthanded or lefthanded? ... We know he batted lefthanded but some references in our Billy Hamilton file state he threw righthanded while others claim he threw lefthanded. Similarly, some record books list righthanded and others list lefthanded. Would you know which is correct?[12]

Mrs. Starr's succinct response clarified an issue that had been unresolved in baseball record books for half a century: "My father threw left-

Line drawing from the *Boston Globe*, June 13, 1900. Hamilton, often inaccurately described as having thrown right-handed, is correctly represented here with a gloved right hand. The accompanying sketch depicts a fine play by Jimmy Collins, the Boston third baseman and future Hall of Famer.

handed. I am glad I can give you this information."[13] For those who may doubt Mrs. Starr's memory on this issue, there is further visual evidence that proves Hamilton was a left-handed thrower. On June 13, 1900, the *Boston Daily Globe* published a sketch that depicted Billy making a spectacular catch in a game the previous day against Pittsburgh. Realizing he could not reach the ball, Hamilton "stuck up his mitt, blocking the ball, and caught it in his bare hand as it came down."[14] The sketch shows Hamilton jumping to block the ball in his *gloved right hand*, leaving his *left (throwing) hand* free to make the grab of the ball when it came down.

Although no records exist of Sliding Billy's earliest teams or baseball mentors, we can begin to get an idea of his approach to basic aspects of the game—hitting, fielding, base running—by examining statements that he made about these topics during and after his career, and from observations made about him by his contemporaries, including players and sportswriters. Since there is no extant photo or film of Billy Hamilton hitting or even taking a swing, we can be thankful that *Sporting Life*, in June of 1898, decided to dedicate a few lines to this topic:

> Hamilton has a very peculiar attitude at bat. Probably no player stands so far away from the plate as he does.... He stands with his right foot well in front of his left, using the former as a pivot. Thus he is able to bunt, to hit to left field, and can also throw his power into a drive.... He is one of the most scientific batsmen in the country.[15]

Billy had a distinct philosophy of hitting. On the surface, his two known statements about the issue appear contradictory. Responding to a *New York Times* reporter's query about how he always seemed to manage to hit "cleanly," he responded:

> It is due to the quickness and the eye action. A batsman, nowadays, must think and act very quickly to make a good showing against the present pitching. Good hitting, after all, is very much of a knack. You will notice the good hitters are comparably few in number, and if a player is not a good batsman when he enters the big league, he rarely becomes one afterward. In other words, a batsman is born. I do not believe there is such a thing as practice in batting. I know I never practice myself. Some players will pass a good part of a morning practicing hitting, using as many pitches as they can get. I think they overdo the thing: they work so much and they wonder why it is they cannot bat effectively in the game. A good batsman must make a study of the pitcher. He must understand his peculiarities and know how to meet his delivery in a style that is conducive to safe hitting.[16]

The previous April, however, commenting on spring training, Billy stated that

> Spring Training is only valuable to me so far as it enables me to cultivate my batting eye.... If a man takes good care of himself during the winter he is ready in a jiffy to field, but it takes time to get back your batting skill. I never hit hard at the ball in the spring, and think it is a mistake to swing too hard at the ball in the beginning. I take it easy and work myself by degrees to the proper point. All I want to do is satisfy myself that I can meet the ball just right.[17]

Perhaps we can conclude that for Billy, even a "born hitter" needs a little time practicing in order to get back in shape after a five-month layoff. His statements, nonetheless, confirm what his record attests to — Hamilton had no interest in setting out to drive the ball over the fence. Succinctly summarized, his approach might read like this: Perfect the timing of the swing, which will vary according to the type of pitch thrown. Know what the pitcher throws and when he throws it, and adjust the swing accordingly. Control the swing. Alter or adjust it as needed to be able to hit the ball cleanly and place it where you want it to go.

Hamilton's legendary patience as a hitter, as epitomized by his "Good Eye Bill" nickname, has been mentioned previously. In 1893, *Sporting Life* offered another observation about one of his plate strategies: "Hamilton is a very tricky batsman. He has a good eye for a ball and if he sees an incurve approaching that is not too speedy, he will let it hit him."[18] A sportswriter's brief comment about a Philadelphia matchup with Washington in September 1892 gives us a clear idea of Billy's bunting skills. "Hamilton's bunting was the feature of the game; three times he pushed the ball gently toward third and sprinted to first before [third baseman Paul] Radford could propel the leather to [first baseman Henry] Larkin."[19]

Despite the fact that he ranks fourth in putouts for nineteenth century outfielders [20] and regularly made spectacular, nearly impossible acrobatic catches, fielding was Billy's weak point, and he knew it. Bob Allen, a Philadelphia shortstop who was Billy's spring training roommate in Jacksonville in 1890, the year Hamilton joined the club, revealed in 1897 that

> it is a fact ... that Billy was in the dumps when he first joined Philadelphia. He would pretty nearly cry because of his fielding. He could hit and run better than any of us but he was afraid his fielding would cause his downfall. I used to cheer him up as best I could. Now look at him. He is one of the greatest in the league, not only in base running and batting, but in fielding as well.[21]

Early on with Philadelphia, Billy played left field, and it was reported that "in the west [among the Western teams in the league, such as Chicago, and St. Louis] they think Hamilton plays the deepest left field in the league."[22] By 1893, however, he had staked his claim to center field, and his positioning there was described in the following manner: "Hamilton plays more of a left-centre field, and thus is enabled to stop hits that might yield two or more bases if he played more nearly in the centre of the field."[23] Also by this time, his depth of play was now determined by his knowledge of the hitters. "Billy Hamilton had [Cap] Anson down pat in the fourth. He came in about 75 feet behind Bobby Lowe [second baseman] and your uncle [one of Anson's many press nicknames] popped up a little fly which Hamilton caught without moving half a dozen feet."[24] In his lengthy obituary in the *Sporting News* in December 1940, one of Billy's unusual positioning styles in center field was recalled.

He often would stand in center field, half facing the left fielder, with hands clasped behind him and head turned over his left shoulder while his eyes watched the man at the plate, then chase off like a flash with the crack of the bat and pull the ball down from an almost impossible angle and position.[25]

Comments about Hamilton's running, as may be expected, are more numerous. Describing his 1889 season with Kansas City, during which he stole 111 bases, *Sporting Life* summarized his running skills in this fashion: "Hamilton combines the three qualities of a great baserunner: he always gets a good start, is a fast runner, and can slide with the best of them."[26] In 1936, Bobby Lowe, who played with Billy in Boston in the late 1890s, and who had the distinction of being the first player to hit four home runs in a game, described his former teammate's running style in an interview. "Billy was very fast, took a good lead off the base, used good judgment, and took advantage of the slightest weakness a pitcher might have had. He was a head first slider, and could go to either side of the base, leaving only his hand for the opposing player to touch."[27] In 1951, Fred Clarke, a Hall of Fame outfielder for Louisville and Pittsburgh in the Hamilton era, confirmed the dangers of Billy's head-first sliding style: "Billy Hamilton of Boston was the most daring base-stealer in the league when I was at Louisville.... He was a head-first slider and I copied his style. But not for long. One day in Washington I stole second but the second baseman, whose name I forget, tagged me to black both eyes and break my nose."[28] The only quote we have from Billy on the subject appeared in a September 1891 number of the *Philadelphia Inquirer*, which itself relied on a long passage from the *Cincinnati Commercial Gazette* that reacted positively to Billy's base-stealing philosophy.

> There is hardly a game that Hamilton doesn't have one or more stolen bases, still there is no one who can say he is working for a record. He always plays to win, but if his club is so far behind in a game that there isn't a possible chance for victory, Hamilton never runs the risk of an injury by stealing a base just to improve his standing in the averages. "They tell me," he said at the Gibson House yesterday, "that [Arlie] Latham is after the base running championship of the league. Well he can have it for all I care. If I can win a game by stealing a base, I'll take big chances to do it, but in a game that isn't close, you'll never hear of me running bases. There is nothing in it for a ballplayer, as he takes too many chances of being crippled."[29]

Ironically, this approach, praised by the Cincinnati press as an example of a player who is not preoccupied with personal records, was, as we shall see, later cited by some Philadelphia sportswriters as being an example of "slacker" behavior. Nevertheless, the dangers of base stealing mentioned by Billy were real in the rowdy era of baseball. Runners like John McGraw regularly spiked defenders, who regularly responded in kind. In an age prior to the discovery and use of antibiotics, the greatest fear of either type of spiking incident was of infection of the wound, which, in a worst-case scenario, could result in amputation. Likewise noteworthy is the fact that team owners of the era were under no contractual obligation to pay a player if he were disabled on the field.

A final area of preliminary consideration of Hamilton's approach to the game deals with his general philosophy with regard to aggressive play. The intense "rowdyism" of the period that has been mentioned previously, has been succinctly summarized by Bill James: "The tactics of the Eighties were aggressive; the tactics of the Nineties were violent. The game of the Eighties was crude; the game of the Nineties was criminal. The baseball of the Eighties had ugly elements; the game of the Nineties was just plain ugly."[30] Given this state of affairs, it is instructive to compare Billy Hamilton's concept of aggressive base running with that of another base-stealing outfielder of a later era, Ty Cobb, whose aggressive tactics are legendary.

In August 1891, for example, during a game against Cincinnati, Billy walked, stole second, and was rounding third after Sam Thompson doubled when third baseman Arlie Latham stood in his way, grabbed him by the shirt, and held him. "Hamilton, however, broke away and reached the plate safely. Latham did some very dirty ball playing, and had it been any other player but Hamilton, Mr. Latham's eye might be in mourning for his conduct."[31] Latham was a base-stealing rival of Billy's, whose claim of superiority in this regard was being challenged by the man from Clinton. Clearly, Billy's tactics did not include violence or retaliation, even when he would not have been blamed for such a reaction. Earlier that same year in a game against Boston, Billy drew a walk, and used an unusual tactic to distract pitcher Harry Staley.

> Once on the bag he danced around in a most tantalizing way, drawing several throws from pitcher to first, but like a flash, Hamilton dropped to the ground on each throw, and with a comical smile, winked at Staley ...

when least expected he dashed off to second, which he stole in safety, and as Staley turned to catch him, he winked the other eye."[32]

Billy's tactic was successful. He later scored on a single by Ed Delahanty.

Ty Cobb's method of "getting into another player's head" was far more radical. During spring training in 1917, Cobb's Tigers were hosting the New York Giants at their out-of-the-way training site of Waxahachie, Texas. Giants second baseman Charley "Buck" Herzog, angered that Cobb had arrived late and caused a delay in the start of the game, made fun of the "big shot" and called him a "redneck from Georgia" in front of the crowd. After the start of the game, Cobb singled to right, and then called down to Herzog from first base, "Now I'm coming, you whore's son."[33] When Cobb made his move, "Herzog, taking catcher Lew McCarty's throw, advanced up the line to tag him. Cobb went for the baseman rather than the bag, ripping Herzog's pants from thigh to ankle. Herzog threw punches. T.C. [Cobb] reciprocated, then both teams got into it."[34]

Despite their relative scarcity and brevity, Sliding Billy's own words about his approach to the game, when coupled with opinions about him offered by contemporaries who played against him or saw him play, paint a clear picture of a player who combined intuition, an analytical approach to the game, and hands-on knowledge to develop his playing strategies. These methods would hold him in good stead years later when he began his long minor league managerial career. They likewise will be useful to recall when examining the specifics of Billy's major league career in chapters three and four.

Back in Clinton, however, the youthful mill worker still had much to accomplish. When not working or playing ball, Billy was known to frequent Dexter's Roller Rink in town, where he developed his skills at roller skating, another Victorian sports fad, on the rink's hardwood floors. For Americans in the early years of the nineteenth century, "there was no obvious merit in sport—certainly no clear social value to it and no sense that it contributed to the improvement of the individual's character or the society's moral or even physical health."[35] By the second half of the century, however, Americans were favoring an "energetic, dynamic style in all aspects of life."[36] Sport was an obvious way to implement such a lifestyle. A "physical fitness mania"[37] seized the country, bringing with it a new interest in general exercise, gymnastics, and overall physical fitness.

Roller skating was the Victorian physical fitness craze of the 1870s; bicycling would replace it in the 1890s. First made fashionable by the New York City elite who discovered it while vacationing in Newport, skating had originated in the 1860s. A decade later the sport spread across the country, with rinks composed of hard maple floors built in nearly every city and town. Typically, "the rinks had a gallery above, where spectators could watch the show below. New York's Casino Rink accommodated one thousand spectators and one thousand skaters."[38] Dexter's rink in Clinton imitated this design, thus enabling it to serve also as the Clinton Opera House, and as an arena for a form of hockey played on skates called roller polo, a sport that enjoyed professional status in New England and one that Billy also mastered. Late in her life, Sliding Billy's eldest daughter, Ethel, suggested there were other attractions for Billy at Dexter's beside the roller rink and roller polo. "Most people don't remember, but my dad was a wonderful skater, and played polo on skates at Dexter's Rink in Clinton. I believe that is where he met my mother, who was an accomplished skater herself."[39]

Few people remain today who knew both Billy and the future Rebecca Hamilton personally. Fortunately for baseball history, one who does, the Hamilton's granddaughter, Phyllis Reynolds, age 91, of Arlington, Massachusetts, remains as perky and vivacious as she was three-quarters of a century ago. Phyllis has been an invaluable resource in the task of constructing an accurate portrait of Billy and Rebecca's personal life.[40]

Billy cut a handsome figure in his late teens. Fair-skinned with large, wide-set eyes and a square jaw, his boyish good looks made him appear younger than his age. He eschewed the popular handlebar moustache of the era for a clean-cut look, with close-cropped, carefully groomed hair parted high on the left side. It was a style he would wear to the end of his days. The accomplished roller skater who stole his heart, Rebecca Jane Carr, was the eldest of three children born to farmer Henry Carr and wife Eliza Jane, of nearby South Lancaster. Like the Hamiltons, the Carrs immigrated from Northern Ireland, although they preceded Samuel and Mary by a decade in this regard. Rebecca Jane, who was known affectionately as "Jen" by Billy, was a petite, quiet, lady-like young woman. Nevertheless, she also possessed the practicality and common sense of a farmer's daughter. Apart from being attracted to each other by the specifics of their personalities, from the moment they met, Billy and Rebecca were aware that they also shared a common ethnic, religious, and class background. It was a good match. It would last almost fifty-three years.

From this point on in his life, events in Billy's personal and professional paths would be inextricably bound together. His first taste of professional ball turned out not to be so "professional" after all. He signed with Waterbury, which had fielded an Eastern League team the previous two years, and whose ranks contained four players from the disbanded Cleveland National League team. In 1887, however, the league disbanded, and the team returned to an amateur state-league status. "In the next year [1887] the league was demoralized and the teams dropped out one by one, but Waterbury held on through the season.... In 1888 the season opened with only local players, which [sic] entered a state league."[41] While the Eastern League was collapsing around him that year, Hamilton played excellent ball. Although he wasn't in the lineup on April 30, 1887, when Waterbury opened the season, his debut the next day against Bridgeport made a statement. Batting seventh and playing right field, he garnered three hits, including a triple, in four trips to the plate. That performance earned him a starting spot for the next game against Springfield, and he celebrated by going two-for-four (a double and a triple) walking twice, and stealing a base. From then on he was fixture in the lineup. Over the next six games he would go 15-for-30, and in the succeeding 47 games, through August 8, he would hit safely in 41 contests. By early July, however, Bridgeport and Springfield had pulled out of the league. New Haven and Hartford soon followed, leaving only Danbury and Waterbury. The two teams played seventeen contests against each other through season's end. The Eastern League was no more, and Billy Hamilton, who had banged out 116 hits in 71 games for a .371 average, was out of a job.

It was an extremely difficult time to make a living in professional baseball. The collapse of the Union League and the downsizing of the American Association from twelve to eight teams after the 1884 season not only eliminated forty percent of the National League and American Association playing slots, but also created a glut of released players from disbanded teams and leagues who were seeking positions on teams in regional associations like the New England and Eastern leagues. In this period of great uncertainty in Billy's professional life, tragedy struck in his personal life. In January 1888, his father, Samuel, died at age 57. The cause of death was listed as "paralysis," a vague description for multiple diseases of the era. Having already signed to play with Worcester of the New England League for the upcoming season, Billy married Rebecca in Clinton, two months after his father passed away. The twenty-two-year-old now was the sole provider for his mother, sister Mary Jane, and his new bride, a responsibility he would continue to assume for the next six years, at which time sister Mary Jane married barber Frederick Walsh and moved to his nearby hometown of Sterling with her mother in tow.

As children of the Victorian era, Billy and Rebecca's actions during this period of their lives would be efforts that represented the best of Victorian virtues: responsibility, perseverance, hard work, self-discipline, thrift.

Rebecca Carr Hamilton, circa 1887 (courtesy Hamilton Starr).

After a banner half-year at Worcester, Billy's stellar performance there and some help, as we have seen, from umpire John Gaffney, would earn him a contract with his first national professional team, the Kansas City Cowboys, in August 1888. The following year he led the American Association with 111 stolen bases in 137 games, and attracted the interest of Harry Wright, manager of the National League Philadelphia Phillies. Joining Philadelphia in 1890, he won the league batting title in his second year with the team, and in 1894 had his greatest offensive season.

The rhythms of his personal life followed those

of his professional life. Celebrating his first year with the Phillies, he and Rebecca purchased a home on the north side of Clinton in December of 1890. It was the first home that anyone in either the Hamilton or Carr families had ever owned. It would remain the family homestead for the next twenty-seven years. In 1891, Billy bought a second, smaller property in town, and in 1894, he partnered with another Clinton resident to purchase a 36,000-square-foot tract of land on High Street, on which they built a multiple-family apartment house. Hamilton must have had an innate compulsion to stay close to a baseball diamond, because all three of his properties were located less than a

Billy Hamilton, circa 1890 (courtesy Howard "Skip" Reynolds).

five-minute walk from Fuller Field. A few years later, Billy bought out his partner and became sole owner of the apartment house. Until its demolition in the late twentieth century, this complex would be known in Clinton as the Hamilton Block.

A brief note in *Sporting Life* gives a good indication that the Hamiltons' self-discipline and famous frugality were paying off: "Billy Hamilton, according to Frank Selee [Boston's manager], has a leery eye for a rainy day, and during his nine years as a professional ballplayer has accumulated $15,000 worth of property that yields him an excellent dividend."[42]

During this same period, Billy and Rebecca would celebrate the birth of two daughters, Ethel and Mildred, but mourn the loss of a third child, Violet. While census records and Phyllis Reynolds' statements confirm this sad event, no birth or death certificate exists for Violet, suggesting she was either stillborn or died during childbirth. To the end of their lives, Billy and Rebecca would celebrate the memory of their lost daughter by planting violets and lilies of the valley in their garden each year.

Over the six-year period from 1888 to 1894, Billy's annual salary averaged less than $3,000 per year. For his four months' work at Worcester he earned $100 per month.[43] His full year in Kansas City (1889) may have earned him as much as $2,000. The 1890–92 seasons were banner years for Billy in Philadelphia, as he was paid between $3,000 and $3,400 per season. League and team-imposed salary caps lowered his annual income to $1,800 for 1893 and 1894. While a $3,000 annual salary average was approximately seven times the amount that a mill worker of the era could earn in a year, Billy at the time was providing for his mother, sister, wife, and two daughters, and paying mortgages on two of his three properties (the 1891 purchase was in cash —$600). Thrift, a respected Victorian virtue, was Billy's middle name during these years, and an awareness of his circumstances at this time in his life adds a dimension to his previously mentioned comment, "I have all that I want," made in response to the taunts of his profligate Philadelphia teammate Ed Delahanty.

The two-story Hamilton homestead at 75 Forest Street still stands today. Although its original windows have been replaced, siding installed, and the front porch glassed in, its foundation suggests the home's real age, and city documents confirm it. The home is located on a large lot on a quiet side street just off High Street, Clinton's version of Main Street. Beyond the backyard, a stand of hardwood trees slopes down to the Nashua River, which at this point is no more than a shallow, swiftly running stream some twenty feet wide. It was a fine place for raising children. The "dominant goal" for both working-class and middle-class people of the Victorian era was the "single-family detached home."[44] With the purchase of the Forest Street home, Billy and Rebecca achieved this goal two years into their marriage. Victorians described such a modest home as a *laborer's cottage*:

> a term that served as a universal description of all types of unpretentious frame (sometimes brick) houses between 1870 and 1910 with modest touches of the Italianate, Eastlake, or Queen Anne styles. Chicago's *Real Estate and Building Journal* listed a one-story, frame cottage with a parlor, kitchen, and two bedrooms for $600 in 1886–87. For slightly more than double this price, a worker might buy a two-story cottage, including an indoor bath, fireplace, and three bedrooms. A Queen Anne–style dwelling of seven rooms (including a sitting room, a parlor, and a tub bath) complete with a tower, cost $1,900.[45]

Eliminate "complete with a tower" from the last sentence and you have a nearly perfect description of the Hamilton house on Forest Avenue

2. Early Innings   55

Billy and Rebecca's "laborer's cottage" at 75 Forest Street, Clinton, Massachusetts. It was purchased in 1890 and remained the family homestead until 1917, when the Hamiltons moved to Worcester.

in Clinton. A block away, on High Street, stand more elaborate, elegant homes from the same period. The Victorians dubbed their style "Eclectic Manse," described as a "massive, asymmetrical collage of a house," that exuded "breadth, depth, and expanse ... the manse ... implied affluence and achievement through its elaborate, monumental façade."[46] After Billy signed with Philadelphia in 1890 for the highest salary that he would ever earn as a ballplayer, one might readily understand he and Rebecca might be tempted to purchase a house of this type, one which would present a clear, external image of success. They chose instead the "laborer's cottage."

Cultural historians have noted the changing role of the home that occurred during this era. Earlier in the century the home was a center of economic production, "but with the decline of the family farm and handcrafts, it was left free to concentrate more than ever upon the socialization of the children. The emphasis shifted from the home as a place of productive activity to the home as a place of family community."⁴⁷ While no photos exist of the interior of the first Hamilton homestead, a remarkable narrative penned by a lifetime resident of Clinton in 1925 provides a unique glimpse inside a typical Victorian home in Clinton like that of Billy and Rebecca.

> Here is a picture of an average home in Clinton about the year 1898. It was a cottage house of five or six rooms, or an apartment of the same size in a double house or a corporation block. The first floor contained the living room, dining room, and kitchen, with two bedrooms or perhaps three upstairs. In the cottage house was an attic, finished or unfinished. The living room had a certain collegiate air about it. It had a cushioned window seat and a box couch with many decorated cushions, a couple of Morris chairs, a desk of the style known as Larkin.... A bright carpet was cut to the size of the room. Walls were adorned with family portraits in crayon ... an engraving of the Colosseum, Millet's "Angelus" or Grace Darling in a boat.... There were a few books, perhaps Dickens, Scott, or Hawthorne in sets, with Longfellow and Whittier for the poets, and always a few library books scattered about the room.... In the dining room a table, round or square, could be made larger by inserting or removing leaves. A lamp hung over it, and a picture of fish, feathered game, or impossible fruit adorned the walls. Perhaps a sideboard had the best silver in view, and souvenir plates showed in a rail on the wall. The room was apt to be a secondary living room when daughter grew up and demanded the living room of an evening for purposes her own. A Glenwood or Crawford range was in the kitchen, with pots of geraniums in the windows. Comfortable wooden chairs and cane seated rockers were there. Some families used it more than the living room.... Parlors were going out. Some families had them, but those that did seldom heated them in the winter. Bedrooms were apt to be furnished in sets, but iron and brass beds were popular. If the bed was iron, it was enameled white and the lady of the house was apt to get a brush and enamel all the bedroom furniture to match it, to the disgust of later collectors of antiques. Floors were carpeted, sometimes with straw matting, sometimes with braided rugs. The former was cold to the feet. A strange article of furniture known as a "commode" was often seen. It was provided with a china bowl and pitcher, very ornate. Guests were supposed to use them, but in practice, the family washed at the kitchen sink, in relays. Bathrooms were coming in, however.... Most houses had a large entry or hall. It was equipped with a "tree" large enough to hold all the family wraps ... a proper house had a rather large cellar and the family stored large quantities of vegetables and apples....⁴⁸

Fundamental to the Victorian cult of domesticity was a "family centered culture,"⁴⁹ in which the mother was exalted: "The mother was an acknowledged guardian of moral, religious, and other cultural values among Victorians, and the house was her sphere of influence."[50] This practice was new to modern history: "What was innovative in Victorian culture ... was the new importance of the mother's position."[51] The importance of the wife and mother in the Hamilton family was quietly yet significantly endorsed by the fact that the deed to the couple's homestead bore the name of a single person: Rebecca Jane Hamilton. Phyllis Reynolds recalls her grandmother fondly as an impeccable housekeeper, in whose gleaming waxed floors one could see one's face reflected, and as one who always dressed formally, even when she left the house to run errands.[52] Within the home, the particular domain of the Victorian mother and wife was the kitchen. "Even those women who had a domestic servant usually did their own baking, since most considered this culinary art a special demonstration of their domestic skill."[53] Not surprisingly, therefore, Phyllis Reynolds reports that her grandmother's forte in this regard, much to the delight of all, was the preparation of homemade pies and donuts.[54]

Another indication of Billy's own commitment to the Victorian family-centered culture comes from an unexpected source. Each week, numbers of the journal *Sporting Life* contained a section entitled "News and Comment," in which pithy, one- or two-sentence bites of information on players, managers, and owners were recorded. Their content varied widely, dealt with both on-field and off-field activities, and was frequently self-reported. During his years as a player and player-manager, a striking element of the comments made in *Sporting Life* about Billy Hamilton is the large number that deal with his family: "Hamilton missed his first game of the season on Friday on account of an interesting event [the birth of his daughter Ruth] that was expected to occur in the family."[55] "It was expected that Billy Hamilton would be on hand, but illness of his children prevented."[56] "Hamilton delayed from Spring Training due to illness in his family."[57] "Manager Billy Hamilton will have the sympathy of his friends in the long illness of his wife, who is a severe sufferer of rheumatism."[58] "Billy Hamilton will have the sympathy of the interested in the recent death of his mother at the age of 76 years."[59]

Victorian values were tools that Billy and Rebecca Hamilton employed to create a stable, loving home life, to become financially secure, and to transition in rapid fashion from the working class to the middle class. Some of these same qualities — hard work, perseverance, and self-discipline — would also be the virtues that would help establish Billy as a premier baseball player on the national professional scene.

Back in early spring of 1888, Billy still had a lot to prove, and a desperate need to succeed in his career with Worcester of the New England League. Even Mother Nature refused at first to cooperate. On March 11, a classic nor'easter, dubbed "The White Hurricane" and "The Monster Storm," dropped forty to fifty inches of snow from New York to Maine. The storm prevented most players from getting in shape and delayed the start of the season until April 28. Billy Hamilton, however, was ready. In his first game as a professional, he played center field, hit fifth in the order, banged out two doubles, stole a base, and scored a run against Lowell. The stolen base, curiously absent from his repertoire at Waterbury the year before, became Billy's forte in the New England League. He averaged one per game through June, stealing four against Portland on May 24, and three each against Portland and Lowell on May 29 and 30, respectively. By July 28, when he played in his last contest in the league, he had 87 hits and 70 stolen bases in just 61 games, and was hitting a sizzling .352. At Worcester, he briefly would also have the opportunity to do what few professional players would be able to do for the next seventy years — play defense behind an African American pitcher. Armed with a sharp pick-off move and a devastating array of breaking pitches, left-hander George Washington Stovey, son of a white mother and a black father, had joined catcher Moses Fleetwood Walker of the Newarks of the International League the previous year (1887) to form the first African American battery in organized baseball.[60] He started at Worcester on June 9, 1888, and in a month of service won six games and lost five, with an earned run average of 2.30. Apparently, Stovey's petulant, temperamental nature, and not his race, was his downfall. He was released by Worcester a few weeks before Billy Hamilton left for Kansas City. Stovey would play most of the remainder of his career with all-black ball teams.[61]

The remarkable numbers that Billy put up at Worcester, and a kind word from Umpire Gaffney, would earn Billy, the teetotaling Sabbatarian who didn't curse or smoke, a spot on a team in the American Association, a major league organization that played Sunday ball, sold liquor at its games, and had lowered the standard National League ticket price from fifty cents to twenty-five in order to attract a less-genteel crowd. Few matches between player and league could have been less likely. On July 31, 1888, Billy packed his bags, kissed his new wife, said goodbye to his quaint, quiet New England hometown, and headed to Baltimore to catch up with his new team, which, though on the road at the time, played their home games in the wilds of eastern Kansas. Sliding Billy was now a Kansas City Cowboy.

3

Cowboys and Ponies

"Oh! He could run like a shot!"
— Millie Prior, Billy Hamilton's daughter

The American Association, of which Billy Hamilton's Kansas City team was a member, owed its existence in large measure to the imperial arrogance of the National League. In 1876, the National League, by a bloodless coup, successfully eclipsed the player-controlled National Association by rigorously addressing its predecessor's worst failings: irregular schedules, and gambling and game-fixing by players. Once it became the sole professional league on a national scale, the thereafter aptly named National League sought to consolidate its power through a series of restrictive, unpopular, and openly monopolistic measures that managed to anger players, owners, and many baseball fans alike. Players objected to the implementation of the reserve clause, "a continuing option on the services of a player,"[1] and to the practice of blacklisting any man who violated the league constitution. Many fans and owners on the other hand objected to league rules that limited the number of teams, mandated an admission fee of fifty cents in order to exclude undesirables, and prohibited both Sunday games and liquor sales at ball games.

In banning Sunday ball and liquor sales, National League president William Hulbert was appealing to prevailing cultural parameters of the mid–Victorian period, during which the sabbatarian and temperance movements flourished. By the 1880s, however, millions of European immigrants with somewhat different values had flooded the country's great industrial centers. A large portion of these were German Protestants and Italian and Irish Catholics, most of whom viewed the Sabbath not as a day to be given over exclusively to prayer and meditation, but rather as an opportunity for leisure and recreation. They likewise did not find the consumption of alcohol necessarily to be evil. These first- and second-generation working-class Americans could not afford a fifty-cent admission fee for a ball game, and their six-day workweek left them only Sundays for enjoyment of leisure activities, including spectator sports. President Hulbert's strictures were intended to maintain decorum, propriety, and traditional values in baseball, and thus attract an exclusively middle-class clientele. The restrictions' actual result was to alienate and frustrate a burgeoning class of new Americans who were eager to follow the national pastime. The new fans found a home as rooters for teams in the new American Association. President Hulbert never comprehended the irony of the fact that National League players were initially drawn almost exclusively from the working class — the same class he strove so vigorously to exclude as spectators from league parks.

Player dissatisfaction with Hulbert's rules led to the formation of the Union League in 1884, an experiment that would last only a year. Dissatisfied team owners and prospective owners had better luck. In 1880, Hulbert's National League suspended the Cincinnati franchise for violating its liquor and Sunday baseball codes: "Thus it happened that the city that just twelve years earlier had been the cradle of professional baseball ... found itself excluded from the one and only league in 1881."[2] Representatives from several large cities that had been excluded from the National League responded to Cincinnati's censure by founding the American Association, the first league to stand up to the National League successfully. The association began play in 1882, fielding teams in Cincinnati, Pittsburgh, Philadelphia, Baltimore, St. Louis, and Louisville. Dubbed initially the "Beer and Whiskey League" by its National League detractors, the association functioned through 1891, at which time it merged with the National League.

The influence of association values on the new, consolidated, post–1891 National League, known by the amalgam term "League Association," would be significant. Among the amendments to its revised constitution were a twenty-five-cent admission price in cities that desired it, the right to sell alcohol, and permission for Sunday ball in all cities where it was allowed, "although no club would be compelled to play on Sunday."³ Additionally, of the twelve teams in the new, consolidated League Association, only four—Chicago, Philadelphia, Boston, and New York—did not originate in the American Association. William Hulbert died of a heart attack in 1883 at age 50, and thus never lived to see all the "social ills" that he fought against become guidelines for his own National League teams when the merger with the American Association was formalized. Only one of his Draconian restrictions would last more than a decade, but that one, the hated reserve clause, would not be overturned for nearly one hundred years. Unfortunately, too many association players took their derogatory nickname, the "Beer and Whisky League," seriously. Philadelphia's Jerry Dorgan, Judd Birchall, Curt Welch, and Bob Matthews, for example, all died early deaths due to alcoholism, as did Toad Ramsey and Pat Beasley of St. Louis.

During the American Association's ten-year existence, twenty-five cities fielded teams for at least one year, with the number each year varying from six to thirteen. For two years, 1888–89, Kansas City, Kansas, was a host city. Located at the eastern edge of the Great Plains and at the junction of the Kansas and Missouri rivers, Kansas City functioned historically as a gateway leading both east and west. In the pioneer era it was a westward-bound stopping point on the Santa Fe and Oregon trails. After statehood (1861) and the completion of the Transcontinental Railroad (1869), the stockyards of such Kansas towns as Abilene, Wichita, and Dodge became final destination points for Texas cattlemen driving their herds to the railhead. All southern and western railroad lines through these cities and towns ultimately merged at Kansas City before heading east, and for this reason, it was often referenced in newspapers of the 1880s as "New Chicago."

In 1888, a group of Kansas City businessmen headed by John Speas successfully petitioned the American Association to establish a team in their city. Kansas City had experimented with major league teams twice in the past. In 1884 it fielded a team in the Union League. Of the eight teams that completed the 1884 Union League season, the Kansas City entry finished dead last, with a dismal record of 16 wins and 63 losses. An 1886 National League team produced similar results by finishing seventh in an eight-team league, with a record of 32 wins and 89 losses. Mindful of these previous failures, John Speas and his investors spent more than $18,000[4] on player contracts in 1888 in an attempt to finally bring the city a winning team. The majority of their first-year recruits, however, proved to be castoffs from other association teams. At midseason, Speas acquired the contract of a young player from the New England League for the bargain basement price of $200.[5] The player was outfielder Billy Hamilton, who would not single-handedly be able to turn around the Kansas City team. He would, however, become the only player who began his major league career with an American Association team to be named to the Baseball Hall of Fame.

Although Billy Hamilton had gained experience and maturity in his travels about New England while playing for Waterbury of the Eastern League and Worcester of the New England League, nothing could have prepared him for Kansas in the 1880s, where the Wild West still began at the city's limits. Only a decade earlier, lawman Wyatt Earp had resigned from the Dodge City police force and headed for Tombstone, Arizona, where in 1881 he and his brothers would have a fateful encounter with the Clanton gang. Kansas was still making news across the country as cowboy and gunslinger territory well beyond Hamilton's stay there. In 1892, the Dalton Gang rode into the town of Coffeyville and robbed two banks. In the ensuing gun fight with the townsfolk, all but one of the Dalton clan were shot dead. The jubilant defenders of Coffeyville commemorated their victory by taking grotesque photographs of the unsuccessful robbers' corpses posed alongside their smiling intended victims.

Although Kansas City was making strides toward modernity, a dispatch to *Sporting Life* in the spring of 1889 regarding a Cowboys home game against the Columbus Solons, during which Billy Hamilton played right field, provides a vivid example that the Wild West still made an occasional visit to town. "At the game yesterday—in deep centre field—a band of Indians stood guard over a herd of buffalo. Now and then the 'last of the race' stampeded, and it took Chief Orr and his men several minutes to round them up again.... The noble red men grew tired of the sport in the third inning and withdrew."[6] It may not be overly presumptuous to assert that this may be the only recorded incident of buffalo roaming center field during a game in the history of major league baseball.

On July 28, 1888, Billy Hamilton played his last game with his

Above and below: "Billy Hamilton, the Kansas City Cowboy, 1889. These originals were later used commercially in the Old Judge Tobacco baseball card series. Note the 12 inch square home plate of the era. Billy fields barehanded, as he would for nearly half of his major league career (courtesy Howard "Skip" Reynolds).

Worcester teammates against Lowell, going one-for-three and stealing two bases. At midpoint in the season, the New England League was in the process of falling apart. Portsmouth had disbanded in June, and Lynn and Salem would do the same in early August. For the second year in a row, Billy played in a professional league that would collapse and disband before the season ended.

Happy to have a job, Hamilton joined his new Cowboy teammates on the road in Philadelphia, and was in the lineup for the first time on July

31 against the Athletics at the Jefferson Street Grounds. It proved to be a rude awakening to the major leagues for the young man from Clinton. Leading off and playing left field, Hamilton went hitless in three plate appearances against Gus Weyhing, a lanky right-hander who hailed from Louisville. Billy's performance, however, was no worse than the rest of the team that day against Weyhing, who hurled a no-hitter, and added insult to injury by hitting a double and a triple in a 4–0 winning cause. The journeyman pitcher, who would be Hamilton's teammate a few years later on the Phillies, won 264 major league games in his career, although his production decreased significantly after the 60' 6" pitching distance was established in 1893.

From his first day in the league, Billy's chief challenge during his abbreviated 1888 stay with Kansas City was adjusting to the caliber of the major league pitching he was facing for the first time. For example, Gus Weyhing's partner on the Athletics that year, Ed Seward, would go 35–19 with an earned run average of 2.01. Brooklyn, Cincinnati, and St. Louis also had their aces. "Silver" King of St. Louis, thus nicknamed for his prematurely gray hair, was the league's dominant hurler, finishing with 45 wins and a remarkable 1.64 ERA. Bob Carouthers and the diminutive 5' 4" Mickey Hughes of Brooklyn would combine for 54 wins. Cincinnati had three 20-game winners, including Irish-born Tony Mullane, baseball's first ambidextrous hurler, whose good looks earned him the nickname "The Apollo of the [Pitcher's] Box" for his ability to attract ladies to the ballpark. In contrast, Kansas City's top three pitchers, Bill Fagan, Henry Porter, and Tom Sullivan, were a combined 31–64 for the season, and by the end of the following year, all were out of major league baseball. The difference in the pitching quality that Billy would experience from his team's opponents in this first year in the majors led to his posting the lowest batting average of his career (.264), although it was the second-highest mark on a team that hit just .218 overall. However, after going two-for-three and scoring two runs in a victory against Cleveland on August 10, the mid-season rookie was warmly praised by the Kansas City press when the Cowboys returned home from their road trip.

> Hamilton, the new fielder of the Cowboys, if he keeps up the playing of yesterday, is by far the strongest man the club has signed this year. He has everything necessary for a great ballplayer in his makeup. He is strongly built and is the best sprinter on the team.... He takes an excellent position at

bat and strikes out free and quick, throwing his body into the blow, and he has a good understanding of the game and is by far the best coacher the club has had this year.[7]

In a complimentary but factually inaccurate summary of Billy's career that was published by the *Sporting News* in 1940, the anonymous author offered the following explanation for Billy's low stolen base total (19) for Kansas City in 1888:

> On beginning his major league career at Kansas City, Hamilton came under the managership of Dave Rowe, veteran outfielder.... Rowe placed Hamilton, who had not reached his twenty-second milestone, in right field.... Southpaw Matty Kirby picked Hamilton off three times in a series.... Manager Rowe put a quietus on the ambitious burglar.[8]

In actuality, Billy had already turned twenty-two on February 15, 1888, five months before joining the Kansas City team. Additionally, neither David Nemec's *The Great Encyclopedia of 19th-Century Major League Baseball* nor Macmillan's *The Baseball Encyclopedia* lists a Matty Kirby in the league in 1888. Indeed, the only Kirby in the association that year was right-hander John Kirby, who played on Billy Hamilton's team. Most importantly, as indicated by the *Kansas City Star* on June 30, 1888, Dave Rowe was fired as manager of the team a month before Billy played his first game with the Cowboys. Hamilton played most of his games that year under the tutelage of Rowe's replacement, player-manager Sam Barkley. Billy stole nineteen bases in thirty-two games for the '88 Cowboys. (Official records state that he played in thirty-five, but my own review of the box scores indicates that he did not play on August 13, 14, and 26.) Had he had the opportunity to play for the entire season and maintain such a stolen-base pace, he would have finished with seventy-five, a total that would have placed him in the top ten of the league.

Before completing his first week with Kansas City, Billy did something that in all probability he had never done: he played an official ballgame on a Sunday. On August 5, Kansas City played the Athletics in Gloucester, New Jersey (the Athletics circumvented Philadelphia blue laws that prohibited Sunday ball by playing some of their Sunday home games in New Jersey). Later in his career, Billy was adamant about not playing on Sunday. While with Boston in 1898, for example, he "refused to play in Weehawker [sic] Sunday because he is opposed on principle to playing ball on the Sabbath."⁹ In 1902, *Sporting Life* reported that Hamilton turned down a player-manager position for the Eastern League's Providence team "because he doesn't want to play on Sunday."¹⁰ Whether his sabbatarian views were not yet solidified at age 22, or whether for simple financial expediency, Billy played Sunday games when required in 1888 and 1889, starting on August 5, 1888, when he went one-for-four in a losing cause versus the Athletics.

Hamilton's first full month in the major leagues was a shaky one. He was moved from lead-off to the sixth position in the order, and went one-for-twenty-eight between August 9 and August 30. He caught fire, however, in the first thirteen games of September, getting nineteen hits and batting .422. The local press attributed his improvement to the instruction of manager Bill Watkins, who also was new to the team, having taken over on September 8 for interim player-manager Barkley. "Hamilton is showing the effect of Watkins's coaching more than anyone else, and is improving rapidly."¹¹ Although Canadian-born infielder Watkins had only thirty-four games of playing experience in the big leagues (with Indiana in 1884), as a manager he led the Detroit Wolverines to their only National League pennant in 1887.

In what unexpectedly would be his last full game of the season, Billy had his best offensive performance, going four-for-six and scoring four runs in an 11–3 win over Louisville on September 18. In the first inning of the following day's game he suffered a serious injury that ended his season and had the potential to jeopardize his career. While two published accounts chronicled the injury, they differed significantly with regard to specifics. *Sporting Life* reported on September 26 that "Hamilton sustained a serious injury in sliding to second in the first inning. He spiked himself on the left ankle, severing an artery, and had to be carried from the grounds."¹² The *Kansas City Star* account of September 20, the day after the incident, provided more details:

> Day before yesterday Hamilton hurt himself so that he was not able to practice yesterday morning, but he went in yesterday afternoon only to receive another injury that will probably lay him off for the rest of the season. In the first inning yesterday he cut his ankle joint so badly that it had to be put in a plaster cast, and while the cast will have to stay on but a short while, he will hardly be able to play this year.¹³

After only six weeks in the major leagues, Billy returned to his Massachusetts home a month earlier than he had expected, unsure of

Kansas City Cowboys, 1889. Billy Hamilton is seated on the far right. Seated to the left of manager Bill Watkins (in formal attire) is shortstop Herman Long, who would later be Hamilton's teammate in Boston (courtesy Transcendental Graphics).

his baseball future. With Hamilton absent from the lineup, Kansas City went 5–14, finishing the season with a record of 43–89, forty-seven games behind the league champion St. Louis Browns, who took the pennant for the fourth consecutive year. The dominance of the Browns underscored a major weakness of the American Association. Like the National League, it too employed the reserve clause, which required a player to sign with the team he played with the previous year unless he was released. Therefore, the league's older, more established teams like St. Louis, Philadelphia, Brooklyn, and Cincinnati, were better able to maintain a rich pool of seasoned veterans, and consequently, ended up in the highest rankings of the league.

Over the winter, the Kansas City management tried to find a winning formula by replacing most of the 1888 starting lineup. The newfound talent proved to be less than talented. For newly signed rookie catcher Charlie Hoover and first-year pitchers Parke Swartzer and John

McCarty, the 1889 season would be their only season in the major leagues. For three other Cowboys with experience under their belts — pitcher Tom Sullivan, first baseman Dan Stearns, and utility man Jim Manning — it would be their last season. The need for the return of a healthy Billy Hamilton was pressing. One bright spot among the new acquisitions was rookie shortstop Herman Long from Chicago. After his apprenticeship-by-fire with the 1889 Cowboys, Herman would spend a decade with the Boston Nationals, where from 1896 to 1900 he once again would team up with Sliding Billy. Long, a solid .289 lifetime hitter with great fielding range, nevertheless holds one of baseball's least-coveted records.

> In the 1890s Boston's hard working Herman Long became an idol among Hub [Boston] baseball fans. There's little doubt that Long was an aggressive fielder. He still holds the major-league lifetime record for average chances per game by a shortstop. However, Herman was something less of surehanded. He has the unenviable distinction of having been charged with more errors — well over a thousand — than any man who has ever played the game.[14]

The Cowboys received good news in March of 1889: "W. R. Hamilton, one of the outfielders of the Kansas City baseball team, arrived in the city this morning, and he and his wife are at the Centropolis.... He is in good condition to take part in tomorrow's [exhibition] game."[15] The press undoubtedly was unaware that there was a special motivation for Rebecca to accompany Billy on the long return trip to Kansas City. The young couple were celebrating their first wedding anniversary.

A momentous national event occurring a few hundred miles south of Exposition Park in Kansas City also coincided with the opening of the 1889 baseball season. April 22, 1889, marked the start of the Great Oklahoma Land Rush, the official opening to settlers of a portion of former Indian Territory. At noon on April 22, while the Kansas City Cowboys were warming up for their game at Cincinnati, thousands of future homesteaders in wagons, on horseback, and on foot entered Oklahoma territory, staked out a parcel of unclaimed land, and then raced to file a claim of ownership. The Cowboys would lose their game that day, but in Oklahoma thousands of pioneers would win a chance at a new life on the Great Plains.

Billy Hamilton, showing no ill effect from his past year's ankle injury, was literally "off and running" as the season started. Batting second and playing left field, he went three-for-four, scored a run, and stole two bases in his first game against Louisville. The Cowboys went on to take four straight in the opening series against the Colonels. Leading off for Louisville and playing third base was a familiar figure — "Mr. Louisville Slugger" — Pete Browning, who was playing in his last season with Louisville's American Association team before moving on to the Cleveland Infants of the Players' League in 1890. Browning was one of the most eccentric players of the era. "The Gladiator," one of the game's most talented hitters, was an alcoholic semi-literate who was plagued by ear infections that could not effectively be treated and ultimately caused him to become almost completely deaf. His auditory condition, his frequent inebriation, or a combination of both, "made him sometimes appear to be in another world on the ballfield."[16] Pete hit over .300 in eleven of his twelve full seasons, and reached .402 in 1887. He is one of few to lead two leagues in hitting — twice in the American Association and again in the Union League during its only season (1884). Despite his remarkable hitting credentials, Browning has never been elected to the Baseball Hall of Fame, most probably, as William Curran suggested in 1985, due to his horrendous fielding.

> When Pete arrived in the majors he was tried at every position except catcher to determine where he would do the least harm.... The decision was moot. In 1886, for example, when Browning was well established as one of the American Association's top power hitters, he fielded .791. So far as I can determine, it is the lowest fielding average ever compiled by a major-league player for a full season at any position.[17]

As has been demonstrated by the cases of Mike Kelly and Ed Delahanty, illnesses or accidents, when combined with alcohol, exercised a deadly effect on many ballplayers of the era. This was true also for Pete Browning. He regularly sought relief in alcohol from his relentless ear pain, actually a condition called mastoiditis, and the illness in turn affected his balance and damaged his brain. He died in a mental hospital in 1905 at age forty-four.

Early in the Cowboys' 1889 season, Sliding Billy's head-first style of base stealing nearly sidelined him again. On April 20, in the fourth inning against Louisville, "Hamilton, in trying to make second, was hit in the head by Shannon [the Colonels' second baseman] and his jaw was badly hurt."[18] He recovered sufficiently the next day to go three-for-five in a ten-inning loss to Cincinnati in the Queen City's home opener. Billy brought a .400 average back to Kansas City for the Cowboys' home opener. In the first game he played there after being carried off the field with an ankle injury the previous September, he scored four runs and stole five bases, including a swipe of home, as the Cowboys again pounded the Colonels, 16–5. After stumbling in it next three series, going 2–9, Kansas City caught fire again, winning five straight series, including three of four games against the defending champion St. Louis Browns. Their fine start prompted *Sporting Life* to praise the "unexpectedly splendid showing made by [Manager] Watkins' kids."[19] Billy Hamilton was lauded for his success on the base paths: "Hamilton's base-running is something marvelous. On a slow catcher he will steal second every time, and third every other time."[20] Any doubts, either by himself or his team, about his major league abilities had now vanished. After thirty-five games, Billy led the team in hitting at .337, had scored forty runs, stolen twenty-four bases, and hit two home runs. During the Cincinnati series, April 30 through May 2, umpire John Gaffney did the officiating, and thus got a first-hand look at how his young referral from the Worcester team was progressing. Also in late April, Billy defensively was moved from left to right field, and quickly began demonstrating another aspect of his game. On May 1 he completed two double plays from that position with second baseman and former player-manager Sam Barkley. Soon afterward, he doubled up a man at first with Dan Stearns and teamed up with shortstop Herman Long on another double killing.

During these early months of the season, Billy also began to showcase a previously unheralded aspect of his baseball talents, one that highlighted both his bunting abilities and his selflessness as a player—the sacrifice bunt. Over the course of the season he would advance runners in this fashion three dozen times. The major league record for sacrifices in a game, four, is considered to have been set by "Gentleman Jake" Daubert, on August 15, 1914.[20] In reality, on that date in 1914, the fine hitting and fielding first baseman of the New York Superbas *equaled* a record set a quarter-century earlier by Billy Hamilton. On July 3, 1889, during a 19–10 rout of Columbus, Billy sacrificed four times, went two-for-three including a triple, scored three runs, and, playing in right field, executed a double play with second baseman Jim Manning. Jake Daubert's 1914 mark came in the first game of a doubleheader. In the second game, Daubert sacrificed twice, thus ostensibly setting a record of six sacrifices in consecutive games. In Billy Hamilton's next game after laying down four sacrifices, the first game of a doubleheader, he sacrificed three times, thus exceeding Daubert's mark of six sacrifices in two consecutive games by one. For good measure, Billy also laid down a sacrifice in the second game of the doubleheader, giving him a total of eight in three games.

Meanwhile, Exposition Park in Kansas City continued to be a venue that offered unique challenges to professional ballplayers. In addition to the buffalo stampede in center field that was previously mentioned, tornado-prone Kansas added spring weather challenges to the players' worries. During the May 6 game versus St. Louis, for example, "There was a small cyclone blowing, and the dust was so thick at times that players in the outfield could not be seen from the grandstand."[22]

The Cowboys' bubble began to burst in late May. Third baseman Jim Davis was laid up by injuries, rookie pitchers Swartzer and McCarty were ineffective, and veteran Tom Sullivan was getting pounded in almost every game he started. In one unfortunate outing, he walked four and hit two in the sixth inning against the Athletics, and all six men scored. In mid–June, they went 1–9 in series against Philadelphia, Columbus, and Cincinnati before returning to Kansas City for a homestand.

On June 28, in the first game of a doubleheader against Louisville, Billy Hamilton had a day that should be — but as yet is not — recorded in the record books. He banged out four hits and scored three runs. All four hits were triples. The feat was recorded the next day in the *Kansas City Star* in the following fashion:

> The feature of the game was the wonderful batting of Hamilton, who went to bat five times in the first game, and made four 3 base hits, being given his base on balls the other time.... The visitors played a strong game except in the fifth inning, when the club got rattled, and stupid playing allowed one of Hamilton's triples, and singles by Manning and Burns to net Kansas City five runs.[23]

By the time the game was reviewed in *Sporting Life*, in its July 3, 1889, number, the description of Hamilton's feat had changed significantly: "The feature of the game was Hamilton's great batting. He was four times at the bat, made four hits, three of them three-baggers."[24] One can only conclude that between the time of the *Kansas City Star* report the day after the game and the *Sporting Life* report, which was published four days later, the reporter for the latter publication, having read in the original description that the Colonels "by stupid playing allowed one of Hamilton's triples" and two singles to net a run, interpreted the triple instead as a muffed single or double that allowed Hamilton to take third base. The basis for such an interpretation remains unexplained. However, regardless of whether we consider Billy to have hit four or three triples that afternoon, a problem still exists in the record books.

Only two players — George Strief in 1895 and Bill Joyce in 1897 — have hit four triples in a game in the history of baseball, according to *The SABR Baseball List and Record Book*.[25] If the initial Kansas City report of the June 28, 1888, game is accurate, Billy's name should appear on that list as the first player to do so. SABR records list numerous players who have hit three triples once in a game (including Billy, who did so with the Phillies in 1891), but lists the name of only one player (Dave Brain, 1905) who has done so twice. If we believe the *Sporting Life* report, i.e., that Billy hit three triples in the game on July 28, 1888, then his name should be added to the list of those who have done it twice (1889 and 1891). In either interpretation, Hamilton shares a record, a fact that to date has not been acknowledged.

The Cowboys' downward slide continued through mid–July. They were in sixth place, with a record of 30–38. Rookie pitcher McCarty, who could not get along with Manager Watkins and was continually fined, was sold to the minor league St. Joseph, Missouri, team, leaving Kansas City with just four pitchers. They closed out July with seven straight losses on the road. Billy continued to do his part. He stole four bases, scored two runs, and completed a double play with first baseman Dan Stearns at Brooklyn on July 24, and hit a ninth-inning home run the next day in a losing cause. Errors, inexperience, and bad pitching took their toll. Herman Long was temporarily replaced by former Toledo infielder Billy Alvord at shortstop, and the new man committed two successive errors against Philadelphia in the ninth inning, opening the door for the Athletics to score six unearned runs and win the game, 12–10. At Columbus on August 4, an error by third baseman Jumbo Davis in the last inning allowed three runs to score in a 6–4 loss. The *Kansas City Star*, which in June had stated that "the big clubs may look out for us now,"[26] now proclaimed the team "a sore disappointment this year."[27] Home attendance, rarely more than a few thousand, dropped off dramatically in late August, when the team lost seven of eight games.

By September, Brooklyn had seized the lead in the association from perennial champion St. Louis, and Kansas City had fallen to 49–71, going 2–10 in its last dozen games. The local press lamented, "The big pot of money which Kansas City has spent strengthening has not enabled the team to rise above seventh place."[28] Although Billy Hamilton's batting average had dropped to .301, he was eighteenth in the league in that category at the end of the season, with 161 hits in 137 games. His 111 stolen bases led the league, he was fourth in runs with 144 and fifth in on-base percentage at .413. The Cowboys may have faltered, but the man from Clinton had come into his own as a professional player.

Just before Thanksgiving, President Speas announced that Kansas City was resigning its membership in the association. Poor attendance, an inability to attract a sufficient number of quality players, and the city's great distance from East Coast teams were all factors that contributed to the demise of major league baseball in Kansas City. Until the Dodgers and the Giants left New York for California seventy years later, Kansas City remained the farthest western outpost ever attempted by the major leagues.

In three years of professional baseball, Billy had seen the first two leagues he played in collapse and disappear, and the first major league team he played for resign from its league and disband. As difficult a situation as this may have seemed for him, his experience was quite common for players in the early years of baseball, as leagues, cities, owners, and players struggled to assume control of the national pastime. By the time Hamilton ended his major league career in 1901, that struggle would be over.

Sliding Billy received an early Christmas present in 1889. On December 21 he was sold to the National League Philadelphia Phillies for $3,000.[29] First reviews of him by the Philadelphia press were favorable: "Hamilton is modest. He is reported as wanting only $2,200 of the purchase money paid for his release, $3,000 in salary per season, and a five-year contract."[30] Purchased by the Cowboys from Worcester for $200 in July of 1888, he was purchased by the Phillies for $3,000 seventeen months later. His contractual value had increased fifteen-fold in seventeen months, and he had established himself as a highly regarded player:

> Hamilton of the Kansas City's ... is one of the finest outfielders in the profession, champion base runner of the Association, and a good, reliable hitter — one of your tricky bunters and sacrificers, a la [John Montgomery] Ward and [Arlie] Latham.[31]

The Christmas holidays must have been joyous for Billy and Rebecca. Although 1889 had been financially rewarding, Billy's salary would jump by at least one-third in Philadelphia. Most importantly, Billy would be much closer to home for a greater part of the season. Playing for the Cowboys, the closest opponents to home were in Brooklyn and Philadelphia. While Billy was competing at these venues, Rebecca might have been able to attend games, but Billy, in all probability, would not have been able to get back to Massachusetts for the entire season. With the Phillies during the upcoming 1890 season, Billy's home base would be a half-day's train ride from Rebecca. The team would make visiting stands in New York, Brooklyn, and, most importantly, in Boston, just thirty-five miles from Clinton. Playing for the Phillies, Billy would make more money and be much closer to his widowed mother, his sister, and his new bride. Rebecca and Billy also now could begin thinking about having a family of their own.

Baseball roots in the "City of Brotherly Love" run deep. As early as 1831, the Olympics amateur club was playing a version of the game in Philadelphia. The preamble of their constitution, published in 1837, provides a glimpse of a time when professionalism was the furthest thing from a player's mind:

> Whereas — Field Sports having from time immemorial been the favourite [sic] recreation of all classes of men, not only for the amusement they afford, the bracing and healthy vigour [sic] they impart to the human frame, and the hilarity and good feeling they promote; but for their manly and athletic character, and the generous and friendly emulation they encourage and uphold ... the undersigned, therefore, well assured that these characteristics ... have in no manner degenerated, and that the present age is not behind the taste for their enjoyment, when exercised with decorum and moderation ... hereby unite ourselves in a social compact for purposes hereafter specified....[32]

Forty years later, the Athletics, Philadelphia's entry in the professional National Association, won the first-ever professional circuit pennant by virtue of achieving the highest winning percentage (.759), even though the Boston Red Stockings had won more games. In the final three years (1873–75) of the National Association's five-year existence, Philadelphia fielded two teams in the league, the Athletics and the White Stockings (who changed their nickname to the Pearls in 1874). Both teams held their own, finishing third, fourth, or fifth in a league that at times had as many as thirteen squads. In 1874, diminutive (5' 8", 120 pounds) William "Candy" Cummings, the putative inventor of the curveball, won twenty-eight of the Philadelphia Pearls' twenty-nine season victories.

Upon the demise of the National Association, Philadelphia's Athletics joined William Hulbert's National League, and had the distinction of hosting the new professional circuit's first game on April 22, 1876. They lost the contest to the Boston club — now nicknamed the Red Caps — by a 6–5 margin, after having committed eleven errors. Unfortunately, their stay in the new league would be brief. After struggling with a 14–45 record, the team elected for financial reasons not to make their final road trip to play Western club rivals. They were expelled from the league for this offense by President Hulbert, and the city subsequently endured a half-decade without a professional baseball team.

In 1882, Philadelphia investors eagerly organized a team for the upstart American Association, which had challenged the National League's monopoly of professional ball. They chose to name their team the Athletics after its historic National Association predecessor. In their first season, the American Association Athletics garnered second place. The following year they took the association pennant on the strength of Philadelphia native Harry Stovey's offensive performance. Stovey set a home run record of 14 in 1883, hit .306, and led the league in doubles (31), runs scored (110), and games played (112).

Threatened by the American Association's success, the National League withdrew its circuit's ban on baseball in Philadelphia, and in 1883, the new National League Quakers took the field, vying with their American Association cross-town rivals, the Athletics, for the support of the city's fans. Competition briefly became more intense in 1884, when a new, short-lived association, the Union League, established yet another professional team, the Keystones, in town. Although the eighth-place-finishing Keystones and the Union League disappeared at the end of the 1884 season, two professional teams continued to represent their leagues in Philadelphia until the merger of the American Association and the National League in 1892. In 1885, the Quakers adopted a new nickname, the Phillies. It seemed to do some good, as they finished third, fourth, and second in the first three years following the change, after having finished eighth and sixth, respectively, in their first two years as the Quakers upon returning to the National League.

With the 1892 merger of the National League and the American Association, Philadelphia again became a one-team town. The Athletics disbanded, and the Phillies, for a brief moment, reigned supreme. In 1901 the National League monopoly in Philadelphia and across the nation ended with the formation of the American League, which established a new franchise with an old name — the Athletics — in Philadelphia to compete with the National League Phillies. Former Pittsburgh catcher Connie Mack was hired to manage the team. This new version of the Athletics would last longer than any of its predecessors, from 1901 to 1954, after which the franchise was sold to investors from Kansas City. Connie Mack would last longer than any manager in history, retiring from the A's in 1950 at the age of 87.

When Billy Hamilton arrived in Philadelphia in 1890, the Phillies were owned by Colonel John I. Rogers and Alfred J. "Al" Reach. It would be difficult to imagine two men who were greater opposites. Reach was born in London, England, in 1840, and his parents immigrated to New York when he was one year old. A left-handed second baseman credited with being the first to position himself off the base in shallow right field, he grew up playing baseball in Brooklyn and starred with the city's famous Eckford club. In 1863, Reach agreed to a professional contract with the Philadelphia Athletics for a salary of $25 a week, thus gaining him recognition as baseball's first "professional" ballplayer.[33] When the Athletics joined the first professional league, the National Association, in 1871, Al led them to a pennant with a .351 batting average. By the time he retired as a player five years later, "Reach's reputation as the greatest second baseman in baseball history was solidified by his selection to the first All-American team."[34]

A quiet, gentlemanly individual with prudent habits, Al Reach opened a retail, wholesale, and mail-order sporting goods business in 1874, and gradually built it into a lucrative enterprise. In 1883, buoyed by his economic success, he teamed with local lawyer John I. Rogers to purchase the Worcester Ruby Legs and brought the franchise to Philadelphia, first as the Quakers, and two years later as the Phillies. Beginning in 1883, he also began publication of the *Reach Official Baseball Guide*, an annual review of major league statistics.

John I. Rogers, co-owner of the Phillies, was a Philadelphia native. Admitted to the bar in 1865, he was elected city controller in 1880. Active in the state militia, Rogers served in a Philadelphia contingent that quelled the Pittsburgh labor riots of 1877, during which 20 workers were killed. After being appointed Judge Advocate General of the Pennsylvania National Guard with the rank of colonel by Governor Robert Pattison, Rogers' preferred appellation in the press thereafter was "Colonel Rogers." Contentious, contemptuous, and litigious, the Colonel, who served as the National League owners' legal counsel, also had a reputation for stinginess with his players. In 1894, Sam Thompson, the normally quiet and non-argumentative Phillies outfielder, openly criticized the team's owners "for providing the players second-rate railroad and hotel accommodations, and vowed to quit unless things improved. They did."[35]

Such rare concessions, however, did little to change Rogers' basic approach to his players' complaints: "When late 19th century Phils complained about management's skinflint ways, co-owner Colonel John Rogers snapped, 'If you're looking for a soft job, you should work in a sponge factory.'"[36] Despite being a lawyer, Colonel Rogers was not above the use of underhanded tactics on the ball field. During a September 1900 home game, for example, it was discovered that a wire had been run between the Phillies' center field clubhouse to a metal plate buried in the third base coaches' box. From the clubhouse, backup catcher Morgan Murphy would read opposing catchers' signals through a telescope and

> relay them, via electrical impulse, to the coaches' box, where the third base coach could pick them up via his metal spikes ... the National League requested that this new form of communication cease and desist immediately.... As for the Phillies' owner, the devious Colonel John Rogers (well, he was a Philadelphia lawyer) ... he thought this ploy was perfectly fair and legitimate.[37]

As unsavory as some of Rogers' tactics and attitudes appear, they were standard fare for the magnates of the era.

Each club owner operated his ball club like a medieval fiefdom. If the owners did little to improve their players unruly behaviors, they also did little to improve their circumstances ... the owners wouldn't try to curb spectator rowdiness, wouldn't do anything to improve umpiring, wouldn't build dressing rooms for opposing teams, and of course, wouldn't consider modifying the reserve clause.[38]

Rogers and Reach built or rebuilt several parks for the Phillies. The first, Recreation Park, built for the 1883 season, was located at Twenty-Fourth Street and Columbia Avenue, with seating for 6,500. In 1887, a second park seating 12,500 and popularly known as the Huntingdon Street Grounds, was constructed at Huntingdon and Broad streets in North Philadelphia. It was rebuilt after burning to the ground in late 1894, after which it was renamed the Philadelphia Ball Park. At the end of the 1902 season, Rogers and Reach sold the Phillies but retained ownership of the park. During a game there on August 8, 1903, a portion of the left field grandstand balcony gave way as a large number of fans congregated to view a disturbance on the street below. Several hundred fans fell thirty feet to the street. "In the twinkling of an eye the street was piled four deep with bleeding, injured, shrieking humanity struggling amid the piling debris."[39] Twelve were killed and more than two hundred injured in the city's deadliest sports disaster. Rotten beams were cited as the cause of the accident, and further investigation revealed that in the eight years that had passed since the park was constructed, the structure had not once been inspected by the City Bureau of Inspection. More than 80 lawsuits were filed over the incident. Although Rogers and Reach were originally found culpable for not having the wood structure inspected, the final U.S. Supreme Court ruling on the tragedy found that "neither the ballpark nor the ballpark's landlords were responsible for the accident. Both were absolved of all blame and financial responsibility."[40]

Philadelphia had finished second, third, and fourth, respectively, during the three seasons prior to Billy Hamilton's arrival — a refreshing change for Billy from the seventh- and eighth-place finishes during his seasons with the Cowboys. The Phillies had a solid fan base in a major eastern city, and had been in the league since 1883. "Big Sam" Thompson, a power-hitting outfielder whom they had acquired from Detroit the year before, had led the league in home runs (20) and RBIs (111) in his first year with the team. Pitchers Charlie Buffinton and Ben

Sanders combined for 63 wins. Speedster Jimmy Fogarty in center field led the league with 99 steals. Although struggling defensively at shortstop and second base, promising second-year man Ed Delahanty banged out 72 hits in 56 games. The team had speed, power, and pitching. All they needed, perhaps, might be a spark in the form of a pesky hitter who could run like the wind.

The Phillies pilot since 1884 had two decades of managerial experience and was a legend in the sport. Harry Wright was born in England in 1835 and came to the United States at the age of three, when his father was named cricket professional at New York's St. George Cricket Club. Young Wright grew up playing both cricket and baseball, and as an adult played both sports professionally. Trained as a jeweler, he applied the best qualities of his profession — patience, precision, and attention to detail — to his baseball playing and managing career. After seasons with the Knickerbockers and the Gothams in New York, Wright moved on to Cincinnati, first as a cricket pro and then as a baseball pitcher and outfielder. Hired to develop and manage the 1869 Cincinnati Red Stockings professional team, he scouted and signed team members, designed their uniforms, and organized their famous cross-country tour. He later managed the Red Stockings in the National Association and Providence in the National League before coming to Philadelphia. Although his code of good sportsmanship and gentlemanly conduct seemed anachronistic when compared to the rowdy style of play that prevailed in the sport during his later years, his teams were models of efficiency and discipline. Players, fans, and owners referred to him affectionately as "Uncle Harry," and the Philadelphia press, not known for its courtesy, showed their own respect for "the father of the game" by referring to his team often as "Harry's Ponies," or "Harry's Colts."

Despite the rosy outlook in Philadelphia for the 1890 season, storm clouds had been gathering among players in the league since before the end of the previous season over the threat of the imposition of a salary cap of $2,500. While John Montgomery Ward, president of the Brotherhood of Professional Base Ball Players, was out of the country on a world tour organized by sporting goods magnate A.G. Spalding, the league passed the salary restrictions. Once again, however, the league underestimated the determination of those whom it had antagonized. Ward took insults from no one. Expelled in his first year at Penn State

University for attacking upperclassmen who had been feuding with him,[41] he went on to a stellar baseball career, first as a pitcher and then as a shortstop for New York's Gothams and Giants. In the off-season he took courses in political science and earned a law degree at Columbia University. His response to the National League's salary cap was to form a new association, the Players' League, for the 1890 season. "Entire rosters switched allegiance from the National League to the Players' League, and almost every great star threw his lot with the Brotherhood."[42]

Despite fielding a fine product, Ward was unable to convince his financial backers to hold on for a second year, and the Players' League disbanded at the end of the 1890 season. The league's pilfering of established players did, however, manage to create havoc in the National League's presumed lineups at the start of the season. After leading the last player uprising against major league baseball in the nineteenth century, "Monte" Ward played four more years in the National League before establishing a successful law practice, often representing players in grievances against the league. In later years he became a crack amateur golfer, competing in Europe and across the United States. John Montgomery Ward was elected to the Baseball Hall of Fame in 1964. "His plaque mentions neither the Players' League nor the Brotherhood."[43]

The tumultuous state of baseball affairs at the start of the 1890 season proved beneficial for Billy Hamilton as he began his career with the Phillies, but bad for the Phillies as a team. Both pitching aces, Buffinton and Sanders, jumped ship and would pitch across town for the Players' League Philadelphia Quakers. All the infielders except second baseman Al Myers had made the same move, as did center fielder Jimmy Fogarty. Ed Delahanty also broke the reserve clause in his contract and went back to his hometown to play for the Cleveland Infants of the Players' League. Thus, when the Phillies gathered in Jacksonville, Florida, for spring training, the only starting positions that were taken were those of the three returning men who had remained loyal to the Phillies: Myers at second base, Sam Thompson in right field, and hometown favorite Jack Clements behind the plate.

Surprisingly, Philadelphia came out of the gate quickly, winning 22 of its first 35 games and vying with Cincinnati for the league lead. Pitcher Kid Gleason and rookie hurler Tom Vickery started well, taking up the slack for the team aces that had jumped to the Philadelphia Players' League team, the Quakers. Billy Hamilton, starting in left field, adjusted rapidly to National League pitching. In a three-game series with Brooklyn in May, he garnered seven hits, walked five times, scored four runs, and stole three bases. In game two of that series, he served notice to the league about his speed by advancing to third from first on an infield putout.

"Wright's Ponies" were riding high until the end of June, winning a team-record sixteen straight games. A series of setbacks and the team's near total reliance on rookies soon changed the course of their season. Two key veterans were sidelined — catcher Clements with a hand injury and second baseman Myers with malaria — leaving Thompson and Hamilton as the only position players on the field who were not rookies. Manager Wright developed a serious eye disease that left him temporarily blind. With Wright incapacitated, team owners John Rogers and Al Reach unaccountably placed the team in the hands of rookie shortstop Bob Allen as player-manager for 34 games until Wright's return late in the season. Hoping to provide some stability, they sent rookie center fielder Eddie Burke and pitcher "Phenomenal" Smith to Pittsburgh for veteran outfielder Billy Sunday. Sunday played well in what would be his last month in the major leagues, but it would not be enough to halt the Phillies' slide. An outstanding defensive outfielder and base stealer, Sunday would gain national fame thereafter, but not as a ballplayer.

Billy Sunday began his baseball career in Chicago, where he came under the bad influence of Mike "King" Kelly, and soon was spending his free time drinking and gambling with Kelly and his friends. Returning home early one Sunday morning after a drinking binge, Sunday overheard a mission choir singing hymns. Bursting into tears, he announced that he was changing his ways. He kept his promise. Sunday quit drinking, smoking and gambling, and refused to play ball on the Lord's day. A few years later he became an evangelical preacher. Proselytizing across the nation for several decades, he was the country's most recognized evangelist, and a true precursor of Billy Graham. Sunday drew on his experience in professional baseball to add a unique flavor to his sermons.

> One oddity of Sunday's rhetorical style was his frequent use of baseball imagery. In his sermons, Christ throws fast balls at temptation and calls the

devil out; sinners are left on base; and those who repent their sins slide — Billy Sunday would slide headfirst across the stage to emphasize this point — into salvation. Billy Sunday never entirely severed his connection to baseball; he was frequently a spectator at major-league ballparks, and loved to serve as a volunteer umpire in minor-league games.[44]

In the waning days of the 1890 season, Billy Sunday had come to a crossroad in his life. Prior to signing with the Phillies late in the season, he had accepted an offer to become national secretary for the Young Men's Christian Association and had planned to retire from baseball. Under the headline "Story of Sunday's Contract," the *Philadelphia Inquirer* [45] reported that Billy Sunday was given an option to renew with Philadelphia through the 1893 season. Which path should he follow? Evidence from Mildred Prior, Billy Hamilton's daughter, suggests that while the two Billys were roommates with the Phillies, Billy Hamilton provided Billy Sunday with advice on the issue.

> Billy's ear was sought even by Billy Sunday, another outfielder who left baseball at the top of his game to become a preacher. "Mr. Sunday and my father were roommates at Philadelphia," Mrs. Prior revealed. "One day Mr. Sunday told my father he was thinking of quitting baseball for a religious life. They talked a long while about it and my father told him it was a wonderful idea if he was prepared to make the financial sacrifice.... Later, Mr. Sunday told me it was this talk that convinced him he should become a preacher."[46]

The popularity of 1920s "Tin Pan Alley" songwriter Fred Fisher's catchy tune, "Chicago (That Toddlin' Town)," would forever assure Billy Sunday's place in American cultural history as an evangelist, and not a ballplayer, when the song described the Windy City as "the town that Billy Sunday couldn't shut down."

Short on pitching, the Phillies in 1890 overused their top two hurlers, Gleason and Vickery, who collectively started 101 of the season's 133 games. Predictably, these two ran out of stamina by mid–August. The third starter, "Phenomenal" Smith, proved less than phenomenal (eight wins, twelve losses) and moved on to Pittsburgh with Eddie Burke in the Billy Sunday trade. The Phillies ended the season in third place, behind Brooklyn and Chicago, after losing a doubleheader to Cleveland on the last day of the season. A remarkable aspect of the doubleheader loss is the fact that Cy Young, who would win more games than anyone in the history of the sport, pitched and won both contests for the Spiders, hurling two consecutive complete games and giving up only four runs.

The two bright spots of Philadelphia's season were the performances of Sam Thompson and Billy Hamilton. "Big Sam" hit .313, tied for the league lead in hits (172), and led the league in doubles (41). Hamilton led the team in hitting (.325), and was second in the league in that category behind Giants shortstop Charlie Glassock, who compiled a .326 average. Billy was second in the league in on-base percentage, third in runs scored, and he led the circuit in stolen bases with 102 in 123 games. Hamilton collected many of his steals and hits in bunches. He stole three bases in a game seven times, and in one game stole four bases. He collected three hits in a game five times during the season. His best combination of base running and hitting occurred against Pittsburgh on July 21 and 22, when he stole six bases in two games and collected five hits, the last being a triple over the head of Billy (soon to be a Phillie) Sunday in the fifteenth inning, winning the game. Late in the season, the Philadelphia press, which largely had ignored his offensive prowess during the campaign, paid Hamilton a left-handed compliment on his improved defense:

> Hamilton has always been a hard hitter and the best base runner in America, but at the start he was ranked as a rather poor fielder. Old-time players said, "Never mind, as long as he can hit and run, the fielding will come to him." They told the truth, for Billy has constantly improved his fielding, and is now almost a sure fly-catcher.[47]

Sliding Billy's introduction to the National League had been an unqualified success, but there was even more to be grateful for as the season drew to a close. On October 5, 1890, Billy and Rebecca's first child, Ethel Carr Hamilton, was born in Clinton, Massachusetts.

Although significant changes were coming to the National League in 1891–92, Philadelphia's position in the standings changed little. In both years the team finished in fourth place. The 1891 season began with a tragedy that shocked the city's baseball faithful. In May, Jimmy Fogarty, the slick center fielder from San Francisco who had spent a half-dozen years with the Phillies before jumping to the Players' League, died in Philadelphia of tuberculosis. The graceful outfielder was just 27 years old. Grief-stricken, the team wore black armbands in memory of Fogarty for a month. Despite the collapse of the Players' League at the end of the 1890 season, the Phillies were unable to sign any proven performers from its ranks for the 1891 campaign. Their three starters, Kid Gleason, Duke Esper, and John Thornton, combined for a disappointing 59-53 record. The collective batting average of the infield was an anemic .226, and the only players who hit over .300 were Billy Hamilton and left-handed catcher Jack Clements. Clements, a burly native Philadelphian who carried two hundred pounds on a 5' 8" frame, played sixteen years in the big leagues, and would become "the first man in the majors to catch 1,000 major league games. No left-hander since his departure has caught as many as 100 games in the majors. Clements also holds the all-time record for highest BA [batting average; Clements hit .394 while playing 82 games of a 133-game season in 1895] in a season by a catcher."[48] Ed Delahanty, who spent 1890 with the Cleveland Infants, did return to the Phillies but hit a disappointing .243, the worst full-season average he would register in his career.

Billy Hamilton proved without question that his fine first season with the club was not an aberration. Healthy, and playing in all but five of the season's 138 games, he had one of the most prolific offensive years in the game's history. He won the batting crown with a .340 average and led the league in on-base percentage (.453), hits (179), runs (141), walks (102), and stolen bases (111). An offensive highlight of the season, one that recalled a similar effort while at Kansas City, came in a July game at Cincinnati, when three of Hamilton's four hits were triples.

Patterns in Billy's offensive and defensive strategies were beginning to be noticed by the press. His trademark head-first slides and bunting skills were lauded. After a May game against Brooklyn, he was praised for bunting, and the manner in which he then "reached first base in safety by fast sprinting and a headfirst slide."[49] His ability to hit to the opposite field, and occasionally to do so with power, also was highlighted: "Hamilton opened the third inning with a tremendous hit to the left field fence, and made a circuit of the bases."[50] In the outfield, he drew frequent praise for his "brilliant" and "phenomenal" catches. Over and over, details about Billy "making the grand circuit" revealed the patterns by which he wrangled his way to first base and then worked his way around the diamond to score: a walk, a steal of second, a move to third on a passed ball, then scoring on a sacrifice fly[51]; reaching first on a error, stealing second, going to third on a sacrifice, and scoring on a passed ball.⁵² Some descriptions of the process were even cast in a humorous light, as in the case in an August game against Cleveland. "[Pitcher] Gruber's first act was to send Hamilton to first on balls. Now that's the sort of thing we can stand all day, and Hamilton showed his appreciation by stealing second, which drew a wild throw from Zimmer [catcher], enabling the runner to reach third."⁵³

Billy later scored on an Ed Delahanty single.

One aspect of Hamilton's 1891 statistics was inadvertently overlooked by the press of the era. Nevertheless, this unheralded performance still stands today, nearly twelve decades later, as a major league record. On July 23 in New York, Billy stole a base off future Hall of Fame pitcher "Smiling Mickey" Welch. The following day he stole another off Amos Rusie. He stole a base in the first game of Philadelphia's next series against Brooklyn on July 25, and then stole another in each of the concluding games of the series. The Phillies returned home to face Boston on July 31, where Billy stole two more bases against future Hall of Famer John Clarkson in the teams' first contest. Rain shortened the series, but Billy managed to steal a base in the second game, a 1–0 loss. Chicago then came to town and Hamilton's thievery continued, with one steal secured in each of the three-games. Cincinnati followed Chicago to Philadelphia for a three game series. The Reds lost all three contests against the Phillies, and Hamilton once again stole a base in each game. Sliding Billy's larcenous consecutive-game streak finally ended on August 10 against Cleveland. When the dust had settled, he had stolen at least one base in thirteen consecutive games.

Lou Brock, who ranks second all-time in stolen bases with twelve more (938) than Hamilton, never managed a steal in more than six consecutive games. (He did this twice, in 1971 and 1974.) All-time stolen base king Rickey Henderson once had an eleven-game thievery streak (August 14–27, 1983), and he stole a base in nine consecutive games twice (1980 and 1986). No one else has come closer to Billy Hamilton's 1891 mark of steals in thirteen consecutive games.

No longer content with being known as a good base stealer, Hamilton now wanted to establish himself as the best. "Billy Hamilton has challenged Arlie Latham to a hundred-yard dash for $100 a side, but Arlie has been slow in accepting."⁵⁴ Latham, a brash third baseman for Cincinnati and St. Louis who performed vaudeville routines in the off-season, was also a showman on the field. A major proponent of on-field "rowdyism," Latham, as a third base coach, would run up and down the baseline screaming obscenities at the pitcher and the defense in order to distract them. His predilection for this type of heckling is credited with leading to the establishment of the coaching "box," within which coaches were expected to stand. As previously mentioned, Latham earlier in the 1891 season attempted to prevent Hamilton from scoring by grabbing him by the shirt and holding him as he rounded third base. Instead of responding to this interference with a punch, Hamilton challenged Arlie to an athletic match, using a time-tested Latham tactic. Early in his career, Latham issued a challenge to all comers, offering a $100 prize for anyone who could outrun him in a hundred-yard dash race. At the time, Billy Sunday (who as yet had not renounced gambling) took him up on the offer and beat him badly.[55] Now in his eleventh season, Arlie could never have taken on Hamilton in this type race and emerged victorious, and he therefore refused the latter's challenge. The press reported that "Latham's claim to the title of champion base runner has been successfully disputed by Billy Hamilton of the Phillies."[56] Arlie, however, would get his revenge. After retiring as a player, he spent one year, 1899, as a league umpire. That year, he ejected Hamilton from a game for arguing a call. It was the only time Billy was ejected from a major league game in fourteen seasons, and almost certainly resulted from the longstanding bad blood between the pair.

At the close of the 1891 season, the American Association ended its ten-year run and merged with the National League, forming the "League Association." Louisville, Washington, Baltimore and St. Louis from the old association were added to the National League, while the remaining five teams were disbanded. In an attempt to ameliorate the cumbersome nature of the new twelve-team league, a split season was initiated, with league leaders at the season's midpoint and end both recognized as champions. The concept was so unpopular that it was jettisoned after one season.

Chafing from their inability during the previous year to attract significant veteran players from the defunct Players' League, the Phillies acquired three solid performers from the disbanded Philadelphia Athletics association team: Billy Hallman, a steady .280 hitter who would play second base for them for the next half-dozen years; Lafayette

Napoleon "Lave" Cross, who would defend the hot corner for the Phillies over the same time period; and, premier hurler Gus Weyhing, 31–20 for the 1891 Athletics, the same pitcher who blanked Billy and the Cowboys with a no-hitter during Hamilton's debut with Kansas City in 1888. Third baseman Cross holds the distinction of playing in four leagues — National, American Association, Players' League and the American League — during his twenty-five-year career. Additionally, the Phillies signed aging slugger Roger Connor, a 6'2" 220-pound power hitter from Waterbury, Connecticut, who had played the majority of his previous thirteen major league seasons with New York.

Philadelphia opened the 1892 season with Hamilton in left field, Delahanty in center, and Thompson in right. Billy's successful two years on the team had made him popular in the press, and on April 15, the *Philadelphia Inquirer* published an extremely flattering biography of him, accompanied by a line-drawing portrait with the caption, "The Fleet-Footed and Popular Member of the Philadelphia Team."

> Billy Hamilton is the phenomenal left fielder of the Philadelphia club. As a base runner Hamilton is considered the peer of any player in the country, and this is borne out by the fact that last season he led the entire profession in stolen bases. As a fielder, Hamilton stands in the front rank, he being a sure catch, and owing to his sprinting powers, is able to cover an unusual amount of territory. Few ballplayers have become so universally popular as this famous Knight of the diamond, who has made himself worthy of all the kind words of praise accorded to him.[57]

Ironically, in the course of three years, the same paper that issued such words of praise would be vitriolic in its condemnation of Sliding Billy.

After a sluggish start, the Phillies found themselves in second place behind Boston in late June. Hamilton was on a tear offensively, leading the team in hitting, but a particular feature of his early-season work, his fine fielding and throwing, drew regular press attention.

> Hamilton made a wonderful catch of a foul fly in the sixth inning that brought applause from the crowd[58]; ... he scooped in Smith's fly after a long run, and, recovering quickly, by a neat throw, caught Comiskey at first[59]; Hamilton ... distinguished himself, making three difficult catches in left field, each of which seemed to be a clean hit[60]; Billy Hamilton made the star play of the game. In the fifth inning, Lowe sent a foul fly apparently into the left-field seats, but Hamilton, by a great run, jumped into the railing and caught the ball.[61]

By late June, the Phillies were 41–24. Over a four-game stretch during this period, Billy banged out 13 hits. A few days later, however, he suffered an ankle injury that would plague him for the remainder of the season and result in a drop in his stolen base total, from his previous high of 111 to 57. The injury laid him off for a dozen games in July. When he returned to the lineup late in the month, he still seemed tentative. "Hamilton's ankle makes him a little timid about stealing bases, but he is liable to make the best of the catchers hustle in a few days."[62] Two weeks later, his inside-the-park grand slam against Boston served notice that he was back in form: "Hamilton drove the ball on a dead-line to the left field terrace and when the dust had cleared away Hamilton was sitting on the players' bench with a home run to his credit and three other runs had come in."[63]

Later in the month the Phillies' injury list got longer. Catcher Clements went out with an arm injury, as did third starter Duke Esper. Sam Thompson suffered a series of hand injuries that affected his offensive game. Consequently, from mid–July to season's end, the team barely played .500 ball, a record not strong enough to overcome Boston's near-.700 winning percentage for the season. Billy again led his team in hitting at .330, and was second in the league in this category. His 17 three-hit games and 39 two-hit games were a clear indication of his potent bat. Even though he was slowed by the ankle injury, he still placed third in the league in on-base percentage, fourth in hits, and second in runs.

The National League owners, who now referred to themselves as "magnates," ought to have been feeling ecstatic with regard to their recent victories over the upstart Players' League and the pesky American Association along with their re-establishment of a monopoly in professional baseball. In fact, however, the recent "league wars" had left them financially weak. They were made yet more vulnerable by the weakening national economy, which was hovering at near-recession levels. One of the first signs of the economic downturn was seen in a steep decline in game attendance around the league. The Phillies were no exception. "On some September afternoons, the talent-laden Phillies played before only a few hundred people. The majority of the 188,000 spectators drawn in 1892 attended the first half-season."[64] Philadelphia owners responded by lowering salaries for the 1893 season by 50 percent. "The Phillies' best athletes were awarded contracts in the neighborhood of $1,800."⁶⁵ After complaining bitterly, all 1892 regulars, with the exception of Roger Connor, who was traded to New York, ultimately recognized their weakened position due to the league's re-established monopoly, and grudgingly signed their dramatically reduced contracts.

Amid bitter recrimination and bleak economic news, the 1893 season began with a significant rule change. Reasoning that poor attendance in 1892 was linked to an excessive number of low-scoring games, the Rules Committee eliminated the pitchers box, and pitchers were now required to throw from a rubber plate, 60' 6" from home. One foot was required to be in contact with the plate during the delivery of the ball. As a result of the rule change, 1893 league batting averages rose 35 points, and teams scored 1.47 more runs per game.⁶⁶ Increased offense achieved its desired effect: "Attendance rose markedly in almost every city."⁶⁷Although Philadelphia's offense was the most explosive in the league in 1893, weak pitching, a key player sidelined by serious illness, and the team's inexplicable inability to fare well against several weaker teams left them at the end of the season precisely where they had ended up the two previous seasons — in fourth place. Hamilton, Thompson and Delahanty placed 1-2-3 in league hitting, with Del, who at last was coming into his own, taking the slugging, total bases, RBI, and home run crowns. Counterbalancing the outstanding offense, however, was the grim fact that the earned run average of the three starting pitchers Weyhing, Carsey, and Keefe increased by an average of nearly two runs per game, from 2.70 to 4.60. "Wright's Ponies" lost their season series to powerful first-place Boston, but won them against second- and third-place Pittsburgh and Cleveland. They had losing records against the fifth-and sixth-place teams, New York and Brooklyn, and unaccountably, lost eight of their twelve contests with tenth-place St. Louis. David Nemec, dean of nineteenth-century baseball studies, aptly describes such behavior on the part of the Phillies as the "strange proclivity to do well against the team above, but flounder against the team right beneath it."⁶⁸

The illness that would end the team's hopes for a championship was suffered by the league's leading batsman — Billy Hamilton.

Sliding Billy started the season with wonderful news: his second daughter, Millie, was born in April. By the end of July, he was on a pace to match the remarkable statistics of his signature 1891 season. In

82 games he had collected 135 hits, scored 110 runs, and stolen 43 bases. On a given day, he could be virtually unstoppable offensively, as was the case in a late July blowout against the Senators, when he went four-for-four, including a triple, scored four runs, walked twice, and stole two bases. He was hitting the ball harder and longer with greater frequency than at any time previously in his career. During the week of May 17–23, Billy smacked four "out-of-the-park" home runs, hitting a pair of them twice in that period. The first pair, hit against Washington, prompted an unusual headline for a team blessed with the likes of power hitters Ed Delahanty and Sam Thompson: "Hamilton Swings His Little Bat: Billy's Home Run Hitting Enables the Phillies to Down the Senators."[69] In a major league career that spanned fourteen seasons, Hamilton totaled 40 home runs. In a week in 1894, he hit ten percent of that total. It would also be his best defensive year.

Playing in left field and occasionally in center, he averaged .964 on a team whose fielding percentage was .926. His outfield heroics included a feat against Louisville that would become a regular feature of his defense — a barehanded grab [in his throwing hand] made while on the dead run. "He made the star play of the day. In the second inning Bill Brown sent a ball on a dead line far into centre field. Had it not been intercepted it would have struck the fence, but Hamilton, while on the dead run, managed to get his left hand on the ball, and it stuck there. The crowd cheered Billy to the echo."[70]

This stellar year would end unexpectedly for the twenty-seven-year-old Hamilton in early August. With the Phillies in second place and beginning a three-game series with the Senators, on Thursday, August 3, a brief note appeared in the press: "Hamilton was sick and had to lay off today."[71] Unable to recover, he missed the next series with Baltimore, prompting a second press notice that expressed greater concern, not for his health, but for what his loss would mean to the team. "Hamilton's absence is missed [sic] more ways than one and the team will not be in good trim until he plays again."[72] Finally, a longer article revealed the serious nature of his affliction.

> William Hamilton, the famous baseball player and centre fielder of the Philadelphia League Club, is lying seriously ill with typhoid fever at his residence, on Dauphin Street above Broad. Hamilton played his last game with the Phillies at Boston a week ago yesterday. He complained of being unwell at that time and played while advised not to. Returning to this city Thurs-

day, Hamilton was unable to play, and on Friday took to his bed.... Dr. Boger, the physician of the Philadelphia Club, has been attending Hamilton since Thursday last, and another physician was called in consultation yesterday. Hamilton's condition was so critical on Tuesday that his wife was telegraphed for and she arrived from her home in Clinton, Massachusetts, yesterday.... Hamilton is one of the most noted batsmen and baserunners in the country and at this time he is leading the league. His absence from the team is a sad blow just now when his services are most needed.[73]

Typhoid, also known as "nervous fever" for the delirium it caused in its victims, struck most frequently in cities that used untreated lake or river water in their water supply systems. Although the first effective vaccine to treat the disease was created in 1897, it did not become widely available until after World War I. Approximately 35,000 deaths were attributed to typhoid in 1900.

Billy would survive his illness, but Philadelphia could hardly survive in his absence. By August 17, the team had dropped to fourth place. Losing six of their last eight games in late September assured them of this standing, and Boston won its third consecutive league championship. In an October *post mortem* of the disappointing season, Manager Wright acknowledged the critical significance of Hamilton's loss to the team.

> Hamilton's sickness was our first blow. The loss of Billy, both at the bat and in the field, has been a very disastrous one for us. Turner [Billy's substitute] is a good man, and I have only praise for his work, but he could not be expected to fill Hamilton's shoes. Delahanty and Thompson were not accustomed to his style of fielding, and many balls went for two-baggers and triples which would have been caught had Hamilton been on the team.[74]

The National League supplied a new twist to the expression "adding insult to injury" by adding insult to *illness* in Billy Hamilton's case by awarding the 1893 batting title to Hugh Duffy of Boston. Hamilton completed two-thirds of the season, hitting .380 before contracting typhoid fever. Duffy played the full season, hitting .363. In David Nemec's words, "Many ... authorities are unhappy that major league baseball still credits him [Duffy] with the 1893 batting title, even though Billy Hamilton outhit him by 17 points."[75]

Shocking as it may appear to the modern observer, the presence and persistence of life-threatening diseases in nineteenth-century baseball, like the presence and persistence of severe alcoholism, was a commonplace occurrence. The Phillies had already seen enough of it. Jimmy Fogarty's death from tuberculosis was a terrible start to the season. Hamilton's typhoid fever was an equally terrible way to end it. Charlie Ferguson, a Virginia-born pitcher with an overpowering fastball, joined the team in 1884 and in four years won 96 games, including a stretch of sixteen victories in a row. In the spring of 1888, Ferguson contracted typhoid fever; He never made it back to the ball field. On April 29, 1888, nine days into the season and just twelve days past his twenty-fifth birthday, Charlie Ferguson died.

At the close of the 1893 season, Philadelphia owners John Rogers and Al Reach were frustrated by Harry Wright's inability to bring them a pennant in a decade as manager. They fired "the father of baseball" and handed over control of the club to Arthur Irwin, a former light-hitting journeyman infielder with three years of managerial experience. Irwin, who had guided the Boston Reds to the last American Association championship in 1891, was a skinny, bug-eyed Canadian with large, protruding ears and a healthy ego. He was an impeccable dresser, and fancied himself to be a savant in the art of "scientific baseball"— that is, bunting, place-hitting, base running, and sacrificing, so much so that he published a book on the subject in 1895. Irwin had also patented his own model fielder's glove, and enjoyed a sideline career as a promoter of prize fights, bicycle races, and other sporting contests. Later in life he owned and managed minor league teams.

In his two years as the Phillies' skipper, he posted a respectable 149–110 won-lost record, but in the process managed to create considerable dissention among players, fans, and local sportswriters, who constantly compared him unfavorably to his predecessor, the beloved Harry Wright. Irwin irritated fans by arbitrarily changing the team uniform colors, placing red and black bars on their stockings,[76] and was accused of not being "strict enough with the team" by owner Rogers.[77] Irwin also befuddled his players by instituting a complex system of signals and strategic position moves that proved impractical. "Irwin's coaching tactics are apparent but not always successful. At times the boys get badly mixed up in the signals and make stupid plays."[78] His own strategic moves were likewise panned. "Mr. Irwin has on several occasions himself shown poor judgment in handling his runners, and the loss of one game at least can be traced to this."[79] Finally, the flippant observations and underhanded tactics of the Phillies' pilot infuriated other teams. In September 1894, he was accused of violating the terms of the 1883 National Agreement, which prohibited signing players who had been reserved by other clubs, when he illegally signed a minor league pitcher. In July of that year, he came under fire for insulting the entire Louisville team, calling them "a lot of antiquated stiffs."[80] By September, the inevitable comparison to his predecessor was being suggested: Irwin was "not popular with the players," while "Harry [Wright] was universally liked."[81]

Years later, after Irwin's disappearance and apparent suicide at the age of 63 in 1921, it became clear that his unusual antics were not limited to the baseball field. It was discovered that he had been leading a double life for decades, with a wife and grown children in two separate cities, Boston and New York. In a written correspondence dated the year after Irwin's "death," a pitcher who had known him added an ironic footnote to the Irwin saga: "How can Arthur Irwin be dead? I just saw him in Oklahoma."[82]

Although Baltimore would rise from eighth place in 1893 to first place in 1894, top individual performances of the year would be accomplished by players on other clubs. "The Hoosier Thunderbolt," Amos Rusie, won 36 games for the second-place Giants, and the bat of diminutive 5'7" Hugh Duffy was the major feature of a Boston team that would slip from first to third place in the standings. One hundred and fourteen years later, Duffy's .440 mark in 1894 still stands as the highest season average in baseball history. A Rhode Island native, Duffy "first hit Boston in 1888 and last rapped the ball around during infield practice in 1953, at age 86."[83] A line drive hitter with occasional power — he hit 18 home runs in 1894 — Duffy was a speedy outfielder who studied opponents' hitting patterns and positioned himself accordingly. After his Major League debut season with Chicago (1888), his batting average rose every year, from a respectable .282 to the meteoric .440 in 1894.

Hugh jumped to where the money was; between 1889 and 1891 he played in three different leagues (American Association and the Players' and National leagues). In 1901, he increased that number to four when he led the Beaneaters' exodus to the American League. Such restlessness left him with a second record that will never be broken. He is the only player to hit .300 or better in four major leagues.[84] During the off-season, Duffy operated a bowling alley and saloon with former teammate and future Hall of Famer Tommy McCarthy. In 1893 and 1894, McCarthy played left field and Duffy center for the Beaneaters. Their combined batting average during those years was .354 and .394, respectively, earning them the nickname of the "Heavenly Twins."

Duffy's individual offensive performance was nearly matched in 1894 by a trio of Phillies who made up their outfield that year: Delahanty in left, Hamilton in center, and Thompson in right. Their status in baseball history is succinctly summarized in the title of a 1982 *Sports Illustrated* article, "The Best Outfield Ever? Why, Del, Big Sam and Sliding Billy, For Sure."[85] Sam and Del both hit .407 in 1894; Billy hit .404. The trio's combined batting averages for 1893–95 were .372, .404, and .395, and during these three years they also garnered a total of ten individual league offensive honors.

Ed Delahanty was a kid who never grew up. One of five baseball-playing brothers from Cleveland, the high-strung, quick-tempered "Del," at 6'1" and a slender 170 pounds, was the "original bad ball hitter, waving a long heavy bat that would reach any pitch thrown anywhere."[86] After a little more than a year in the minors, he signed with the Phillies in 1888. Originally a catcher, he was tried at shortstop and second base before settling in left field for the majority of his dozen years with Philadelphia. Famous for his "high living and low judgement,"[87] Del aroused the consternation and enmity of players and owners alike in 1890. That year, he accepted a $1,000 advance to jump to his hometown Cleveland club of the upstart Players' League. Two weeks later, concerned over the non-guaranteed nature of his Spiders contract, he accepted a $500 advance to return to the Phillies. While at spring training with the team, he accepted another advance check and contract from Cleveland, snuck out of his rooming house, and rejoined the Spiders, his third team in five months, for the remainder of the year. His conduct earned him the nickname "Triple Jumper," a moniker he never lived down.

Del's impetuousness and petulance off the field never affected his hitting. He batted over .400 three times, and led the league at least once in batting average, doubles, triples, home runs, RBIs and on-base percentage. His lifetime .346 average still ranks him among the top five hitters of all time.

Sam Thompson played right field to Ed Delahanty's left field for the 1890s era Phillies. In terms of personality and disposition, the two men were as far apart as the distance that separated them on the ball field. A quiet, folksy, tobacco-chewing gentle giant (he was 6' 2" and weighed more than 200 pounds), Big Sam was seven years Del's senior. Prior to his major league years, Sam earned his living in the construction business in his native Indiana. According to the legend, "a scout from the Detroit Wolverines coaxed Thompson down from a roof he was repairing with an offer to play baseball for the same $2.50 per day that he was earning as a carpenter."[88] In his second year with the Wolverines, Thompson helped lead them to their only pennant, taking league honors in batting average (.372), slugging (.571), RBIs (166), and hits (203).

Arriving in Philadelphia in 1889, Sam played a steady right field for a decade. His patented one-bounce throws to home plate cut down many a runner attempting to score. In 1890, unlike most established stars that jumped from their National League teams to the Players' League, Sam remained loyal to Philadelphia. Deceptively speedy for his size, he hustled for 159 triples in his 15-year career, while coming in second to Roger Connor for nineteenth-century long-ball honors, hitting 127 home runs to Connor's 138.

Despite the Phillies' disappointing fourth-place finish under Art Irwin, 1894 was a season of personal milestones and records for the third member of the "best outfield ever," Billy Hamilton. His .404 batting average was a career high, placing him among two dozen others who had or would reach the .400 plateau. His 196 runs scored in a 129-game season remains the high-water mark in this category. On August 31, in a game against Washington, he entered the record books for base-stealing:

> A feature of the game was the all-around work of Billy Hamilton. He made three runs, three hits, one a two-baser, accepted four chances and stole seven bases, establishing a new record. The base stealing record up to yesterday was five, held by several players. Hamilton equaled this record in the fifth inning. In the seventh he bunted the ball and beat it to first. Both Wynne [pitcher] and Dugdale [catcher] tried to keep Hamilton from beating the record, but he slid into second under a good throw, and threw up a cloud of dust sliding to third, causing Dugdale to make a bad throw, on which he scored. Hamilton stole second base four times, and third base three times.[89]

While faithfully providing the details of Billy's performance that day, the article errs in declaring that the previous record was five stolen bases. On this date Billy actually *equaled* a record of seven steals in a game set by George "Piano Legs" Gore of the Chicago White Stockings in 1881. Gore and Sliding Billy remain the only two players who have accomplished this feat.

Hamilton set another record in 1894 that went unheralded by the league and by the press of the era. Between July 6 and August 2, he scored at least one run in every contest, thus establishing the mark for consecutive games scoring a run (24), a record that still stands today. For good measure, Billy scored in 20 consecutive games in a second streak that began two weeks later, on August 15, and ended on September 3. That effort, and an 18-game scoring streak in 1893, rank fifth and sixth, respectively, all time. Other outstanding offensive performances of the year included a five-hit, five-run, four-stolen base game against Boston on August 8, a four-hit, four-run tally against Chicago on September 6, and a blistering streak of 25 hits and 16 runs scored in eight games between August 15 and August 22.

In the outfield, Billy continued to excel. On successive days in early May at the Polo Grounds he made a sensational "circus" catch. In the first game, "[Jack] Doyle rapped out a hummer to deep centre. It looked good for two bases at least, but Billy was after it like a shot and took it off the scoreboard."[90] In the next day's contest, Giants catcher Duke Farrell sent a deep shot to center, "but Hamilton, by a desperate effort, got under the ball and held it after falling clear of the ropes.... It was a beautiful catch and perhaps saved the game."[91]

As explained in Chapter One, no outfield fences existed in many cavernous parks of the era like the Polo Grounds. Simple ropes cordoned off the playing field, with the areas beyond them designated for overflow seating.

Playing at home against Boston in mid–July, the Phillies beat the Beaneaters by forfeit in a game that would have been considered hilarious were it not marred by incidents of "rowdyism" by players and fans. A Billy Hamilton steal in the first inning proved to be the catalyst for the chaos that transpired afterward. After drawing a walk, Billy stole second, went to third on a Bill Hallman out, and scored on Ed Delahanty's sacrifice fly. Using a stream of profanity, Boston first baseman Tommy Tucker had loudly protested the safe call at second on Hamilton. Livid after Billy had scored, Tucker proceeded to engage in "colorful banter" with the Phillies fans until the eighth inning. With Boston behind in the score and a thunderstorm approaching, Beaneaters captain Billy Nash instructed his players to use delaying tactics in the hope of having the game called due to inclement weather. The Bostons then began refusing to field balls, thus deliberately letting the Phillies get on base. In response, Philadelphia's Sam Thompson, in order to be called out and retire the side, ran from first base to third without bothering to go near second base. Boston then refused to bat, and Hugh Duffy grabbed the game ball and ran around the outfield with it in his grasp. At this juncture the umpire declared the game a forfeit, giving Philadelphia a 9–0 victory.

Events now turned ugly: "The crowd then surged onto the field and assaulted first baseman Tucker, who had been cursing them all day."[92] Staggered by a blow to his left eye, Tucker was placed under the stands for protection, while fans began attacking other Boston players. After finally being escorted to safety outside the Huntingdon Street Grounds, the Bostons' horse-drawn omnibus was stoned by enraged Phillies fans at Broad and Cumberland streets. The rowdy era had arrived in the "City of Brotherly Love."

While the season ended disappointingly for Irwin's Phillies, Billy Hamilton went home to his growing family having completed one of his most impressive seasons in organized baseball. Back in Clinton that fall, life was rich and rewarding. The cottage on Forest Street was filled with the laughter of Hamilton's two young daughters, and before the end of the year, Billy would buy a large tract of land and begin construction of his apartment house. As Hamilton's twenty-ninth birthday approached, he and Rebecca had turned the corner financially and could look forward to a secure future. Their lives were in sharp contrast to the tragedy of Mike "King" Kelly that November — his career over, shipwrecked by alcohol, financially ruined, dead of pneumonia at 36.

By 1895, the frustration of the Philadelphia club's owners, fans, and city sportswriters had turned to anger, one that frequently was directed at two members of the team: manager Art Irwin and Billy Hamilton. The Phillies played well enough to earn third place, behind Cleveland and first-place Baltimore, but the coveted league championship continued to elude them. Other than replacing Bob Allen at shortstop with Joe Sullivan, skipper Irwin made no changes either in the infield or the outfield, and kept two of his starters from the previous year, Kid Carsey and Jack Taylor. "Brewery Jack," whose nickname is self-explanatory, was a 6'1" right-hander from Maryland who was in the middle of three consecutive twenty-win seasons. He had been recruited and hired by Harry Wright, and, like many of his teammates, found it difficult to adjust to Manager Irwin's quirky strategies and dictatorial manner. Jack Taylor's life would be tragically short. Five years after completing the 1895 season, he died of Bright's Disease at the age of 27. Third starter Willie McGill, new to the team, was a journeyman hurler who had played with five different clubs in the previous five years. He spent 1894 with Chicago, where he logged an unimpressive 7–19 record.

By mid–June the Phillies were in seventh place, and the press was openly criticizing the team's owner for refusing to spend the money to develop a strong pitching staff: "The Phillies' weakness in pitching is apparent to all but one man, Colonel John Rogers, who owns controlling interest in the club."[93] In all probability, even if Rogers had wanted to improve the staff, he would have been financially unable to do so. The improvement in attendance from 188,000 in 1893 to nearly 400,000 in 1894 was largely negated by the aforementioned disastrous fire that completely destroyed the Huntingdon Street Park in early August 1894. The park was rebuilt in a remarkable twelve days, but its cost, and the fact that its predecessor was only partially insured, left Rogers in financial difficulty.

A series of maladies that befell the players did nothing to soothe the team's frustration. Carsey began the season out of shape and was ineffective through May. Taylor developed a sore arm, and newly acquired shortstop Sullivan and steady third sacker Lave Cross developed a mysterious illness that left them with chills, fatigue, and body aches. Delahanty sprained his leg, and new pitcher McGill was out for four weeks with an ankle injury. In response to the withering criticism from the press, Art Irwin began experimenting wildly with his lineup. For a few games in April, and for an entire week in June, he assigned Hamilton, now the league's premier leadoff man, to hit in the cleanup spot.

The *Inquirer* soon began an extraordinary campaign to effect change on the club. Rather than present its views in a sports column, the paper began placing brief, one- or two-sentence comments in bold print above, beneath, or alongside the daily box scores: "Just think what service one more first class pitcher would be to Philly."⁹⁴ After stating that "the [Phillies] management does not intend to put up the cash to purchase a first class pitcher,"⁹⁵ it offered to put up its own money to purchase the release of "one or two good pitchers."⁹⁶

In mid–June, after being beaten by Louisville, the weakest team in the league, the *Inquirer* lashed out specifically at Hamilton, criticizing his "indifferent" play and stating that he "seemed to be on bad terms with himself and everybody else."⁹⁷ Clearly influenced by the press, Irwin responded by "laying off," i.e., benching both Hamilton and Lave Cross for the remaining two games of the Louisville series. The *Inquirer* added fuel to the fire by publishing a direct quote made to Billy by Irwin during a closed team meeting: "You lose runs and games by your indifference and foolish base running."⁹⁸ One has to wonder not only about Irwin's motivations at this point, but also about his sanity. Hamilton led the league in stolen bases and runs in 1894 — hardly the record of either an indifferent player or a foolish baserunner. He would lead the league in the same categories in 1895.

Humiliated in front of his teammates as well as in the press, Billy let his playing do the talking for the remainder of the season. From July 1 through September, he scored at least one run in all but eight games in which he played. He led the league in runs scored (166) and stolen bases (97), was fourth in hits (201), second in on-base percentage (.490), and batted .386. At season's end, Philadelphia's grumpy fans demonstrated they had not totally been swayed by Irwin's criticism or the press's campaign against Hamilton. In a contest to determine the most popular players, fans ranked Thompson first, Cross second, Hamilton third, Clements fourth, Hallman fifth, and Delahanty sixth.⁹⁹

The other quiet man on the team, Sam Thompson, also had one of his best seasons. After having the tip of his little finger amputated in mid–1894 to remove bone fragments caused by being hit by a line drive, Big Sam hit .392, led the league in slugging (.654), total bases (352), home runs (18), and RBIs (165).

Despite a season of bickering and internal strife, the ballyard in Philadelphia did provide some unique on-field experiences. One of the most unusual involved Boston's Herman Long during a game against the Phillies in late August. Long, it will be remembered, played his rookie season with Billy Hamilton at Kansas City before moving on to Boston, where he became the most error-prone fielder ever to play the game. On the evening in question, however, he proved definitively that there was nothing wrong with his throwing arm. "A fat rat scampered across the field, in a game last week at Philadelphia.... Long took a hand, and throwing the ball, caught the rodent and killed him outright. It was a great throw."[100]

The Orioles' pennant victory in 1894 symbolically marked the emergence of "rowdy" baseball and the decline of the last vestiges of the "gentlemanly" nature of the sport left from an earlier era. The club's blend of a fast playing style with the outrageous on-field antics of "Mugsy" McGraw and his rowdy teammates had become a winning combination. The 1895 Orioles, although decimated by injuries, including McGraw's season-long bout with malaria, still possessed enough talent and moxie to take the title. A familiar former Phillie took advantage of the Orioles' injury woes to reinvent himself at another position for them and add years to his career. New Jersey–born Kid Gleason, who won 70 games as a Phillies pitcher between 1888 and 1891, played 112 games at second base for the 1895 Orioles, hitting a solid .309.

Hamilton was out due to an unspecified illness or injury for a seven-game stretch in late September 1895, during which the Phillies lost three straight to the champion Orioles. He returned to play in a four-game series with Brooklyn that ended the season. After a five-hit, two-run effort in the first contest, the press observed that "Hamilton's rest did him good."[101] One would have to agree, for in the remaining three games he scored seven runs and added six hits to his season tally.

An ironic counterpoise to the supremacy of Baltimore's rowdy boys in 1895 occurred near season's end, when word came from Atlantic City that Harry Wright, the grand promoter of the "gentlemanly game," was gravely ill with pneumonia. On October 3, the man who played with the New York Knickerbockers and managed the first professional baseball team, passed away. The last living link with baseball's origins was gone. Wright's last words had been "Two men out...."[102]

Two men *were* out at Philadelphia. Arthur Irwin, preferring to resign rather than be fired by the Phillies, signed to manage the New York Giants a few days before his Philadelphia contract expired. After leading the Giants to a seventh-place finish in 1896 and the Washington Senators to consecutive eleventh-place finishes in 1898 and 1899,

Irwin retired from major league baseball. The Phillies would wait another twenty years before winning their first pennant, and then another thirty-five years before winning their second.

At the league's annual meeting in November 1895, a major trade was announced. Philadelphia had traded Billy Hamilton, their fleet-footed center fielder, to Boston for the Beaneaters' third baseman and team captain, Billy Nash.

Sliding Billy was going home.

4

Boston Billy

> *"Hamilton is now playing the finest game of his career, and that means he is the most valuable center fielder, all things considered, today in the game."*
> — T.H. Murnane, *Boston Daily Globe*, June 13, 1898

Although the Bay State's early version of baseball, the "Massachusetts Game," was eventually superseded by the Knickerbockers' "New York Game," Boston possessed a professional baseball pedigree that rivaled that of New York and Philadelphia. Like Philadelphia's Athletics, Boston's Red Stockings were a charter member of the National Association in 1871, a circumstance due in large part to the efforts of Massachusetts industrialist and amateur baseball player Ivers Whitney Adams. Adams, who had made a fortune in the netting and twine business, took it upon himself to contact Harry Wright, player-manager of the undefeated 1869 Cincinnati Red Stockings team, regarding the possibility of forming a professional club in Boston. After Adams' personal visit to Wright, the latter agreed to terms, bringing along with him his brother, shortstop George Wright, first baseman Charley Gould, and hard-hitting catcher Cal McVey. Adams then instructed Wright to travel to Rockford, Illinois, to secure contracts with Rockford's star pitcher, Al Spalding, second baseman Ross Barnes, and outfielder Fred Cone. Soon afterward, the Boston Baseball Association was incorporated, with Ivers Adams serving as its first president. Harry Wright's powerful new team would win four successive pennants (1872–75) during the five-year history of the National Association.

In the middle of the 1874 season, some members of the Boston

Red Stockings and the Philadelphia Athletics, with the association's permission, took a month off to embark on a whirlwind tour of England that was organized by Al Spalding for the purpose of promoting baseball abroad. Although the tour was a financial and marketing failure, during the trip another industrialist and amateur baseball player, Arthur H. Soden, had the opportunity to play center field for the American professional squad during a game at the Kensington Oval.[1] Within three years, Soden would become president of the Boston National team, which he would rule with an iron fist for three decades.

When William Hulbert's new National League debuted in 1876, Boston's Association entry signed on, changing its name to the Red Caps. Most of the stars that Harry Wright had brought to town for the Association Red Stockings a few years earlier, however, had already defected to the Chicago White Stockings, who took the league's first pennant. Wright's first-place magic returned in 1877–78, but when the team faltered afterward, he was released. Boston did not win another pennant until they changed their name to the Beaneaters in 1883. While the team didn't have to compete with an American Association club within the city limits during this era, as did Philadelphia, the nearby National League Providence Grays (1879–83) and Worcester Ruby Legs (1880–82) still provided stiff competition for the local fans' dollars. Additionally, in 1884, the short-lived Union League fielded the Boston Reds. The Reds would return in 1890 as a team in the equally short-lived Players' League, winning their association's only pennant after eight Beaneaters jumped to their squad.

Beaneaters president Arthur H. Soden first made his fortune in the roofing business, and then turned to banking, mining, and railroads. Soden and two partners, J. W. Billings and William Conant, purchased the Boston club in 1877, and in a burst of egotistic bravura, proclaimed themselves the "Triumvirs." Soden's effect on the club would be significant, but it was his overall influence on professional baseball that lasted well into the second half of the twentieth century. In a league meeting in September 1879, Soden proposed the infamous reserve rule (known now as the reserve clause), which granted each team exclusive rights to sign a player from season to season. The new regulation was approved by the owners. The reserve clause would remain in effect in major league baseball until 1975. For his efforts in solidifying the owners' control of the ballplayers' destiny, league owners dubbed Soden the "Dean of the National League."

Despite his enormous wealth, Arthur Soden's reputation for stinginess and aloofness from his players was legendary:

> Boston players took tickets, mowed the grass, and chased foul balls into the stands. They were allowed one pair of shoelaces a year. If the pair lasted two seasons the team would pay the player's horse car fare to the park. Soden revoked free passes for the players' wives, and ripped out the press box to add seats. When Charley Jones ran into Soden and demanded $378 in back pay, he was fined $100 and suspended two years.[2]

Catcher "Boileryard" Clarke, who spent two years with the Beaneaters (1899–1900) and later coached the Princeton University team for three decades, accused Soden of abject indifference toward his players:

> And what of Boileryard Clarke's testimony about what it was like to play for Boston in those years? Upon coming to Boston from Baltimore in 1899, Clarke immediately noticed that along with being notoriously stingy, Beaneaters owner Arthur Soden was a remarkably cold fish. Clarke swore that even though he played with Boston two full seasons Soden never knew he was on the team, let alone his name.[3]

Not surprisingly, Clarke was one of the first Beaneaters to jump to the upstart American League in 1901.

In contrast to his normal, near-maniacal tight-fistedness, Soden occasionally would demonstrate equally radical largesse. At a time when top salaries hovered around $3,000, for example, he paid $10,000 to Chicago to acquire Mike "King" Kelly, and negotiated a three-year contract for $25,000 with the White Stockings temperamental pitcher John Clarkson.

A hint that such wild swings in behavior may also have been evident occasionally in Soden's personal life is revealed in a *New York Times* news item of the era. In January 1909, F.L. Small, a broker, filed a $500,000 lawsuit against Soden, stating that the magnate had often "visited his home, alienated his wife's affections, drugged both him and his wife, and frequently enticed her away from his home."[4] No record exists of the disposition of the suit.

Late in Soden's reign, baseball players and fans were informed of an incident that solidified his unsavory and devious reputation. In 1900, frustrated by years of repression and hostility on the part of the owners, a players' group established a new union, the Protective Association of Professional Baseball Players, and prepared a list of grievances to present to the magnates. The owners' strategy consisted of refusing to meet with the players' delegation. Union representative Cal Griffith, a pitcher for the Chicago club, took matters into his own hands and followed owner Soden into a saloon, "where in the presence of reporters he demanded to know whether Soden had received a copy of the player petition. When Soden replied that he had not, Griffith proved him a liar by grabbing the document from Soden's coat pocket."[5] The incident aroused public sympathy for the players among the fans and forced the owners to make some concessions. While not extraordinary, "the total effect was to free them [the players] from abject serfdom and to elevate the status of the profession."[6]

The tide had turned. After a good portion of his team's players jumped to Boston's American League team in 1901, Soden brashly pontificated, "Many of the men who are jumping the league are saving [us] the trouble of giving them their discharge papers. The public refused to enthuse over their work last season in the big league and is not likely to do so next season."[7] History proved the "Dean of the National League" wrong. Boston's new American League team nearly doubled its National League rival's attendance figures in 1901, finishing second in the new junior circuit, while the Beaneaters finished fifth in the senior circuit.

Arthur Soden sold his interest in the Boston Nationals just prior to the start of the 1906 season.

Boston's National Association and National League teams played their home games at the same location, the South End Grounds at Columbus Avenue and Walpole Street, for forty-four years. During that period the park was built and rebuilt three times. South End Grounds I opened on May 16, 1871. Torn down for improvements in 1876, its second incarnation was a setting "where Sir Lancelot would have felt right at home."[8] The park's Grand Pavilion "was what we now would call a grandstand. After an open space of perhaps six feet sat a third level anchored by six conical spheres made of hand stamped tin.... From each flew pennants that in earlier times might have heralded jousting tournaments."[9]

Although the South End Grounds featured extremely short distances down the foul lines (250 feet in left field; 255 feet in right), outfield depth quickly increased to 450 feet in dead center and left-center, and 440 feet in right-center. This unique configuration is described by Michael Benson, author of *Ballparks of North America*, as "like a bowling alley. It had only one field: center."[10] During his Boston years, of course, it was Billy Hamilton's job to defend this immense piece of real estate.

After burning to the ground in May of 1894, South End Grounds was rebuilt in July of that year, but since this version of the park was under-insured by Arthur Soden, its third incarnation, formally known as the Boston National Base Ball Park, was much more modest. South End Grounds III was demolished after the 1915 National League Bostons, known then as the Braves, built a new 40,000-seat stadium on Commonwealth Avenue.

The November 1895 Billy Hamilton-for-Billy Nash exchange between Philadelphia and Boston is regarded today as one of the more lopsided trades in baseball history.[11] Richmond native Billy Nash, one of the first Jewish players of the game's early era, arrived in Boston midway through the 1884 season after playing on Virginia's short-lived (46 games) American Association team. After five years with the Beaneaters, he jumped to the Players' League Boston Reds in 1890 for their only season. Nash was lured back to Boston's National League team in 1891 by the offer of the title of team captain and a three-year contract at $5,000 annually. A strong-armed third baseman, he led the league in fielding percentage from 1891 to 1893, and was a lifetime .275 hitter.

With manager Frank Selee at the helm, the Beaneaters won three consecutive pennants from 1891 to 1893, but slipped to third place in 1894 and fifth place in 1895, as the rowdy Baltimore Orioles came to prominence. After the fifth-place finish there was considerable turmoil on the Boston team. Nash wanted complete control of field decisions: "It is known that Captain Nash would like to be given the full charge of the club when on the field, with it the selection of the pitchers, etc., but Manager Selee would scarcely allow this to pass out of his hands."[12] While it was common in an earlier era for the captain to be the field general as well, this practice was disappearing in the 1890s. The arrival of future Hall of Famer Jimmy Collins, who threatened Nash with stiff competition for the third base assignment, further soured his relations with Selee. The schism that had developed between the captain and the manager appeared irresolvable.

> The experience of the past season demonstrated to many minds that it was almost impossible for Manager Selee and Nash to be associated together in one team. The lack of entire harmony between the manager and the captain

was plainly visible on several occasions, and it was evidently only a matter of time when the two men would be separated.[13]

While trade rumors involving Nash were swirling, the national press reported that the team in general was "torn with schisms," and that "no team could win with so much working at cross purposes."[14] In November, a front-page article in the *Sporting News* entitled "Trouble in Boston" further suggested that religious differences played a part in the team's "disharmony." "They may talk as they please about religion cutting no figure with the harmony of the team, but I tell you it did last season ... a Boston catcher says a young pitcher, Sexton, was released due to his religious beliefs."[15]

With manager Arthur Irwin out at Philadelphia, the Phillies owners reasoned that trading Hamilton for Nash would net them not only a fine infielder and team captain, but also a player-manager. In Boston, Manager Selee, realizing that Nash and veteran outfielder Tommy "Little Mac" McCarthy were nearing the end of their careers, sold McCarthy to Brooklyn, traded Nash to Philadelphia for Hamilton, and eased Jimmy Collins into the full-time job at the hot corner. Tommy McCarthy retired from baseball after the 1896 season. Nash hit .247 for the Phillies that year while leading them to an eighth-place finish, and spent only one more full season (1897) in the majors, hitting .243. In contrast, over the next three seasons, Collins would average .323 and Hamilton .359 for Boston, and the Beaneaters would win two pennants. In December of 1895, the national press gave the distinct advantage to Boston with regard to the trade, and while doing so painted a picture of Hamilton that had been largely absent from his portrait in the Philadelphia press:

> The trade will certainly hurt the drawing capacity of the [Philadelphia] team, for no one was more popular with the patrons of the game here than Billy Hamilton. He is the best run-getter that ever played ball. Many are the crowds that Hamilton has sent away from the grounds at Broad and Huntingdon Streets satisfied that they had received their money's worth ... there is a dash about his play that inspires the spectator ... that he will be missed both by the team and the patrons is a certainty.[16]

After visiting friends in Boston in January 1896, Billy made his first public comments on the trade, which were paraphrased by a reporter and suggested that he was already in training for the upcoming campaign:

He said he could not but laugh at some of the statements that have been made about him, statements that he preferred to refute by his work on the ballfield rather than by any rejoinder on his part ... in his career of six years in Philadelphia he had made many friends. He liked the city very much and he regretted to sever the ties that had bound him to members of the Philadelphia club.... Billy hopes to show up better in his throwing next season. He has been bowling a great deal and thinks the exercise has benefitted him considerably.[17]

The man responsible for bringing Billy Hamilton to Boston, Frank Selee, did not look the part of a savvy bench manager. Short, frail, and bald, sporting the iconic handlebar moustache and bowler hat of the era, he seemed an unlikely strategist or team builder. In Selee's case, however, appearances were deceiving. Raised in suburban Boston, he recognized early the limits of his own physical baseball talent, and set about instead to succeed as a manager of minor league teams. Promoted to the National League's Bostons in 1890, he led them to five pennants in eleven years. Philosophically, Selee was a throwback to the age of gentlemanly baseball, insisting not only on rigorous training from his players, but also on temperance and good behavior. He believed in place-hitting, sacrifice hitting, and stealing bases, and his teams were said to "resemble a ballet on dirt."[18] The Boston pilot possessed an uncanny ability to assess talent, both on the rise and on the decline, and would dispassionately dispose of players who were past their prime, regardless of their loyalty or years of service. In 1901, after the new American League raided and decimated Selee's Boston roster, the Beaneaters faltered. Released by owner Arthur Soden, Selee spent four years building the fledgling Chicago Orphans (later known as the Cubs), making the same kind of astute hires there that he had made in Boston, including the familiar double-play combination of shortstop Joe Tinker, second baseman Johnny Evers, and first baseman Frank Chance. Selee, however, didn't live to see the Cubs talent he hired come to full fruition. Never in good health, he developed consumption (tuberculosis) and died of the disease in 1909. He was 49 years old.

As the 1896 campaign approached, some Philadelphia sportswriters, not content with having helped engineer Billy Hamilton's departure from the Phillies, tried to influence the perception of Sliding Billy by the Boston press, which, to its credit, chose to take a different view.

A Philadelphia writer kindly gives advice as to the treatment of our new fielder, "Billy" Hamilton, who is considered by him as a disorganizer, a bad man on grounders and throwing, and as being "mulish" [that is, behaving like a mule; stubborn]. Considerate treatment by newspapers is advised by him as an incentive for Hamilton to do good work. It is very evident Hamilton did not get this in Philadelphia, and it is historical of the failure of any manager, even Harry Wright, to land a pennant winner in that city, and it is acknowledged that Irwin was no improvement over his predecessors and was glad of the opportunity to go elsewhere. Mr. Wright was able to go so far with the team and no further. "Mulishness" seems to have been contagious in that team for that is exactly the reputation it had all along the line ... the team had been for years a great batting and fielding team and nothing more, and the way the game was misplayed at times was enough to provoke any fast man. It is just possible that Mr. Hamilton may find conditions in Boston the coming season which will suit his disposition....[19]

Billy Hamilton as a Boston Beaneater, 1897 (courtesy Transcendental Graphics).

In an interview given in late February, Billy Hamilton, reflecting on the trade and his treatment by the press, considered himself to be a lucky man:

> Judging by what they have to say about me in Philadelphia ... I will be anything but a good man for the Bostons, a rank disorganizer and heaven knows what else, but I think that with some in the old city of Philadelphia I had a different reputation. I regret changing sides with the many of my friends in the Quaker City, but think it's time to make a change if you do not have everybody with you. There are players in clubs who would like to change but cannot. I am one of the lucky ones. I sympathize deeply with those who are obliged to stay. Better get away even if abuse follows you than stay and be made a target of. I am just anxious for the season to begin, so that I can get my work in and show my traducers a thing or two.[20]

Billy Hamilton, circa 1896. The original appeared as a "baseball card" handout in a Sunday edition of the *Boston Journal* (courtesy Howard "Skip" Reynolds).

Years later, in an unusual admission of "trader's remorse," Philadelphia co-owner Al Reach conceded that his team's decision to trade Sliding Billy had been a mistake. "We should never have allowed him to go, had it not been for some bad advice that we got ... we made a great mistake. Hamilton is without doubt one of the best players in the country."[21] This admission was reiterated in somewhat stronger terms by *Sporting Life* in 1902:

The acquisition of Collins was the downfall of Billy Nash, and Boston not only secured a wonderful third baseman, but on top of that got one of the greatest batsmen in the country in Billy Hamilton. It was immediately acknowledged that Philadelphia got gold-bricked on this deal, for the absence of Hamilton meant a [great] deal to the Philadelphia club, and his place was not filled for a long time.[22]

On March 19, as the Bostons left Massachusetts for spring training in Charlottesville, Virginia, curious Beaneaters fans got their first close glimpse of Sliding Billy. It is clear that the reputation of his good habits, and not that which was proposed by Philadelphia sportswriters, had preceded him: "Billy Hamilton was eagerly regarded by many at the depot, for [they] seldom had been accorded the opportunity to see him in citizen's clothes. Hamilton is in great trim, as is to be expected of a man of the best habits who has an eye to business all the time."[23]

Billy's individual Boston photo from the 1896 season, which was published as a special insert to a Sunday edition of the *Boston Journal*, presents a marked contrast to his earliest major league photos, previously discussed, which were taken while he was a member of the Kansas City Cowboys in 1889. The earlier photos depict young Billy in several defensive and offensive poses, dressed in bulky, ill-fitting quilted knickers of the day, and wearing a long sleeve shirt that looks suspiciously like a long underwear top under his short-sleeved uniform jersey. He sports a wide belt that is so ill-fitting that its buckle is gathered up behind his back in the photo. The awkward poses, ill-fitting clothing, and earnest seriousness of Billy's expression speak volumes about the team, the era, and the young rookie. The 1896 Boston photo reveals an entirely different man. His mature, muscular body poured into a neatly pressed and creased shirt and knickers, his shoes shined, Billy is pictured in a relaxed, confident pose, right hand on his hip, and left hand leaning casually on his bat. He gazes into the distance with a calm, determined glance. The photo comparison vividly illustrates the fact that Billy's circumstances had changed markedly from his Kansas City days. So had the man.

By the start of the 1896 season, Skipper Selee had only partially completed his reconstruction of the Beaneater team. The "keepers" included team captain Hugh Duffy and newcomer Billy Hamilton in the outfield, Jimmy Collins at third base, Herman Long, Billy's old

Kansas City teammate and rodent killer extraordinaire at shortstop, and reliable Pittsburgh native Bobby Lowe holding down the second base assignment, as he had since his rookie season in 1890. Selee had not yet found replacements for two other current team members — ten-year veteran first baseman Tommy Tucker and thirty-five-year-old right fielder Jimmy Bannon. Just prior to the start of the 1894 season, Selee lost his veteran catcher, Charlie Bennet, to a horrific accident. In January of that year, Bennet, a seven-time fielding percentage league-leader behind the plate for Boston, slipped while trying to board a moving train in Wellsville, Kansas. Both his legs were severed by the train wheels. Bennet survived, but spent the rest of his life in a wheel chair. After using several journeyman catchers for two years, in April of 1896 Frank Selee acquired a new man behind the plate, signing the highly talented but, as we shall see, the highly troubled Western League catcher, Martin Bergen.

Two pitchers that Selee retained, Nichols and Stivetts, would have significant seasons, winning 30 and 24 games, respectively. Ashland, Pennsylvania's 6'2" Jack Stivetts was one of the best hitting pitchers in the history of the game. In 1894, Stivetts "compiled 26 wins, 80 hits, and a .533 slugging average. No other performer since 1893 — not even Babe Ruth — has been both a 20-game winner and so potent a hitter in the same season."[24]

Nichols, a future Hall of Famer, would notch seven thirty-win seasons in the 1890s. One of baseball's premier pitchers, he won 361 games in 15 major league seasons — an average of 24 per season. A Wisconsin native, he first signed with the Western League's Kansas City squad in 1887 at the age of 17. His tender age and youthful appearance earned him the nickname "Kid." Although sources suggest that he threw only one pitch — the fastball — news reports from his Boston years make frequent reference to "Charley's curves." Nearly as remarkable as his seven thirty-win seasons is the fact that he completed 94 percent of the games that he started.

Frank Selee was intent on replacing third starter Jim Sullivan, who had been up and down with Boston and Columbus of the American Association. Two young pitchers would eventually compete for that spot on the roster, but neither was signed until late in the season, and both would not come into their own until the following year. Selee plucked Welsh-born Ted "Parson" Lewis directly from the Williams

College campus, and the college man made his debut with the Bostons in July. After his baseball days were over, Lewis, who acquired his nickname by stipulating in his contract that he would not pitch on Sundays, entered the academic world, and would eventually become president of the University of New Hampshire. The second young hurler, Connecticut native Fred "Kloby" Klobedanz, a left-handed breaking ball pitcher, saw his first action in August.

A "master at putting together a team better than the sum of its parts,"[25] Selee would need another full year to build a championship team. Baltimore took the pennant for the third consecutive year in 1896, with the Bostons ending "a most disappointing season"[26] in fourth place.

During spring training that year in Virginia, Billy Hamilton, who had danced around stampeding buffalo herds in the outfield at Kansas City, had yet another bovine baseball encounter. Players of the 1890s had never heard of windbreaker jackets; they kept warm in early spring and late fall by wearing heavy, oversized, wool cardigan sweaters. *Sporting Life* noted that famously frugal Billy Hamilton had been exercising during spring training with the Beaneaters in his old Phillies cardigan, "the bright red, black striped sweater that Arthur Irwin picked out for the Phillies last season."[27] On a five-mile team run through Charlottesville's farmers' fields,

> Hamilton got the boys in trouble. Several lively bulls were roaming around when one of them caught sight of Hamilton's crimson jersey, the only one of that color in the crowd. Billy was jogging with his head down when [Jack] Stivetts [Boston's pitcher] ... saw Mr. Bull on the dead run, with his head down, making a bee line for Hamilton ... the entire "push" [group of team members] went for the stone fence and got over in time to see the bull come pretty near to butting the fence."[28]

As fortune would have it for Billy Nash and Billy Hamilton, Boston opened the season before 20,000 spectators in Philadelphia. Both men involved in the recent trade accorded themselves respectably on opening day; Nash had a hit, Hamilton had two with a stolen base and three runs scored. The Beaneaters won the opener, but Philadelphia took the series, winning the next two games. Against the champion Orioles in late April at the South End Grounds, Billy provided two early examples of his run-scoring ability for his new fans. In the fourth inning, "the ex–Quaker put in a scientific bunt, stole second, went to third on a short passed ball, and scored on Long's fly to Kelly."[29] Later in the contest, he scored from second base on Herman Long's short single to left to win the game.

In what would be a trying season for Boston, Hamilton proved both his worth and the sagacity of his new manager by hitting .365, leading the league in on-base percentage (.477), and coming in third in stolen bases with 83. Kid Nichols continued his dominance on the mound with a league-leading 30 wins, finishing with a second-best ERA of 2.83. Although Boston statistically was out of the picture in 1896, the champion Baltimore squad was harried all season but not conquered by the Cleveland Spiders, who featured Cy Young, a 28-game winner, and left fielder Jesse Burkett's .410 batting average and 240 hits.

Through May and June 1896, Billy Hamilton had at least one hit in all but four games. In the Boston press, his base stealing ability was now either taken for granted—"Hamilton made his usual steal of second"[30]—or was synonymous with his name: "Stivetts scored in the seventh, leading off with a single and stealing second a la Hamilton, and scoring on a single by McGann."[31]

By the end of May, a *Boston Globe*'s sportswriter was now ridiculing the Philadelphia colleague who had sent him warnings about Hamilton:

> Billy Hamilton continues to play entirely to our satisfaction, and you will now notice that there are no cracks at all about his insubordination, and he has not proven a Jonah or anything like it ... those scribes in the Quakertown [Philadelphia] who were knocking him with huge stones when the Phillies were marching along ... are singularly quiet now. The more conservative are just hitting it up for him.[32]

In a game against Cincinnati during one of his early-season hitting streaks, Hamilton had one of his now familiar multiple-category performances, going four-for-six, including a home run, a double, and two singles, stealing two bases, and scoring four runs. It proved to be an unusually hot summer, punctuated by much political heat as the Democrats and Republicans met to select their candidates for the upcoming fall election: William Jennings Bryan of Nebraska, and William McKinley of Ohio, respectively. Billy Hamilton was hot, too, leading his team in hitting, stealing bases, and making spectacular outfield catches. In August, Billy and Rebecca celebrated the arrival of their third daughter, Ruth. A Boston press recounting of a Saturday mid-month game at Brooklyn began with the headline "Hamilton's Day." Billy went three-for-three that afternoon, including a double, a home run, a walk, five stolen bases, and three runs scored. His four-bagger was described as being "as pretty a home run that ever went tearing through the smoke on the railroad tracks."[33] Boston closed the season winning five out of six from Brooklyn and Washington, but still finished seventeen games behind the Orioles. In an October season summary, the *Boston Daily Globe* put an end to the negative impression of Hamilton created a year earlier by Philadelphia press.

> Billy Hamilton naturally landed first [on the team] in batting, in runs scored, in bases on balls.... Boston has every reason to be pleased with the work of this grand player this year. It was prophesied that he would be a disorganizer and cause trouble on the team, but this has all been disproved and it has been largely through his instrumentality that the team has improved in its record of last year.... He has worked hard and faithfully, and has become a warm favorite with the public. There is no better drawing card in the team than "Billy."[34]

The 1897 and 1898 Beaneaters would return to the championship form they exhibited earlier in the decade, and Billy Hamilton at last would enjoy playing on a league champion team. This period would mark a peak in Sliding Billy's major league performance, before a variety of knee, leg, and ankle injuries began inexorably to erode his skills. Soon afterward, the Boston team and the entire National League were affected by the last great schism in major league baseball with the rise of the American League.

After only a week of spring training in Savannah, Georgia, the 1897 Beaneaters slowly worked their way north, playing exhibition games in Charleston, Newport News, Richmond, and Princeton, before finally opening the season at Philadelphia on April 19. After a short period of experimentation, Frank Selee had finally found his right field replacement in the person of rookie Hoosier Chick Stahl, whom he drafted from the Buffalo Bisons of the Eastern League, where Stahl hit .336 and led the league in triples (23) the previous year. Selee then surprised the press, the fans, and members of his team by moving Fred Tenney, a backup outfielder and left-handed catcher for the Bostons since 1894, to the first base position. Tenney responded by hitting .336 and turning in a quite respectable (for the era) fielding percentage of .988.

With these changes in place, Marty Bergen behind the plate, and Nichols, Klobedanz, and Lewis starting on the mound, the Boston pilot finally had what he thought would be a winning combination. For the first few weeks of the season, however, it certainly didn't seem to have been the right call. The Beaneaters lost their first five games, and arrived in Boston for their home opener with a 1–7 record. Billy Hamilton had an uncharacteristically slow start, hitting only .275 through the end of April, but nevertheless drew high praise from Boston sportswriter and former major league outfielder Tim Murnane: "I was given to understand that Billy was mulish, but I have failed to discover a single instance where this player was not anxious to win."[35]

Selee's new lineup soon jelled, Hamilton and the rest of the team started to hit, and Boston started to win, going 15–5 in May. An account of a fine catch made by Hamilton against Washington that month provides evidence both of Billy's speed in the outfield and his basic defensive philosophy of viewing no ball as uncatchable.

> Hamilton made the star play of the day. Reilly led off in the eighth with a savage rap, the ball going in dead earnest for the left field corner. Hamilton and Duffy went sprinting after the ball, and the former got there in time to take the ball close to the ground after one of the best exhibitions of sprinting ever seen at the grounds.[36]

Jimmy Collins, meanwhile, was revolutionizing third base play by "edging in when notorious bunters were at bat, and staying back for strong pull hitters." [37] Handsome, square-jawed James Joseph "Jimmy" Collins got his start with the Eastern League's Buffalo club in 1893. His performance there the following year caught the eye of Frank Selee, who signed him for the 1895 season. Selee liked what he saw, but thought Jimmy needed seasoning and sent him off by special agreement to last-place Louisville for the remainder of the season. Back in Boston to stay the next year, he became a fixture at third base and averaged well over .300 at the plate for the next half-dozen years. Collins' defensive strategy mirrored that of teammate Billy Hamilton by trying for every ball. The nemesis of opposition "small ball" teams like the Orioles, Jimmy "was a master of charging in on slowly hit balls, scooping them up barehanded, and then firing in one motion to first or second."[38]

Fred Tenney proved to be an excellent second man in the lineup behind Hamilton. Billy "almost invariably has started his team off by reaching first on a nice single, a bunt, or a base on balls."[39] Tenney used his adept bunting ability to advance Hamilton to second or third, and while on base could distract the defense while Billy was rounding the bases. "In the first inning with Hamilton on third, Tenney coaxed a throw to first and let the baseman try for him while Hamilton was scoring."[40] Boston's quick turnaround, including a seventeen-game win streak, sometimes caused the giddy press to take flights of stylistic fancy.

> [Chicago shortstop] McCormic hit the ball hard, and as it went out sailing over the meadow, like a hawk locating its quarry, Mr. William Hamilton, a native of the old bay state, was on his toes timing the flying missile. When it came down he froze to it like eel grass on a jelly fish, and the sun went dancing down behind the railroad tracks, while the large crowd gave three times three and a tiger for the boys, who are playing the national game up to date and three points beyond.[41]

Although by late June Boston had climbed into the lead in the standings after taking two of three games from Baltimore at the South End Grounds, for the remainder of the season the team traded places with the Orioles in a mad dash for the pennant. Strategically, both teams subscribed to a similar philosophy — with one glaring exception. Each played scrappy, smart baseball, relying on the bunt, the steal, and the hit-and-run play to score runs. The Orioles, however, supplemented this approach with a rabid rowdyism that included physical and verbal abuse of umpires and opposing players. Outfielders Joe Kelley and the diminutive Willie Keeler, shortstop Hughie Jennings, and third baseman John McGraw formed a formidable Baltimore quartet of lifetime .300 hitters and future Hall of Famers who were the mainstays of the "rowdy" philosophy. This roughhouse quartet, known as the "Big Four,"

> were the core of the team ... all four were Irish and scrappy ... they were friends who played the same way. On the diamond and off, they had learned to work as one ... they prayed together at St. Ann's church ... they would gather after church and visit some of the girls they knew in most of the cities around the league ... all of them ... belonged to the Maryland Yacht Club.[42]

Born in Truxton, New York, John McGraw had no childhood. At the age of twelve he left home, hardened by the death of his mother and four siblings from diphtheria, and by the regular beatings he received from his father. He survived by selling newspapers and peddling fruit and candy on local trains, playing ball in the off-hours. Despite his size (5'7", 120 pounds), McGraw's move from town ball to the minor leagues was rapid, and he latched on with Baltimore in 1891.

McGraw became close friends with red-headed, freckle-faced Hugh "Hughie" Jennings, a light-hitting shortstop from the Scranton, Pennsylvania, coal mines who had been traded to the Orioles from Louisville. In the off-seasons, the pair coached the Allegany College (later St. Bonaventure College) baseball team in Pennsylvania in exchange for room and board and college classes. McGraw cured Jennings of his tendency to bail out on inside pitches, and afterward, Hughie's Baltimore batting average soared.

Willie Keeler, at 5'4" one of the smallest men ever to play major league baseball, arrived in Baltimore in 1894 after having been up and down with Brooklyn and Eastern League Binghamton. Willie and John McGraw soon became one of the best hit-and-run combinations in the history of baseball. Leading off, McGraw's ability to foul off pitches led to many walks. Once on, he would signal to the second hitter, Keeler, and then take off for second on the next pitch. Keeler's outstanding bat control enabled him to push the ball to a space that the middle infielders had vacated while covering second during McGraw's attempted steal.

Perhaps the least well known of the rowdy four, left fielder Joe Kelley of Cambridge, Massachusetts, was handsome and knew it. Blonde-haired, and the tallest and most sturdily built of the Irish quartet, "The ladies loved him almost as much as he loved himself."[43] A solid all-around player, he hit over .300 in eleven consecutive campaigns. In almost any other season in baseball history, his 167 runs scored in 1894 would have won him league honors. That year, however, Billy Hamilton's 196 runs set a scoring record that still stands.

Frank Selee's Boston team earnestly eschewed the roughhouse approach of Baltimore's "Big Four," and the struggle for the 1897 league leadership, therefore, became described in the press as a battle between "the good guys" and the Baltimore bullies. By 1897, a good deal of the Orioles' contentiousness on the field had turned inward. Manager Ned Hanlon, who had condoned McGraw and company's rough style of playing when it brought the team success, now found himself belittled by McGraw in front of his own team.[44] Mugsy's criticism of Willie Keeler's play led to fisticuffs between the two on the team's dressing room floor. After first baseman "Dirty Jack" Doyle allegedly took a punch at McGraw, only Manager Hanlon's physical restraint of his third baseman prevented McGraw from assaulting Doyle with a bat.[45]

In Boston, Selee's lineup changes, including handing over Sullivan's and Stivetts' starter roles to rookies, ruffled a few feathers, but the team's player interactions, in contrast to those in Baltimore, were in a decidedly lighter vein, as evidenced by a humorous incident involving Billy Hamilton and Hugh Duffy during a mid–July game at Pittsburgh. In the first inning, Billy doubled down the left field line, and then on the first pitched ball to [second hitter] Tenney, "he stole third, sliding a considerable distance. He came in contact with Davis' spikes ... and Boston's great fielder's trousers are now shy a few pieces of flannel. The tear in the trousers caused a great laugh from the crowd and Hugh Duffy made everyone roar asking Donovan to provide Hamilton with a barrel."[46]

With Baltimore leading the league by a fraction of a percentage point (.707 to .706), the league championship came down to a three-game series in Baltimore, beginning September 24. "[Boston's] Nichols won the series opener on Friday, 6–4, but [Baltimore's] Hoffer beat Kobledanz the following afternoon to put the Orioles back in first.... Sunday was an off day ... but on Monday ... Boston bats pummeled Corbett and three other Orioles [pitchers] ... and [Boston] won 19–10 to leave town with a half game lead."[47]

If Boston had lost the series, Billy Hamilton in all probability would have been named its goat. Defensively, it was not his finest hour. In the first game, "the only man to waver was Billy Hamilton, who made two bad errors, allowing a base hit to pass him to the fence, and again by putting his team in the hole by muffing a line drive."[48] In the second contest, "Hamilton's mistakes were in allowing two singles to go for three bases; both were failures to stop easy bounding balls."[49] Billy offered no excuses for these miscues, although ankle and tendon injuries that sidelined him for half of August, severely curtailing his base-stealing efforts and general running ability, may partially have been to blame. He redeemed himself in two ways. After going hitless in the first game of the series, he garnered six hits, stole two bases, and scored three runs in the two remaining contests. Tagged out at home in the second game by Orioles catcher Wilbert Robinson after a botched double steal attempt with Bobby Lowe, Billy made sure such a circumstance would not happen again in the third game, even though catcher Robinson outweighed him by fifty pounds. "Lowe lined a clean single to center, and Hamilton raced home with the lead run. As he had done two days earlier, Robinson tried to block the plate, but Hamilton lowered his shoulder and leveled the catcher, scoring the tying run."[50]

The Beaneaters officially clinched the pennant a week later, beating Brooklyn as Baltimore lost to Washington. Despite his late-season leg injuries, Billy Hamilton hit .343 for the year, led the league in runs scored (152), and was third in stolen bases (66), having, in the opinion of the press, "played as large a part in bringing the pennant to Boston as any player on the Boston team."[51]

At the conclusion of the 1897 championship season, Boston played Baltimore in the last post-season major league series before the advent of the modern World Series in 1903. The Orioles won the event, which was called the Temple Cup Series, four games to one.

Although not officially recognized today by major league baseball, post-season "championships" date from 1884. Prior to that year, since there was only one major league in the fledgling era of the National Association (1871–75) and the early years of the National League, the default champion was the team that finished in first place at season's end. After the birth of a second league, the American Association (1881), a natural rivalry developed between it and the older National League with regard to whose organization was superior. In 1884, Association president H. D. McKnight challenged National League president A.G. Mills to a best-of-three series between the champions of each organization, with the winner being declared champion of both leagues. The National League, which regularly dismissed its rival as a minor league, but which was feeling the financial effect of its popularity (as well as the threat of another competitor on the scene, the Union League), accepted the challenge: "Each team put up $1,000 to go to the winner, with the purse held by the N.Y. *Clipper*, which billed the event as the first 'World's Series.'"[52]

The opponents were the league's Providence Grays and the association's New York Metropolitans. On October 23, 1884, the first-ever World Series game was played at the Polo Grounds. Grays ace "Hoss" Radbourne, whose sixty victories that year will forever remain a major league record, defeated Tim Keefe and the Mets, 3–0. Despite having pitched 678 innings during the season, "Old Hoss" was not finished.

He pitched and won both games of a doubleheader the next day to take the series for Providence. In 1885, both leagues and owners, now aware of a new and lucrative revenue opportunity, agreed to expand the series to a best-of-seven format. The second Series between the St. Louis Browns and the Chicago White Stockings ended locked at 3–3, with a deciding game controversially declared a tie. The same two teams met in the next year's classic, with St. Louis becoming the first Association team to win a World Series when John Clarkson's errant pitch got away from catcher King Kelly, allowing the winning run to score in the tenth inning of the seventh game.

Greed reigned supreme in 1887 and 1888, when the series was extended to fifteen and eleven contests, respectively, with games being played in other parks beside those of the two league's pennant winners, regardless of whether one team had already clinched the championship. St. Louis lost both series, first to Detroit in 1887 and then to the Mets in 1888.

Some sanity returned in 1889, when both clubs, Brooklyn and New York, after scheduling an eleven-game series, agreed to cease playing as soon as a winner was determined. The League's Giants beat the Association's Bridegrooms, 6–1, on the strength of Cannonball Crane's four complete-game wins. The last Association versus League post-season championship occurred in 1890, and it was a sad affair. Most star players had defected to the Players' League that year, and the lusterless series between Brooklyn and Louisville, scheduled for 11 games, was declared a draw at three wins each, with one tie, when poor weather and dwindling attendance persuaded both sides to quit. In 1891, the Association champion Boston Reds, "one of the strongest teams"[53] of the nineteenth century, challenged their cross-town rivals, the League champion Beaneaters, to a series. The Beaneaters, undoubtedly aware that the Reds had led the Association in hits, runs, RBIs, walks, stolen bases, and batting average, declined the offer. The first phase of nineteenth century post-season competition was over.

When the American Association and the National League merged in 1892, the rationale for a World Series disappeared. Owners in the new League-Association, however, regretted the loss of another opportunity for revenue. In 1894, Pittsburgh owner William C. Temple proposed a new version of post-season competition, the details of which contained the seeds of its future failure.

Temple offered a silver trophy to the winner of a best-of-seven-game series between the National League's first- and second-place teams. Players on the winning team would receive sixty-five percent of all ticket sales, while the losing team would receive thirty-five percent. In order to generate interest and enthusiasm, the new post-season competition was dubbed the "World's Championship Series," which, decidedly, it was not:

> The first Temple Cup challenge got off to a bad start, when each Orioles starter made a secret fifty/fifty deal with his counterpart on the Giants. The best of seven series then became a travesty, as the Giants won four straight one-sided games.... Though the [second-place] Giants were now officially the League-Association champions, no one outside of New York bought the fact that their victory meant anything, a problem that would haunt promoters of the Temple Cup series in each year of its short existence.[54]

Ultimately, some of the Giants reneged on the fifty/fifty deal, adding mutual player distrust to the lackadaisical play and low fan interest that plagued the series.

The Orioles played all four Temple Cup series, losing, 4–1, against Cleveland in 1895, beating the Spiders, 4–0, in 1896, and winning, 4–1, against Boston in 1897. Poor crowds in Baltimore and Cleveland in 1896 left the Spiders with a paycheck of just $117 per man. "Even in a time of miserably small salaries and low player morale, the meager payoff for playing in raw weather to determine a winner few took seriously seemed hardly worth the effort." [55]

In Baltimore on September 27, 1897, the largest crowd (25,390) ever recorded to that date watched the last game of the Orioles and Beaneaters series that determined the pennant. Two weeks later, only 2,500 turned out to watch the fifth game of the Temple Cup. At the final game, which was won, along with the series, by Baltimore, the crowd was so small "that management refused to give the exact number."[56]

Soon afterward, William Temple withdrew the Temple Cup, and the second phase of post-season major league competition became history. Waiting in the wings was a new league, whose top team in 1903 would challenge the league leader of the older league, creating a new "Fall Classic" that endures to this day.

The 1898 baseball season was completely overshadowed by the Spanish-American War, which, although of short duration, dominated the news long after the cessation of hostilities. A steep decline in league attendance was blamed on the public's preoccupation with the conflict. League owners instituted several significant rule changes for the campaign. A double umpiring system was initiated, leading to more accurate calls and greatly reducing the most egregious attempts to circumvent the rules. The system's extra cost was underwritten by the extension of the season by 22 contests, for a total of 154 games. Players salaries, however, remained capped at the $2,400 maximum, despite the fact they were now required to play 15 percent more games. The existing rule granting a stolen base to runners advancing from first to third on a single was rescinded. (As a result, Billy Hamilton's stolen base total prior to this year subsequently was adjusted downward.) League batting averages in 1898 fell 21 points, to .271,[57] thanks to the fact that all new and current pitchers were now well-acquainted with the 60'6" pitching distance, and that the pitching rubber, which began as a flat surface that was level with the rest of the playing field, was now perched upon a mound of packed dirt. The era of the physically menacing hurler towering on a pitcher's mound had begun.

Eighteen ninety-eight was a near-perfect year for the Beaneaters, but a problematic one for Billy Hamilton. All the starters returned healthy, and Manager Selee's signing of rookie phenom Vic Willis allowed the Bostons to field a four-man pitching rotation, consisting of Nichols, Lewis, Willis, and Klobedanz. The pitching quartet won all but one of the team's record 102 victories, and Boston, "by a margin of only one victory, missed becoming the first team ever to have four 20-game winners."[58] Although Billy Hamilton started the year in fine form, the knee, leg, and ankle injuries that hampered him the previous season became more pronounced as the 1898 campaign progressed, causing him to miss more than forty contests. In early spring, however, it was the old familiar Billy who put in an appearance.

> Billy Hamilton must have made Philadelphia tired by the work he did in the last game in that city. He went five times to the bat and made four hits and stole two bases ... in four successive games Hamilton made twelve hits in eighteen at bats, and in two games he made seven hits in nine times at bat — a good showing away from home.... There is no discounting the power Hamilton is to the Boston club.[59]

The classic Hamilton style of getting on base and "going the rounds," that is, coming around to score a run, was evidenced as early as the season's opener against New York, when he led off the first inning with a walk, went to second on a wild pitch, tagged up and went to third after a fly to right, and came home on a sacrifice fly to right.[60] In another version of "completing the grand circuit," he bunted his way safely to first against Baltimore on April 22, stole second and third, and scored on a single by Herman Long. In the first inning of a game in early June against Cincinnati, "Hamilton got into the game with a rush, drawing a prize [a walk], stealing second and going to third on [Farmer] Vaughn's poor throw, from where he jogged home on Tenney's fly to [left fielder Elmer] Smith."[61]

Besides his fine early-season hitting and baserunning, Billy once again made the near-impossible look mundane in the outfield, as in a game against Brooklyn on May 17: "Hamilton made a wonderful running catch in the eighth when [Billy] Shindle led off with a drive to right center that was marked for the fence. The ball never was more than five feet from the ground, and was taken by Hamilton on a cross run while he stood out like a banner in a strong breeze."[62]

Billy was also hitting for both average and power, and at a level not seen in his career since 1894. In late May, he interrupted his regular routine of peppering bunts and slash hits to the left side of the diamond by pulling two four-baggers to right, with one blast on May 30 sailing "high over the right field fence."[63]

Such efforts were soon curtailed sharply by injuries. On June 13, Billy turned his knee in a game against Philadelphia, and although he tried to play the next day, he was replaced in the third inning and remained out of the lineup for a week. On July 3 he wrenched his knee again in a game and was out for more than a month. Returning to the field against Cincinnati on August 22, he was injured running into the fence while trying to haul down Dusty Miller's double. In mid–September, the *Globe* reported that "Billy Hamilton will be out of the game for a few days with his favorite sore knee."[64] Finally, he missed a series in October due to a recurrence of this injury.

In August, the surging Cincinnati club, behind left fielder Elmer Smith's hitting and fine pitching by Pink Hawley and Ted Breitenstein, challenged the Beaneaters for the league lead. By mid September, Baltimore had overcome the Reds' charge and captured second place on the strength of the performances of their quartet of future Hall of Famers — Keeler, Kelley, Jennings, and McGraw — who collectively were hitting at a .340 clip. Boston prevailed, however, winning all but one of its series with other league teams, and finishing with the most wins (102) in league history.

The 1898 Boston championship proved bittersweet for Billy Hamilton, whose chronic injuries were forcing him to think about retiring from major league play. "Billy Hamilton has informed [reporter] Jake Morse that two more years on the diamond would end his career."[65]

In 1899, the Brooklyn Bridegrooms broke the stranglehold Boston and Baltimore had on the league championship since the beginning of the decade. Historically, the manner in which they accomplished this feat is perhaps more important than the simple fact that they did so. It was a fairly common practice for wealthy owners of one league team to own stock in other clubs in the league during the 1890s. After the 1898 season, several owners decided to take this practice a step further by uniting two clubs under one management team, an action referred to today as "syndicate ball." Cleveland Spiders owners Frank and Stanley Robison, for example, bought a controlling interest in the St. Louis Browns franchise, moved their offices to St. Louis, and transferred player-manager Patsy Tebeau, batting champ Jesse Burkett, and legendary pitcher Cy Young to St. Louis. The Robisons reasoned that with such talent, the last-place Browns, whose franchise was located in what was then the fourth-largest city in the nation, would enjoy better attendance the following year. Baltimore owner Harry Von der Horst and team manager/president Ned Hanlon followed suit by buying a controlling interest in the Brooklyn team. Prior to being incorporated into New York City, Brooklyn was the second-largest city in the country. After their purchase, Von der Horst and Hanlon transferred most of the best Orioles players to Brooklyn. Such "interlocking ownerships," besides creating bizarre organizational charts (Ned Hanlon, for example, served both as field manager for Brooklyn and president of the Baltimore club), "made a travesty of genuine competition between major league clubs."[66]

John McGraw, who had private business interests in Maryland, refused to join his fellow teammates in Brooklyn, and at 26, was named player-manager of a new Orioles team bereft of experienced players. His genius at discovering new talent helped the depleted 1899 Orioles salvage a miraculous fourth-place finish, but Cleveland became the joke of the league as a result of syndicate baseball, winning just 20 and losing 134. Once again, the National League's short-sightedness, in this case in condoning syndicate ball, would ultimately prove its undoing. At the end of the season, Baltimore, Cleveland, and two other teams with weak attendance, Washington and Louisville, were jettisoned from the National League. The displaced players, owners, and fans of three of these cities' teams would soon find a home in a new professional baseball association: the American League.

Nothing went right for Boston or Billy Hamilton in 1899. After being detained from spring training due to "illness in his family,"[67] Hamilton had another home plate encounter with Baltimore's 235-pound catcher Wilbert Robinson in a May 2 game. "Catcher Robinson and Hamilton were in a mix up at the plate, the runner saving his bacon by a fancy twist in passing the rubber [home plate]. Hamilton caught his toe on one corner and sprained his foot."[68] With the exception of a few pinch-hitting assignments and scattered, infrequent starts, the injury kept Billy out of the lineup until late July. In typical Hamilton fashion, he gave no thought to playing conservatively when he returned from the injury. In his first game back he made eight putouts in center field, including one "of the barehand variety on the dead run, [with the ball] not two feet from the ground.[69] After several weeks of solid, everyday play, he injured his knee going after another fly ball, and saw limited action for the remainder of the season.

In late September, Washington catcher and Clinton native Malachi Kittridge shared his thoughts on Hamilton's injury and the poor showing of the Beaneaters with the *Globe*'s sportswriters, who in turn offered their own analysis for the team's lack of scoring:

> "One of the greatest drawbacks the Boston club ran against this season was the accident to Hamilton," says Kittridge, the Washington catcher.... "Hamilton was the run getter, and the Boston team could win games on fewer hits than any team in the league...." Kittridge's opinion of Hamilton is shared by an army of Boston fans. Only a few days ago Hamilton informed a friend that he felt sure of coming around as well as ever next season, as he now understood how to look after his lameness during the winter.... When the greatest run getter in the business was leading off as well as ever about the middle of the season, it was a noticeable fact that Tenney was not advancing him as of old. The batsman and runner are supposed to work together with signs, but this season Tenney figured out that he could see Hamilton start and know when to hit: the result was bad business all around and the team suffered the consequence.[70]

Kittridge would join the Beaneaters and do the majority of the catching for the team in 1901, Billy's last season.

During the brief period of day-to-day play that in effect comprised his 1899 season, Billy, as noted previously, was ejected from the only game in his career, at the hands of former rival Arlie Latham, prompting the *Globe* to observe wryly, "Think of Hamilton being put out of the game by Latham simply for telling Arlie what most everyone knew!"[71] Although Billy finished the year with a respectable .310 average, he stole only 19 bases, and for the first time since his rookie season did not finish as one of the league's top five performers in an offensive category.

Boston's potent pitching quartet of the previous year stumbled in 1899. Nineteen-game winner Fred Kobledanz developed arm trouble, won only one game in the new season, and was released in mid–May. The remaining trio of Nichols, Lewis, and Willis won 17 fewer games than in 1898. Duffy, Long, Lowe, Hamilton, and Bergen all became the object of the frustrated Boston fans' displeasure.[72] By late September, Herman Long was quarreling with Manager Selee, wasn't reporting for games, and requested to be traded to Chicago, his hometown. Frank Selee then announced his intent to seek a permanent replacement for Billy Hamilton. Hamilton remained with Boston, but Selee was unaware at the time that he would need to find a replacement for catcher Marty Bergen, who, after the season's end, committed suicide at age 28 after bludgeoning to death his consumptive wife and two young children with an axe.

Dubbed the "King of Catchers" by the press, Bergen was "a nimble fielder with a bullwhip arm, who could snap the ball to second base without so much as moving his feet."[73] His erratic, paranoid behavior had been present since his minor league days with Kansas City, but became more prominent after his arrival in Boston and turned severe after the death of his young son Willie of diphtheria in April 1899. Bergen was subject to violent mood shifts, and in his paranoia, imagined that his teammates were trying to kill him, and that the team physician was trying to poison him. Throughout the 1899 season, Bergen would disappear from the Boston team without notice for days or weeks. On January 19, 1900, Marty Bergen slit his throat with a straight razor at his North Brookfield, Massachusetts, farm after brutally exterminating his family.

Only three people attended Marty Bergen's funeral: his brother Bill, a future big league catcher; former Pittsburgh catcher and current manager of the Western League's Milwaukee team Connie Mack; and Bergen's Boston teammate Billy Hamilton.

In an age before mental illness was understood or treated, Bergen's horrific deeds were in the main attributed to his own character flaws, and he was vilified in the press. Nevertheless, years later, after Sliding Billy's playing career was over, he could still recall and admire his former teammate's talent on the diamond:

> Of the many selections made of the 20 greatest ballplayers, "Not one," says Billy Hamilton, the old time Boston center fielder, "has named Martin Bergen. There was a man who, excepting Buck Ewing, was the greatest backstop the game ever saw. He was a wonderful thrower and could hit the ball and run bases."[74]

Nineteen hundred — change was in the air in the new century. The United States, a world power after its 1898 victory over Spain, joined other Western nations to intervene in China's Boxer Rebellion. William McKinley chose popular Spanish-American War hero Theodore Roosevelt as his running mate and handily defeated William Jennings Bryan a second time for the presidency. The U.S. population exceeded 75 million, at least six thousand of whom died when a hurricane surge submerged Galveston Island, Texas, on September 8.

A sea change was also on the way in major league baseball, one largely brought about by the efforts of Byron Bancroft "Ban" Johnson, a former Cincinnati sportswriter. Johnson had assumed command of the Western League, the "strongest minor [league] ever,"[75] in 1894, and quickly made it financially profitable through his keen business sense and absolute prohibition of "rowdy ball." In 1900, he changed the organization's name to the American League, established new franchises in Chicago (the White Sox) and Cleveland (the Broncos, later known as the Indians), and signed many surplus National League players who had been released after the league dropped its Louisville, Cleveland, Washington, and Baltimore clubs. Rebuffed in 1901 after demanding equivalent major league status for the new league from the rival National League, Johnson's American League team owners raided the National League's player rosters, offering to pay the players their worth.[76] De facto major league status thus existed for the new league in its first year, with formal acceptance by the National League following in 1903.

Johnson's coup marked the end of the struggle for organizational control of baseball that had been waged since the beginning of the professional era. The new structure would endure without change for a half-century.

Nineteen hundred marked a significant year of change for the size and shape of home plate. Since 1869, home base had been a 12-inch square, with one corner pointed toward the "pitcher's box," and the opposite corner pointed toward the catcher. In 1900, home plate became a five-sided slab, consisting of a "17-inch square with two of the corners removed so that one edge is 17 inches long, two adjacent sides are 8½ inches long, and the remaining sides are 12 inches and set at an angle to make a point."[77] The new shape, which remains today, gave pitchers a larger strike zone, helping to usher in the "Deadball" era of the game that would last until the end of World War I.

"Syndicate ball" still reigned supreme at the turn of the century. The 1899 champion Brooklyns, whose roster was packed with former Baltimore players, felt so confident of their superior status that they changed their team nicknames from the Bridegrooms (adopted in a year in which several players married) to the Superbas. Bolstered by ex–Orioles pitcher Joe "Iron Man" McGinnity's league-leading 28–8 season, Brooklyn lived up to its new nickname, taking the pennant for the second straight year in 1900. Barney Dreyfuss, owner of the defunct Louisville Colonels, bought a controlling interest in the Pittsburgh club and loaded its lineup with ex–Colonel players. As a result, Pittsburgh, which had not finished higher than seventh place in the previous three years, took command of second place in the league in 1900. Two of the Pirates' former Louisville players were an eccentric left-handed pitcher nicknamed "Rube" Waddell, and a powerfully built, hard-hitting utility man, Honus Wagner, who would eventually settle into the shortstop position. Both remained dominant players well into the new century's second decade and eventually were enshrined in the Baseball Hall of Fame.

While other leagues were forming and other teams radically changing their composition, the Boston Beaneaters, with few exceptions, lumbered on with nearly the same basic personnel. This strategy would prove to be a fatal mistake. Kid Nichols, Bobby Lowe, and Herman Long were now in their second decades with the club, and captain Hugh Duffy, after 13 years as a professional, had played his last full season. The only major acquisitions, two former Washington Senators, performed better for the Bostons than most of their returning veterans. Bill Dineen, 14–20 with the Senators in 1899, turned in the top performance of the Beaneater pitching staff in 1900 at 20–14. Buck Freeman, who replaced Duffy in the outfield, had a career year in 1899, hitting .318, slugging an almost-unheard-of 25 home runs (a quarter of his lifetime production), and rapping out 25 triples. Although he dropped to .301 after joining Boston in 1900, hitting only half as many triples and only six home runs, he still finished third in batting on the team.

After starting more than 500 games with Boston, Kid Nichols' strong right arm was giving out. He fell to 13–16 in 1900. Vic Willis, whose 2.50 ERA was the lowest in the league in 1899, ballooned to 4.19 while winning just ten games, 17 fewer that the year before. On the offensive side, Chick Stahl's batting average fell 58 points, to .293; Fred Tenney's dropped 68 points, to .279. Although Hugh Duffy still held the title of team captain, he argued frequently with Manager Selee, and, much in the manner of Marty Bergen during the previous season, began a pattern of absenting himself from games without excuse. At mid-season he was replaced as captain by Fred Tenney. Weak on the mound and at the plate, hampered by injuries and dissent, Boston finished the 1900 season in fourth place, with a won-lost percentage under .500 for the first time since 1886.

Just prior to Marty Bergen's suicide the previous winter, Frank Selee had unsuccessfully offered Hamilton, Bergen, and Long to Chicago for outfielder Bill Lange and Frank Chance, the future first base star for the Cubs who at this juncture was primarily a catcher.[78] The biggest surprise for the Beaneaters in 1900, therefore, was the performance of Billy Hamilton. Given up for dead, Billy turned in his last great year as a big leaguer. Healthy, playing in all but six games over the shortened 140-game season, he lead the team in hitting at .333, scored more than 100 runs, and placed third in the league in on-base percentage (.449). Although his stolen base total had slipped drastically to 32, it was a respectable total in 1900, given the fact that George Van Haltren of New York led the league with just 45. In July, *Sporting Life* bemoaned the general decline in base stealing by using a specific reference to Sliding Billy's early career exploits. "When Hamilton was in his prime, he could steal more than a hundred bases in a season. Nowadays that is a record for an entire team."[79]

Hamilton's performance still continued to impress, and occasionally, to astound. His lone home run of the season, a "line drive over the left field fence, about one yard fair,"[80] was the only run scored in a June win over Pittsburgh. The next day, facing Rube Waddell, "the terror of the West" (that is, western clubs), Billy went three-for-four, scored a run, and showed again why he earned the nickname "Good Eye Bill." "Hamilton gave a pretty exhibition at the plate. Waddell put the two first balls over for strikes and had Sir William on stilts.... Hamilton turned the tables and put Rube in the hole [ran the count to 3–2], and then getting the ball over the center [of the plate], laced a fine single to right field."[81] In a contest against Philadelphia in late June, "Hamilton reached his base seven times in succession, four times on balls, once hit by a pitch, and two safe hits...."[82] What may be regarded as a quintessential Hamilton performance (a combination of hitting, base stealing, fielding and throwing) occurred in a contest against Brooklyn in early May: "Hamilton played a star game. He hit the ball hard, stole three bases, and made a running catch of Smith's seeming safe hit in the seventh when only a few yards behind second base. Then he made a line throw to the plate and nailed [Jimmy] Sheckard, who tried to reach home from third after the catch was made."[83]

Two weeks before the close of the season, the *Globe* paid tribute to the veteran Hamilton, who, despite the injuries that hindered his base thieving, still knew how to get on base. "Hamilton has cut out running altogether this season ... an accident to his knee has made him timid, and now a stolen base is never looked for ... but when it comes to reaching first base, Hamilton leads them all. In the last dozen games he has reached first base 34 times."[84]

Summing up Boston's dreary 1900 season in October, a national press reporter reserved high praise for Hamilton, commenting at the same time on the outfielder's own statements about retiring.

> Hamilton has been doing splendid stick-work all season ... [his] fielding was extremely brilliant.... Some of his catches were extraordinarily fine, and many a base runner found that he could still throw. Hamilton has made assertions this would be his last season, but I am much inclined to doubt this, especially in view of his brilliant performances of past seasons. His powers are by no means waning and he will be very much wanted in 1901.[85]

In December, Boston's manager disagreed with this opinion, revealing a plan for a wholesale overhaul of the team. "Manager Selee gives out the list of Boston players he is willing to trade. It includes all the outfielders, Duffy, Hamilton, Stahl, Freeman, and Barry; pitchers Willis, [Togie] Pittinger, and Lewis. Selee's course is not calculated to endear him to the players mentioned."[86] Boston's skipper would lose many of these players as well as many others that he wished to keep, not in trades, but in wholesale defections to the upstart American League, which was paying top dollar for veteran players. The consequences would prove disastrous for Boston.

All National League teams were wounded by defections to the American League, but Boston was hurt the most. "From the majors' best team in the 1890s, the Beaneaters descended so cataclysmically that they finished in the second division in 12 of the first 13 seasons in the twentieth century."[87] Jimmy Collins signed with the Boston American League team as player-manager, taking with him Chick Stahl, Buck Freeman, Bill Dinneen and Ted Lewis. Hugh Duffy assumed the player-manager position in Milwaukee, and Boileryard Clarke, who had done the bulk of the catching in the absence of Marty Bergen, moved on to Washington. The Boston Nationals were left with Lowe, Long, and Tenney in the infield, Hamilton in the outfield, and pitchers Nichols and Willis. Within another year, Fred Tenney would be the only remaining Beaneater from the 1897–98 championships. In mid–April, the *Globe* summarized the team's plight: "Manager Selee has added three new catchers, three pitchers, two infielders and one outfielder to the club this season. Several are unknown quantities."[88] The new recruits included castoff seventeen-year veteran Mike Smith, a pitcher-outfielder; light-hitting catcher Malachi Kittredge, formerly of Chicago, who, like Billy Hamilton, had been born in Clinton, Massachusetts; and journeyman infielder Gene Demontreville, who had seen service with five clubs before joining Boston. The Bostons would finish the season in fifth place, coming in last in the league in runs scored, hits, batting average, and on-base percentage. They also would finish last in attendance, with their 146,000 total a full 100,000 behind pennant-winner Pittsburgh.

The calamitous state of affairs in the National League in 1901 found a parallel in the year's national events. It was a year of temperature extremes and political upheaval. In mid–summer the nation was gripped by a heat wave that brought severe drought to the Midwest, and 100-degree temperatures to New England, killing hundreds. On September 6, President McKinley was shot by anarchist Leon Czolgosz. He died eight days later, and Theodore Roosevelt was sworn in as president.

In the National League, a new rule that declared foul balls strikes except after the second strike would give yet another advantage to pitchers as the Deadball Era began. The Phillies' Nap Lajoie's legal struggle to nullify the reserve clause in his contract and play for the Philadelphia American League team was the talk of baseball.

The National League pennant race in 1901 was effectively over on June 15, when the Pirates took over first place, not relinquishing it for more that an occasional few hours for the remainder of the season. By June, Manager Selee in Boston knew that his team was out of contention and began experimenting with players and lineups. With most

The 1901 Boston Beaneaters, which was decimated by defections to the American League. Back row (left to right): Fred Tenney, Fred Crolius, Daff Gammons, Bill Dineen, Vic Willis, Pat Moran, Togie Pittinger, Oliver Faulkner; middle row: Billy Hamilton, Malachi Kittridge, Herman Long, Frank Selee, Fred Brown, Bobby Lowe; front row: Shad Barry, Gene Demontreville, unknown, Kid Nichols (courtesy Boston Public Library, McGreevey Collection).

of his former talent now playing in the American League, his roster card looked like a who's who of unknowns playing a game of musical chairs. Outfielder Fred Murphy, acquired from the Connecticut State League in July, was sold to the Giants in August. Second baseman Daff Gammons, signed as an amateur free agent in March, retired from baseball in June. Right fielder Jimmy Slagle, released by the Phillies in June, was signed by Boston in July, and released by the team in September.

While coaching at Harvard University for a month prior to the start of Boston's season, Sliding Billy suffered a mishap: "Billy Hamilton of the Boston club had his nose broken by a batted ball in the Harvard baseball cage Monday night."[89] Due to the injury, Billy got off to a slow start when the season opened, yet still exhibited flashes of his former glory. "Billy Hamilton made two spectacular catches of balls that had 'hit' stamped all over the cover."[90] "Hamilton made a running catch of [Jesse] Tannehill's hit that seemed good at least for a triple."[91] After sitting out for a week in June with a sore leg, Billy was assigned to hit second behind rookie Fred Crolius when he returned. Hamilton would never again lead off as a major leaguer. With the team in seventh place and the majority of Boston fans frequenting the Boston American team's games across town, Beaneaters owner Arthur Soden lowered the price of admission to twenty-five cents, yet still ended the year with a $25,000 deficit.

After a few weeks hitting in the second position, Frank Selee experimented with Hamilton in the fourth and fifth slots in the batting order. Batting .314 at the end of July, he was benched in favor of Pittsburgh transfer Duff Cooley, who started in center field and hit fourth in the order.

> Hamilton's layoff did not occasion much surprise. His batting is not nearly as strong as it was last season, and it was remarked all around what a good man he would make for the Americans [American League]. Just now it looks as if he would be retained as a utility outfielder. It must be a new sensation for Billy to be a bench warmer.[92]

Despite his embarrassing situation, the veteran Hamilton showed his mettle: "Billy Hamilton was in uniform and livelier that a plucked rooster. William was on the lines, coaching every minute. He was interested in his work although not playing. Few star players feel like working when not in the game, but Hamilton was full of advice and helped matters along."[93]

Although used sparingly for the remainder of the season, and not at all during the final two weeks, Billy found a way to go out in style in his last few games, both offensively and defensively. In a 3–0 win against Brooklyn on August 31,

> William Hamilton of Clinton took the first prize, making a record catch in the ninth inning that was worth the price of admission. William, once started, went like a cyclone down the field ... and by a long stretch and a nice piece of timing took the ball in out of the east wind a few feet from the fence. The crowd cheered as Hamilton went out of sight under the grandstand.[94]

Two weeks later, Boston took a doubleheader from Chicago, 2–1 and 1–0. In the first game, an extra-inning affair, "Hamilton, the first man up in the eleventh, drove the ball over the right field fence and won the game.... Hamilton made all of Boston's runs in the two games."[95]

Billy played his last two games as a Beaneater in a doubleheader against New York on September 16, two days after the death of President McKinley. In his final outing, a 4–2 loss, he batted fifth in the order, doubling in four at-bats. Although reserved by the Beaneaters for the following season, he declined to accompany the team south during spring training. In April 1902, the *Globe* reported that "Hamilton has been released outright by Boston."[96] His major league career was over.

Billy Hamilton was five years old when the first professional baseball league was formed. In the first half of his life, wars for control of the sport were fought, and leagues and associations rose and fell. Players rebelled against management, ultimately settling into an uneasy truce with club owners. Pitchers threw underhand, then sidearm, then overhand. They initially stood in a square area 45 feet from home plate; they ended up pitching off a two-foot long rubber slab perched on a dirt mound more than 60 feet from the plate. The round home plate became a square, and then a pentagon. The bare hands of fielders were gloved, and the weight and dimensions of balls and bats were standardized. Catchers invented metal masks and padded protectors to shield their bodies. The curveball, the bunt, and the steal were invented. The "squeeze play," the hit-and-run, and the sacrifice were born. One umpire became two. Rowdy ball rose to prominence, declining when its practitioners used it against themselves and the public had seen enough. What had been a northeastern regional sport became the "National Pastime." By 1901, Billy Hamilton's last year in the major leagues, the great era of transition and transformation in baseball was over. The rules, the equipment, and the organization of major league baseball had been standardized. The modern era of the game had begun.

Hamilton was both a witness to and a participant in baseball's quarter-century transitional period. Along the way, he played the game like few before or after him have. More than a century after he hung up his spikes, some of the records he set or shared still stand: number of stolen bases in a game (seven); number of consecutive games stealing a base (13); number of runs scored in a season (196 in 129 games); number of triples in a game (four); number of sacrifices in a game (four); number of consecutive games scoring a run (24); and career runs scored per game average (1.06). In other all-time record categories, while not leading the pack, Billy has remained close to the leaders, ranking third in stolen bases (912) and on-base percentage (.455; minimum 5,000 plate appearances), and sixth in batting average (.344). He is one of twenty-five men ever to hit higher than .400 in a season. He led his league once in batting average, once in hits, and four times each in singles, runs, on-base percentage, and times on base. He was the circuit leader in stolen bases and in walks five times. His career times-on-base average per game is 2.1; his highest single-season times-on-base average was 2.5 in 1894. His 355 times on base that year has been topped by only three men — Ruth, Bonds, and Williams — all of whom accomplished their marks in significantly longer seasons than did Hamilton.

Only six men in the history of the game have equaled or bettered Hamilton's lifetime .344 batting average. In a fourteen-year career, he averaged 1.3 hits and nearly a walk per game. One of the sport's premier bunters, he has been credited, in all probability erroneously, with inventing the drag bunt.[97] In reality, the majority of Hamilton's bunt hits or sacrifices were pushed down the third base line, not dragged down the first base line. When swinging away, he was predominately an opposite-field slap hitter, but he could also pull the ball occasionally for power. However, eighty-two percent of his hits were singles (1,782).

Despite Hamilton's low lifetime fielding percentage of .926, he ranks fourth in pre–1900 outfielders in putouts,[98] and as we have seen, regularly made the spectacular and at times seemingly impossible catch a commonplace event in Boston and Philadelphia. The fielding average can be partially but not completely explained by Billy's defensive philosophy that no ball was uncatchable, and by the fact that during perhaps half his career, he roamed the outfield gloveless. Hall of Famer Tommy McCarthy, Hamilton's contemporary, is regarded today as an "outstanding fielder,"[99] even though he posted a lifetime fielding average of .887. Accurate assessment of a player's fielding ability, therefore, as Paul M. Gregory reminds us, is an inexact science:

> Fielding ability is perhaps the most difficult to assess quantitatively, and it cannot be gauged accurately simply by computing a man's average of errors in proportion to the number of chances. One outfielder may have a better fielding average than another and yet the second man may be a superior outfielder; he may run faster, have a faster break in going after a fly ball, and may have greater ability to turn the right way in order to convert fly balls into putouts. Accuracy and judgment in throwing are hard to appraise: a good outfielder will not make useless throws to the plate; he will ignore a runner who is almost sure to score and will throw to another base to prevent the batter or other runner from getting an extra base.[100]

With all of Hamilton's fielding faults, Bill James ranks him as the ninth-best all-time center fielder.[101] All things considered, such a ranking seems appropriate.

Although Billy Hamilton's lifetime stolen base count of 912 has been adjusted downward to compensate for the fact that during most of his career a steal could be awarded for advancing from first base to third on a single, he still ranks third all-time in that category. This, despite the fact that until 1898, the pitcher, whether throwing from the pitcher's box, or later, from the pitching rubber, did not have to turn a leg in the direction of first base when throwing to check a runner there. While Lou Brock and Rickey Henderson have subsequently exceeded Billy's adjusted stolen base total, Hamilton's overall base-stealing ability is statistically superior to that of both Henderson and Brock when comparing each speedster's frequency of steals. Henderson averaged a steal every 2.49 games during his career, while Brock averaged one every 2.78 games. Billy Hamilton averaged a steal every 1.74 games, and his closest competition in this regard comes not from Henderson or Brock, but from St. Louis Cardinals outfielder Vince Coleman, who averaged one every 1.82 games. A second measure of superior stealing ability is the number of steals per at-bat over a career. Henderson averaged a steal for every 7.79 at-bats, while Brock averaged one for every 11.00 at-bats. Billy Hamilton's average is one steal for every 6.8 at-bats. In this category, as in the case of that of average steals per game, Billy's closest competition is from Vince Coleman, who averaged a steal for every 7.1 at-bats. Hamilton is one of eight men who have stolen 100 or more bases in a season. He is one of three who have done so three times (along with Henderson and Coleman), and only Hamilton and Coleman have performed this feat in three successive seasons. Henderson is the undisputed leader in the number of steals in a career, with Brock second, but Hamilton far and away exceeds both of them in his lifetime average of steals per game and steals per at-bat. In these categories, Billy Hamilton remains the best base stealer who ever played the game.

Today, William Robert Hamilton is popularly known as "Sliding Billy" in tribute to his prowess as a base stealer. In his *Baseball Nicknames: A Dictionary of Origins and Meanings*, James Skipper notes this usage, but does not provide its source or comment on its origins.[102] Upon Billy's election to the Baseball Hall of Fame in 1961, the *Sporting News* likewise asserted that he was "known affectionately to the fans of the 1890s as 'Sliding Billy.'"[103] Later in the same edition, the *Sporting News* used the nickname in a biographical sketch: "Through the mists of many years they [older fans] can still see Sliding Billy dash around the bases."[104] Nevertheless, a problem exists with regard to the origin of this fond appellation. While playing for the Kansas City Cowboys, Billy Hamilton was known, rather formally, as either William R. Hamilton or simply "Hamilton." During his Philadelphia years, either the informal diminutive "Billy," initially set off by quotation marks, which eventually were dropped, "Good Eye Bill," or, once again, simply "Hamilton," were employed. At Boston, he was known either as Hamilton, Billy, William, or occasionally "Sir William." In 1900, the Boston press added another moniker, "the symmetrical center fielder,"[105] presumably (and unflatteringly) due to his stocky frame. Twenty years after Hamilton's death, the *Sporting News* added a posthumous epithet to the list by referring to him as the "Fast Flyhawk."[106]

A careful review of Billy's playing history, however, does not reveal the use of "Sliding Billy" in any of the Billy's game accounts in the *Kansas City Star*, *Philadelphia Inquirer*, or *Boston Globe* of the era, nor is it a term used to refer to Hamilton in the two most prominent baseball publications of the time period, *Sporting Life* and the *Sporting News*, either during his major league playing years or during his years as a minor league player or manager.

How and where, then, did Hamilton's most well-known nickname originate? The first known use of the term appears nearly four decades after Billy retired from major league baseball.

In December of 1937, seventy-one-year-old Billy Hamilton wrote a letter to the editor of *Sporting News*, commenting on a recent article in which they had mentioned his name. The text of the letter is as follows:

> Dear Sir:
>
> In the November 16th issue of your paper you made reference to Billy Hamilton, of the old Philadelphia and Boston NL clubs of the 1890s as one of the prolific base stealers of the 19th century. I'll have you know sir that I was and will be the greatest stealer of all times. I did stole [*sic*] over 100 bases on many years and if they ever re-count the record I will get my just reward.
>
> Very Truly
> Sliding Billy Hamilton.[107]

The apparent source of Billy Hamilton's most famous and accepted nickname, therefore, is none other than Billy Hamilton.

Hamilton's signature in his letter to the *Sporting News* clarifies how he most wanted to be remembered, but the subsequent use of this colorful and appropriate nickname has most likely tended to obscure his many other baseball talents for modern students of the game. In his *Stolen! A History of Base Stealing*, for example, Russell Roberts includes Billy Hamilton as "one of only six players"[108] inducted into the Baseball Hall of Fame for base stealing. In actuality, Billy's plaque at Cooperstown contains considerably more information about his hitting and run-scoring abilities than his base stealing. Sliding Billy was not only an exceptional base stealer, but an extraordinary ballplayer in almost every aspect of the game.

Back home in Clinton, Massachusetts, in the spring of 1902, Billy Hamilton, age 36, was about to embark on a second baseball career as a minor league player-manager, bench manager, and owner, and as a major league scout. It would be a career that would last longer than his major league playing years. While Billy's first sports love clearly was baseball, he was not a one-dimensional sportsman. When asked what he did in the offseason, Hall of Famer Rogers Hornsby responded, "I look out the window and wait for spring." That was not the Hamilton way. During the off-season during both his major and minor league career, Billy was actively engaged in numerous other regional professional and amateur sports, several of which exist today only in the memory of the very old or in the yellowed sports pages of century-old newspapers. This previously undocumented aspect of Hamilton's life, which will be discussed in the next chapter, adds a depth and dimension that baseball historian Bill James and others claimed was lacking in earlier portraits of the Hall of Famer, while at the same time linking him inextricably to those Victorians of his age who advocated "an energetic, dynamic style in all aspects of life."[109]

5

Home to Clinton

> *"After all, there isn't so much luck in owning a horseshoe as in owning a horse."*
> — Billy Hamilton, *Sporting Life*, 1907

The off-season pursuits of major league ballplayers in the Hamilton era were many and varied. While the average player's salary, as we have seen, frequently was triple that of a skilled laborer, baseball acumen did not necessarily imply money management skills. The age of sports endorsements as a second income source had not yet begun. Those with the least talent in managing their financial affairs found themselves requesting advances on their next year's salaries before the start of the season. Some baseball star extroverts, like Mike Kelly and Arlie Latham, capitalized on their notoriety by becoming vaudeville performers or actors. Songs, skits, or poetry recitation (frequently "Casey at the Bat") were mainstays of the vaudevillian ballplayer. A few famous figures, such as Cap Anson, could satisfy a paying audience simply by giving brief talks about their careers. Entrepreneurial types, like John McGraw, invested in high-profile male-oriented businesses, such as bars and billiard halls, where their off-season presence helped to bring in customers. Others clerked in stores or undertook a variety of other occupations.

> Cy Young worked in a real-estate office. William Hassamaer helped with his father's coal business, and Joe Quinn lent a hand in his father-in-law's undertaking concern. Some went hunting, or played winter ball for nominal salaries and the chance to spend the cold months in a warm climate. Others, one newspaper said, were experts at doing nothing.[1]

5. Home to Clinton

By the late 1890s, Billy Hamilton had paid off his home mortgage, purchased several properties, and was enjoying a steady income from rental fees. While he certainly had the means to be able to rest and relax in the off-season, his personality was averse to the thought. A series of brief notes about Sliding Billy that appeared in *Sporting Life* and the Boston press over a decade-long period provide clues about how he structured his late fall and winter vacation time both during and after his major league career. Not surprisingly, it all had to do with sports and competition.

Hamilton, we recall, greatly enjoyed the Victorian sports fad of roller skating, and, as his daughter Ethel affirmed, he "played polo on roller skates at Dexter's Rink in Clinton."[2] Roller polo, a spinoff of the period's skating craze and the progenitor of modern hockey, became a popular winter sport in New England and the Midwest during Billy Hamilton's teenage years. The configuration of most roller rinks of the era — a first-floor hardwood skating area with a spectator gallery on the second floor — provided a perfect environment for the development of roller polo, initially as an amateur amusement and later as a professional spectator sport. In roller polo, as in some other European and Native American folk games, players hit a ball with a short stick toward or through a goal. The stick, called a "hawkey" (the origin of the term "hockey"), was about the length of a cane, with a crook at the lower end. Performing these actions on skates gave roller polo its name and added a unique dimension to an old pastime. The following is one set of 1884 rules:

> Each team had seven players — goalkeeper, goal-cover and point-cover (the defenders), two backers (midfielders), and two rushers (forwards). Goals were six feet wide and from three to four feet high. The stick had a maximum length of four feet and a diameter of one inch.... The ball was three inches in diameter. The game started with each team forming an inverted wedge. At the referee's signal, opponents rushed the ball placed at center ice. The game was on. There was no rule about offsides, but attackers could not stop within a 5-foot radius around the goal. Two or three fouls, depending on location, equaled a goal for the opponent. Matches were best-of-three or best-of-five goals.[3]

An evening at the polo matches provided welcome diversion during the long New England winters in pre-television and radio years. As an 1895 *Boston Herald* advertisement put it, "Roller polo can arouse the sluggish blood, make the business man forget his troubles, and afford much food for heated argument."[4] Within a few years, the sport's popularity helped to move it from an amateur to a professional pursuit, with game accounts and league standings figuring prominently in the region's newspapers. The "Roller Polo Notes" section of the *Globe's* sports page on February 14, 1896, observed that "a few years ago a polo franchise was of little account. Now it will take big money to get an opening and a good team together."[5] Attendance at these contests was remarkable, considering the size of the towns and the difficulty in simply getting to the rink on snowy evenings. In January of 1896, a paying crowd of five hundred attended the Clinton versus Waltham match at Clinton. A week earlier, more than two thousand home fans watched the Pawtucket, Rhode Island, team defeat New Bedford.[6] Two years later, a crowd of similar size packed the Chapel Street Polo Rink in New Haven, Connecticut, to watch the home team defeat Fall River "in the series of three for the National Championship."[7]

For baseball players of the region who had grown up with the sport, roller polo was a natural attraction in the off-season. The multitalented Arlie Latham, Billy Hamilton's old nemesis, was a goal tender for his hometown Springfield team when not performing vaudeville skits.[8] Catcher Malachi Kittridge, Billy Hamilton's 1901 Boston teammate and also a Clinton native, became a polo team owner: "After he joined the American Roller Polo Association and secured a rink in Clinton, Massachusetts, he organized a roller polo team."[9] Billy Hamilton, roller polo player and "one of the warmest rooters at the roller polo games in Clinton,"[10] assumed a different role in the sport in 1900. "He is to handle the Clinton roller polo team for his friend, Coughlin. Billy knows the game well and ought to make a first class pilot."[11] In 1959, Clinton's John E. O'Malley, known as "the chronicler of Clinton history," asserted that after his major league career had ended, Billy also donned skates to referee polo matches. O'Malley attributed some unusual behavior to the typically mild-mannered Hamilton when functioning in this capacity: "One of the players got mad and threatened Hamilton with a stick.... Well they had to carry that player off the floor."[12]

A modern variant of roller polo made a comeback as a demonstration sport in the 1992 Summer Olympics in Barcelona. Its official Olympic designation is now "rink hockey."

One news note regarding Billy Hamilton's involvement in roller polo was prefaced by an observation that provides clues to another of his off-season passions. Its author observed that due to Billy's work as a polo manager, he "will have something besides a fast nag [horse] or two to take up his time the coming fall and winter...."[13] Nearly a decade later, a *Sporting Life* article affirmed Hamilton's continued interests in such endeavors by making another reference that connected Billy with horses and horse racing. "Frank Connaughton [a former Boston Beaneater shortstop] will put in time in Clinton next season, the same town where Billy Hamilton courses with a fast trotter."[14] Such oblique references are clarified in a 1897 *Boston Daily Globe* entry entitled "Driver Billy Hamilton: Boston's Center Fielder Pilots Winning Horse at Field Day in Clinton."

> The fall field day took place at the Clinton-Lancaster driving park, this afternoon [October 16] when several local races were run off.... A large crowd gathered and the races were very interesting. The race for the 2:30 horses was the feature of the day, and brought out much enthusiasm. "Billy" Hamilton, the clever center fielder of the Boston nine, showed his ability in a new sphere, a driver, winning the race in good form from horses reputed to be faster than his.[15]

Hamilton's home "driving park," as such race tracks were called, was considered "the most costly and the best half-mile track in New England."[16] Municipalities with competing facilities included Springfield, Lawrence, Waltham, Lynn, and Taunton, further attesting to great public interest in the sport.

The *Globe*'s report of Billy's first harness race victory also suggested that it came as a result of expertise developed in another equine sport: "Hamilton drove a clever race, for his initial appearance, although he has for years been among the leaders in the brushes on ice."[17] Virtually unknown today, the sport of sleigh racing on ice ("ice brushes") or snow ("snow brushes"), was another popular winter pastime in Hamilton's era. Single-occupant sleighs known as "cutters " were raced on a mile or half-mile course, either over packed snow on long, straight city streets or on the frozen surfaces of local rivers and ponds. In Clinton, such races took place "on Main Street or the cleared surface of Lancaster Mills pond."[18] The "brush" terminology associated with these contests derived from the custom, in each type of race, of marking the end of the makeshift course "with a piece of brush which would blow in the direction of the horses as they trotted toward it."[19] The sport's popularity is evidenced in the fact that "sleighing news" items appeared frequently in the Boston press's sports pages during winter months. An 1896 entry described the construction of a new harness racing "speedway" built at Haverhill, specifically for "snow harness racing," and asserted that there, "many brushes are sure to occur among the owners of the fast horses in this city and its suburbs."[20] "Ice brushes" required special racing shoes for the horses: "The sport was a dangerous one. Not only was there the risk of the horses falling on the ice, but of the animals wounding themselves with their racing shoes and of being overdriven."[21] A description of a typical "snow brush" in Wilmington, Delaware, captures well the interest and excitement generated by the event:

> The "brushes" were unofficial sport with no set rules or formal starter. As the sleighs gathered near the starting line one horse would break and the others unrein in frantic pursuit. Plumes of snow exploded far into the air from charging steeds as they raced between wildly partisan supporters....
> Fans described sleigh racing on French Street as the most exciting sport they had ever seen. [22]

Given such a longstanding involvement with several types of horse racing, it is not surprising that Billy would also be actively involved in another aspect of the sport — the breeding and selling of horses. "Billy Hamilton had two steeds in the consignment of horses at the big combination sale here [Boston] last week. He is an expert on fast horse flesh."[23]

After Billy's place at Cooperstown was secured, one of his daughter Ethel's reminiscences hinted broadly at her father's love affair with horses. "Dad was an excellent horseman.... I can remember him riding the horses over at Thayer's stable and recall many happy times we spent over there."[24] Ethel's comments further suggest that Billy's off-season adventures, harness racing, sleigh racing, roller polo, or simple horseback riding, most likely were events that the entire family attended.

Life in Clinton upon Hamilton's return from the big leagues, like life in the rest of the country, was much different than it had been fourteen years earlier when Billy left for Kansas City. Worcester County's population more than tripled between 1890 and 1900, from 280,000 to 846,000, and 117 Massachusetts businesses were engaged in the

5. Home to Clinton   147

Postcard of Clinton, Massachusetts, Billy Hamilton's hometown, which depicts three common methods of transportation at the turn of the twentieth century: horse and buggy, bicycle, and the town's trolley tracks. Interurban trolley lines greatly facilitated the growth and popularity of New England League baseball from 1900 to 1913 (courtesy Clinton, Massachusetts, Historical Society).

manufacture of cotton goods.[25] The nation's first subway opened in Boston, and electric trolleys, called "interurbans," provided a new mode of fast, cheap transportation that was outstripping Billy's favorite method of getting around, the horse and buggy. Before Hamilton would retire from his second baseball career in the minor leagues, it would be possible "to move by interurban [trolley] transport from New York to Boston for a fare of four dollars."[26] The electric trolley came to Clinton in 1893, competing with horse, carriage, and pedestrian traffic on High Street, and linking the tiny town to a great system of tracks covering New England. Coincidentally, the "interurban" would help usher in a brief golden era of New England minor league baseball, an era in which Billy Hamilton would take part.

The telephone, present in many Clinton businesses by now, was still rare in individual households, where kerosene lamps and coal stoves continued to provide light and heat. Another new transport mode also made its debut at this time: "Clinton owned one automobile in 1900, possibly a few more, but they were a danger to their owners then."[27] In 1909, the town's Lancaster Mills became the first local industry to be powered by electricity, which was generated in Connecticut and transmitted by way of high tension wires. Billy Hamilton's return to Clinton also coincided with the construction of the Wauchusett Dam and Reservoir, built to provide Boston and its suburbs with a permanent water supply. Still regarded as the largest "hand dug" dam ever completed, the structure forever changed the city's landscape and symbolically epitomized the coming of a new age. "We might say that at this time Clinton passed definitely from the nineteenth century into the twentieth."[28]

Although he was the tenth-oldest player in the National League when released by the Beaneaters,[29] thirty-six-year-old Billy Hamilton could have sought and received a contract from another major league team, given both his experience and the fact that the success of the American League had swelled the number of big league teams to sixteen. He reportedly received an offer to play for the New York Giants, but turned it down.[30] Why did Billy not return to the majors? Fourteen years riding the rails in Pullman cars and three young daughters at home were good reasons, but the most significant one was that "his wife did not want him to play ball any longer and he told her he would not go out of New England."[31] When the 1902 season began, he "accepted an offer from the [independent] Woonsocket [Rhode Island] team," doing "fine work both at the bat and in the field."[32] In late spring he interviewed for a captain-manager position on the Haverhill New England League team. Billy cited a dollar figure for his services that "he thought would be prohibitive, but to his surprise, it was accepted."[33] In early June, Sliding Billy played in the first game of the new era of his career as captain and manager for the Haverhill Hustlers.[34]

In the early years of professional baseball, the terms "major" and "minor" leagues were unknown. Since half of Billy Hamilton's playing years were spent with minor league teams, the distinction between "major" and "minor" requires clarification. Professional leagues that sprung up around the time of the founding of the National League (1876) were properly designated as "regional" leagues or associations, as their names often implied: New England Association, Western League, Eastern Association. The oldest regional leagues, established in 1877, were the International Association (consisting of teams from Canada, New Hampshire, Massachusetts, Ohio, New York, and Pennsylvania), the New England Association (teams from Maine, New Hampshire, and Massachusetts), and the League Association (teams from six states, including New York, Tennessee, and Minnesota). As the popularity of baseball increased, other leagues formed, reaching a total of 19 by the early 1890s. Many such regional organizations regularly played exhibition games with National League teams in order to garnish the pay of players from both sides. It was common on such occasions for the National League teams to sign on the spot the best players from their opposing regional league teams after their contest. Such roster raids played havoc with entire teams and regional leagues.

An 1883 pact among three leagues, two national and one regional, soon would have an impact on nearly all regional professional leagues. The "Tripartite Agreement," commonly called the "National Agreement," was signed by the National League, the American Association, and the Northwestern League. In the pact, the National League recognized the upstart American Association as an equal league of national proportions (a major league). All three leagues also agreed to respect each other's reserve contracts. The agreement provided some needed roster protection for the regional Northwestern League, but most importantly, de facto, categorized it at a second or "minor" level in comparison to that of the National League and the American Association. Most other regional leagues, eager to protect their own players, soon signed on, thus implicitly agreeing to a secondary or "minor" status in comparison to that of the American Association and the National League. The major and minor leagues were now a reality.

In August of 1901, the National League, whose best players were defecting to Ban Johnson's upstart American League, abrogated its agreement with all minor leagues regarding the reserve clause in a desperate attempt to find players for their depleted rosters. The minor leagues countered by forming a protective agency, the National Association (of Professional Baseball Leagues), which, though unable to restrict occasional raiding parties from the Major Leagues on their players, at least reasserted a strict reserve clause policy among its members. Additionally, the National Association, known today as Minor League Baseball, established a basic classification system for minor leagues (Class A, B, C, and D), which, with slight alterations, still exists today.

Peace between the minor and major Leagues finally came in 1903 with the signing of a second "Tripartite Agreement" between the National League, the American League, and their minor league counterpart, the National Association. Under the pact, the National League recognized the equality of the American League, and all three organizations "were to be considered as equal partners in administering the professional game."[35] This major-minor league agreement, which protected all player contracts and territorial rights, remains a key governing instrument of Organized Baseball today.

While the second Tripartite Agreement provided the minor leagues with an important organizational structure and recognition as a partner in professional baseball, it did not guarantee any league's viability. In this regard, the minors at the beginning of the twentieth century had changed little from the time of Billy Hamilton's years with Waterbury of the Eastern Association and Worcester of the New England League. By 1907, there were 36 such leagues and 244 clubs,[36] but they remained fluid and precarious enterprises, dependent on the financial climate, the whims of their fan base, or even the whims of the weather. Leagues changed names and added or dropped franchises at a dizzying pace. Teams disbanded, moved from city to city, or changed ownership, management, and ballparks from season to season. This was minor league baseball's state of affairs when Billy Hamilton took the field as captain-manager of the New England League's Haverhill team in June of 1902.

The majority of Hamilton's playing and managing years after the completion of his major league career were spent in the New England League, the successor to the original 1877 New England Association. Founded in 1885 as the Eastern New England League (in order to distinguish it from the Connecticut-based Southern New England League), it fielded teams from five cities in Massachusetts and Maine during its first season. Its early years were characterized by financial and structural instability, with teams joining, dropping out, or switching cities. The league itself disbanded twice. Its collapse in 1888 paved the way for Billy Hamilton's contract to be sold to Kansas City, jumpstarting his major league career.

The league was back in a reconstituted form in 1890, and its viability in the coming years was improved by the dawn of the electric "interurban" trolley era in New England:

Interurban trolley lines connected cities and towns throughout the region, enabling business men and residents to easily travel from one city to another to conduct business or shop. Baseball fans could conveniently travel from one city to another to attend a ball game. This transport system was a major reason the New England League was able to survive through the entire first decade of the twentieth century.[37]

Coincidentally, the first decade of the twentieth century was the same period in which Billy Hamilton plied his trade in the minor leagues on New England's ballfields.

New England League president Tim Murnane, sports editor for the *Boston Daily Globe*, successfully courted former major league players during this era to pilot his teams in order to increase the organization's fan base and improve the quality of play. Between 1902 and 1910, all New England League pennants were won by teams whose player-managers were former major leaguers. These stars, such as Billy Hamilton, Jesse Burkett, Fred Lake, "Phenomenal" Smith, and Frank Eustace "brought not only high caliber skills (even at an older age) and understanding of Big League strategy, but also used their status to establish a connection with local fans."[38]

Billy Hamilton played for and/or managed the Haverhill New England League team from 1902 to 1904, part of 1906 and all of 1907 and 1908; he did the same for Lynn's league entry, the Shoemakers, in 1909 and 1910. After a two-year stint as a scout for his former Boston Nationals team, he returned to the New England League to bench-manage the Fall River team, in reality, the former Haverhill team of

Player-manager Billy Hamilton of the Lynn Shoemakers New England League team, raising the flag on opening day, 1910, his last season as a player (courtesy Howard "Skip" Reynolds).

the year before, which had transferred to Fall River for the 1910 season. Haverhill was a charter member of the Eastern New England League. Haverhill, located on the Merrimack River, prospered by carving out a niche for itself as a manufacturer of men's shoes. (Lynn, in contrast, manufactured only women's shoes.)

In large part, baseball history owes its ability to chronicle the New England League period in Billy Hamilton's minor league career to a friendship and mutually beneficial business relationship that developed between Sliding Billy and Jacob C. "Jake" Morse. The son of Jewish Bavarian immigrants, Morse was a Harvard and Boston University Law School graduate who became the sports editor for the *Boston Herald* in 1885. Contemporaneously, he contributed regular articles to *Sporting Life*. In 1892, he was named secretary of the New England League, working there under league president Tim Murnane. After being ousted from the *Herald* in 1907 because of a management shakeup, Morse founded *Baseball Magazine*, the first monthly national journal dedicated to the sport. Jake Morse had no qualms about using his position at *Sporting Life* to report as much positive news about his New England League as possible.

Despite Billy Hamilton's outstanding play during his major league career, news items about him in the national press were few in comparison to the attention that flashier players received. Upon his transfer to the New England League and assumption of managerial duties, Hamilton and his team received regular sports coverage from Jake Morse in *Sporting Life*. Thanks to such coverage, much about Billy's activities during that period can be studied today. There was an obvious friendship between Morse and Hamilton that transcended simple expediency. Billy wrote to Jake frequently, and Morse often prefaced his news items on Sliding Billy with the expression "our favorite center fielder, Billy Hamilton." On one occasion, he even referred to Billy as "my dear friend."[39]

Early on, Billy Hamilton exhibited traits that suggested he would make a good manager. His observations on hitting, running, training, and conditioning provide evidence of an analytical, strategic dimension to his play. As early as his Kansas City years, he was described as "the best coacher the club had this year."[40] Similar abilities were noted in Philadelphia as early as 1892.[41] His willingness to help young players improve is exemplified by his coaching of utility infielder Charlie

"Piano Legs" Hickman in Boston: "Billy Hamilton was as much responsible as anyone for the way Hickman banged that ball. The fleet runner and fine hitter took hold of the youngster and showed him a thing or two about meeting the ball and stepping into it...."[42] One report of how Hamilton reacted after being benched by Boston in 1901 would prove prophetic the following year. "To watch him you would think he was the manager of the club. He hustles about in great style, keeps a constant fire from the bench, does a good share of coaching, and is in the game as much that a man can be that is out of it."[43]

As manager of the Haverhill Hustlers, Billy spent his shortened 1902 season sizing up his squad's talent and that of his competitors. By late July, he was declared "a first class minor league manager. Hamilton's Haverhill club has held its own with the top notchers since William took hold."[44] As team pilot, he also began manifesting an aspect of his personality—an occasional bad temper—that had remained hidden as a player: "Billy Hamilton is said to be a hard loser since taking the management of the Haverhill club."[45] Although still hampered by the knee and leg injuries that ended his Major League career, as well as a "strained stomach,"[46] Billy the ballplayer found New England League pitching to his liking, banging out 82 hits (including 23 doubles) in 66 games for a .337 average, and stealing 26 bases in his first minor league season.

In March of 1903, he began what would become an annual relationship with Dartmouth College, spending a month early in the spring coaching the school's baseball team candidates prior to the start of New England League competition. Hampered again by leg injuries, he played in only 37 games for Haverhill in 1903, but garnered sixty hits, averaging a blistering .455. Although former big league journeyman catcher Fred Lake piloted the Lowell team to the pennant in 1903, Hamilton still had something special to celebrate. On August 30, his fourth daughter, Dorothy, was born in Clinton.

Billy's year-and-a-half managerial apprenticeship paid off in 1904, when he took Haverhill from last place to first place in the league. He had retained only four men from the 1903 season, selecting the remaining eight players from 29 candidates, "some of them known to be good, and others of them not known at all."[47] Billy's ability to judge baseball talent did not go unnoticed. A few years later, former Boston teammate Fred Tenney, then the manager of the Boston National team, signed Hamilton as a scout for his squad. Early in 1904, however, a prescient Jake Morse noted, "I never saw Billy Hamilton look better in his life."[48] Even with a bad leg, Sliding Billy, now 38, put up some of the most impressive offensive numbers of his career in his only pennant-winning season as a manager. He hit a league-leading .412, with 168 hits in 113 games, and scored a run per game (113). His 74 stolen bases broke the record set by fellow New England Leaguer Archie "Moonlight" Graham. Graham, who appeared in a single major league game with the Giants the next year, became part of American cultural history as a character in W. P. Kinsella's *Shoeless Joe* (1982), and later in the film *Field of Dreams* (1989).[49]

With the pennant assured in September, Billy felt confident enough to suggest that "he would like to have a run with his Haverhill champions against the Boston Nationals. He thinks he might come out at the long end."[50] While this might appear to have been a boastful assertion, the 1904 Beaneaters finished in seventh place in the National League with a record of 55–98. The Bostons and other teams, aware of the numbers that Sliding Billy was putting up in New England, had approached Billy late in the season, unsuccessfully trying to entice him back to the major leagues. "Billy Hamilton refused to accept an offer from the Boston Nationals to finish the season with that team. He has recently received numerous [major league] offers to play ball for the balance of the year."[51] Mired at the bottom of the league, the Beaneaters, like the Phillies before them, regretted having let Sliding Billy go.

> One who is close to the National League [Boston] management said recently that the two biggest mistakes made by the club were the release of Hamilton and Lowe. "Hamilton has no superior in the country today in all departments," said he, "and while not quite as speedy as in the nineties, can show his heels to three-quarters of the base runners in the country."[52]

Given his managerial success in 1904 and the invitations from major league teams, it came as a great surprise in January 1905, when Billy signed to manage the Harrisburg, Pennsylvania, team from the Tri-State League. Tri-State was an "outlaw" league — one of numerous circuits that did not abide by the regulations of the National Agreement and signed players who were already reserved by other clubs in other leagues. The Tri-State League fielded teams from Delaware, Pennsylvania, and New Jersey from 1904 to 1914. The Harrisburg franchise was the league's most stable team, fielding squads for every year of the association's existence. Billy's primary reason for making the change, and for breaking his promise to Rebecca not to play outside New England, appeared to be financial:

> It is said that he will receive $600 per month from Harrisburg, which is just double the sum he got from Haverhill. "Bill" wasn't half desirous to go and put his figure at what he considered to be a prohibitive price, but Harrisburg had to have him.[53]

The move to the Tri-State League would in all probability be the worst baseball decision that Billy Hamilton ever made in his long career.

According to the minor league classification system begun with the founding of the National Association in 1901, Tri-State was a Class D league, the lowest class in the minors. The New England League, in contrast, was classified as a "B" league, with others such as the Eastern, the Western, and the Pacific Coast leagues designated as "A" leagues.[54] Class D leagues were characterized by inferior players, playing conditions, and, perhaps most importantly for Billy Hamilton, inferior umpires. All of these factors would provide challenges for the former major leaguer and Class B minor league manager. Signing players reserved by other clubs who were part of the National Association created antipathy for Hamilton among managers who respected the reserve rule. An example of such enmity occurred in March of 1905, while Billy was spending a month with the Dartmouth team prior to the start of the Tri-State season:

> Billy Hamilton has flown to Dartmouth with the execrations of Manager Tom McDermott of Fall River. It seems that Hamilton has snatched first baseman Weddige, of that team, and McDermott claims he has also taken a battery — Jerger and Peterson — and another pitcher in Gilroy. These young men cannot be aware that by leaving the Fall River Club they burn their bridges and cannot again play in organized ball.[55]

The Tri-State's inherent instability (Camden, New Jersey, folded after the 1904 season; Coatesville, Pennsylvania, was shifted to Shamokin in midseason 1904 and subsequently folded; the Lebanon, Pennsylvania, team shifted to Wilmington, Delaware, in mid-season, 1905) played havoc with scheduling and revenues. When the money became tight, all remembered the salary that Hamilton was pulling, thanks to Jake Morse's notice in *Sporting Life*.

Problems at home compounded Hamilton's stress. Rebecca, left to care for the four girls, including baby Dorothy, experienced a severe bout of rheumatism. In February, Billy's mother, Mary Hamilton, passed away. His personal distress and his frustration and impatience with the quality of umpiring in the Tri-State league led to a series of run-ins with league arbiters, a behavior highly uncharacteristic Hamilton in the past. "Harrisburg's president refused to accept Tri-State president Theodore Creamer's ruling suspending for five and ten days respectively manager Billy Hamilton and first-baseman Calhoun for rowdy actions and abuse of umpires."[56]

The turmoil in Harrisburg did not immediately affect Billy's play. In 1905 he hit .342 in 110 games and stole 45 bases. By September, it seemed as if he had enough of Class D league play. Jake Morse reported that "Billy Hamilton writes me that under no circumstances will he be back in the Tri-State next season."[57] Billy did return to Harrisburg in 1906, but lasted just two months, hitting an unimpressive .277. In June he resigned his position and went home to lick his wounds. In typical Hamilton fashion, he recovered quickly, and by July was making "a bit of coin by playing for independent clubs occasionally."[58] August 1906 found him back in the New England League, playing for the same team he had managed to the pennant two years earlier. "Billy Hamilton, formerly of Harrisburg, formerly captain and manager of the Haverhill team, resumed play with the local team."[59] Sliding Billy was home in New England again — this time to stay. In January 1907 he signed again as player-manager of Haverhill: "Billy Hamilton, the Haverhill manager, is delighted to be back in the New England League, and will make an effort to hold the top clubs down to a hot race."[60] A photograph of a smiling and seemingly contented Billy with his 1907 Haverhill team confirms the news report. Jake Morse also was pleased. "It will seem like old times to have William around once more."[61]

During his brief stay at Harrisburg, Billy shared some caustic opinions with *Sporting Life* regarding the abilities of players of the new century as opposed to their nineteenth-century counterparts. In an article entitled "Brains in Ball: Famous Billy Hamilton Thinks the Old Timers Employed More Gray Matter than the Moderns," Sliding Billy observed:

> There may be more good mechanical players in the business today than there were ten or fifteen years ago, but when it comes to showing real intelligence — inside work on the field — the present style of player is an empty-

5. Home to Clinton

Haverhill Harriers, New England League, 1907. Billy Hamilton, player-manager, seated top row, center. At age 41, Sliding Billy led the league in hitting in 1907 (.333) (courtesy of Howard "Skip" Reynolds).

skulled animal compared to the brain-bearing player of the National League ten years ago ... you don't see the inside work — the hit and run game, the base stealing, the place hitting, the trick fielding now that you did when the Baltimores were in their prime — every man a star in his position.... I'll grant that the modern player is better at the mechanical game ... but when it comes to thinking — well, he's not in it.[62]

With the absence of Hamilton from the New England League in 1905 and the retirement from baseball of John "Phenomenal" Smith, the journeyman big league pitcher who had led Manchester to the pennant in 1902, league President Murnane "needed another former major leaguer as a crowd pleaser for the 1906 season, and during the winter he found one in Jesse Burkett."[63] The hard-hitting West Virginia native had starred with Cleveland and St. Louis, hitting over .400 twice before retiring from big league ball after 16 years with a .339 average. Like Billy Hamilton, he had invested his earnings well. Married to a Worcester native, Burkett bought the Concord team, moved it to his wife's hometown, and named himself player-manager. A pleasant family man off the field, Burkett was ferocious when a ballgame began, and was "legendary for his outbursts in the New England League."[64] His intimidating on-field comportment and fine hitting paid off in the league, as Worcester won four consecutive pennants (1906–09), the only consecutive-win streak since the league's 1885 reconstitution. Burkett was a talented promoter, using his major league connections to arrange numerous exhibitions games, which often attracted more fans than the league's games.

Now that Sliding Billy was over 40, some wondered if Hamilton's playing skills were fading. In May of 1907 he responded, "My baseball days are by no means over yet. I realize that any ballplayer cannot play forever, and my day will come just as everyone else's does. But I don't feel this is my year by a long odds. I am in fine condition."[65]

He wasn't joking.

Although Hamilton could not match Burkett's league record as a manager, he moved the Hustlers from seventh to fourth place. He did, however, best Burkett offensively in his first full season back in the league, winning the batting championship in 1907 with a .333 average and stealing 29 bases. Burkett and Hamilton, the aging former National Leaguers, were two of only four New England League players who hit over .300 in 1907. Billy slipped to .290 in 1908, but still banged out more than a hit per game and stole 39 bases, prompting Jake Morse's comment that "the veteran Billy Hamilton is still slugging the ball and runs the bases finely."[66] The temper that had flared often while at Harrisburg returned occasionally at Haverhill: "Billy Hamilton was fined in the ninth inning for disputing a decision of umpire M. O'Brian."[67]

Even though Sliding Billy moved the Hustlers up a notch to third place in 1908, his inability to field a pennant-winning team caused the Haverhill ownership to release him at season's end, and he subsequently signed with Lynn, Haverhill's sister city in the production of shoes, for the 1909 campaign. There he would complete his last superlative offensive season. As an old man of 43, he led the league in hitting for a third time at .332 and stole 23 bases.

Billy's Lynn Shoemakers finished in second place in 1910, but injuries plagued Hamilton, now 44. Playing in only 41 games in his last season in professional baseball, Sliding Billy hit .250 and stole just five bases. His complete minor league offensive record, nevertheless, speaks for itself. In 841 games he averaged more than a hit per game, stole 379 bases, and batted .343, virtually the same average as in his major league years.

Baseball historian David Pietrusza suggests that Billy's minor league success at base stealing while in his late thirties and early forties, and while playing under modern rules, "gives us a clue as to just how skillful he would have been under 'modern' conditions in the major league."[68] While acknowledging that Billy's abilities were aided by certain conditions under the old rules, Pietrusza questions the impact of one of the most significant of them on Hamilton. Although until 1897 a runner could be credited with a stolen base for advancing an extra base on a hit, Pietrusza notes that after 1892, such a steal could only be credited if there were a possible chance and clear intent to retire the runner. Furthermore, citing a 1975 study that examined such attempts made by the Philadelphia team during a *pre–1892* season (1887), he observes that of the twenty-three cases of such an advance, "not a single one was credited with a stolen base."[69] Pietruzsa concludes his analysis by noting that Billy was also hampered during the first five years of his major league career by what *Spalding's Base Ball Guide* described as "neglect on the part of the majority of the umpires to strictly enforce the rules applicable to balks."[70] Before the advent of the pitching rubber in 1893, this laxity was abetted by the "pitching box," since while standing within it "the pitcher had too much freedom of movement allowing [*sic*] him in throwing to bases, and especially in regarding feints to throw, in doing which he stepped out of what should be his box boundaries."[71] With or without such considerations, Hamilton's three minor league batting championships and 74 steals in 1904, feats accomplished while in the twilight of his career, remain impressive accomplishments.

David Pietrusza concludes that Billy Hamilton in his prime would have fared well stealing bases in the major leagues under modern rules. How would Sliding Billy have performed in the categories of fielding and hitting in baseball's modern era?

There can be little doubt that his fielding would have improved under modern conditions. In his day, outfielders had to contend with irregular playing surfaces and park dimensions, tall grass, rocks, holes and depressions, soggy footing in spring and fall, and spectators standing directly behind the players on the field during games. For Billy, other exotic outfield hindrances included buffalo stampedes and small tornadoes. Hamilton's most obvious and important disadvantage, however, was the fact that for about one-third of his career he played the outfield barehanded. When he finally put on a glove, it was home-made, and of the flat "pancake" variety that was designed more to dull the force of the ball than to catch it.

Billy Hamilton retired from the major leagues nearly two decades before the first significant improvements in the quality of the fielding glove were made.

> In 1919 [Cardinals pitcher Bill] Doak went to the Rawlings Company ... in St. Louis ... with some suggestions for improving the effectiveness of the fielding glove. Doak's glove featured a multithonged web laced into the thumb and index finger, and a preformed, prelubricated pocket.... By 1920, Rawlings was marketing the Bill Doak Model and it revolutionized the design of all gloves.[72]

Today, modern outfielders' finger-laced, deep pocketed, oversized gloves make the Bill Doak model look primitive. Few would challenge the observation that without the modern glove, many of today's spectacular over-the-fence catches that appear on game highlight tapes would be home runs. For as many examples of remarkable catches described in this volume that were made by Billy Hamilton while playing for Philadelphia or Boston — efforts that included last-second bare-handed grabs and snatches made a foot off the ground on the dead run — there are nearly as many instances in which he managed to get to the ball but could not hold onto it. If Hamilton were wearing a modern glove, even one as primitive to us as the Doak model, the majority of these attempts would have been outs.

Average fielding percentages for outfielders in the National League during the 1890s hovered in the mid-.920s. In the 1990s, playing under near-perfect field conditions and using basket-sized gloves, the league's outfielders averaged a fielding percentage in the mid-.980s. Fielding barehanded or with a primitive glove and playing regularly under poor field conditions, Billy's lifetime fielding average was .928, just a bit higher than the 1890s average. Under modern field conditions and using a modern glove his fielding average in all likelihood would have exceeded the mid–1980 average of National Leaguers who played a century after he did.

Hamilton may have had one defensive advantage over modern-day outfielders. In 1959, summarizing Billy's career for Paul S. Kerr, then secretary of the Baseball Hall of Fame, Lee Allen, the organization's historian, noted that "[Billy's] position was center field, and he was one of the few 'aural' outfielders of the early days, racing at the crack of the bat to the spot where the ball would come down."[73] Although Allen provided no documentation for this assertion, William Curran, in *Mitts: A History of Fielding*, cites two Hamilton contemporaries who allegedly relied on the same skill:

> It was widely reported at the time [the 1880s] that [the Saint Louis Browns Curt] Welch judged fly balls by the sound of the bat. And early in this [twentieth] century, George Burns, the Giants' legendary ball hawk, claimed that he too relied on the crack of the bat to tell him where the ball was headed. Burns said that based solely on the sound he could confidently turn his back on the ball and run to the spot where it would come down.[74]

Physics professor Peter Brancazio's 1983 study of an outfielder's ability to determine where a fly ball will go after it leaves the bat suggests that such a skill may indeed involve the vestibular apparatus of the inner ear.[75] If, however, this ability was already becoming rare in Hamilton's era, as Lee Allen suggests, it would be almost non-existent today, given the enclosed stadia, larger crowds, public address systems, and blaring music prevalent in every contemporary big league park.

One of the greatest hitters for average in the history of baseball, Billy Hamilton would have been a successful hitter in the modern period. By the early years of the "lively ball" era, many of Hamilton's contemporaries and successors who had gained their fame as "forearm hitters," and who had practiced "inside baseball" as he did, were managers of major league teams. Despite their continued regret over the demise of the old-style game, their managing strategy had to take into account the changes that had occurred in baseball. John McGraw, for example, admitted in 1923 that he

> no longer managed the old way. Now, with ... the ball being hit all about the lot the necessity of taking chances on the bases has decreased.... A manager would look foolish not to play the game as it is.... There is no use in sending men down on a long chance of stealing a bag when there is a better chance of the batter hitting one for two bases, or, maybe, out of the lot."[76]

Ty Cobb viewed the fundamental shift in game strategy and techniques that had occurred "as a personal offense.... Yet despite his contempt for the new 'power game,' Cobb, as player-manager of the Detroit Tigers from 1921 to 1926, found himself managing basically according to its dictates, as McGraw did."[77]

Some slap hitters, though rare, survived in the twentieth and twenty-first century power-game era. In 1959, Lee Allen compared Billy Hamilton to a then-modern counterpart and future Hall of Famer: "He was a fine lefthanded hitter of the Richie Ashburn type."[78] The comparison, while apt, reveals as many differences as it does similarities between the two players. Although Whitey Ashburn played in over six hundred more games and batted over two thousand times more than Billy, the latter's number of walks and triples were almost the same as those of the Whiz Kids center fielder, and Hamilton, batting in the dead-ball era, hit eleven more home runs than Ashburn. Billy's lifetime slugging percentage is fifty points higher than Ashburn's, his on-base percentage is fifty-nine points higher, and his batting average is thirty-six points higher. Weighing the same as Ashburn but four inches shorter in stature, Hamilton was the more powerful slugger, even though he never enjoyed the luxury of swinging regularly at clean, new baseballs.

Could Hamilton have handled the speed of today's pitchers' fastballs? While it is impossible to determine accurately how fast pitchers threw in Billy's era, a review of pitching distance rules and a few mathematical calculations strongly suggest that he would have had no more problem hitting today's pitchers than he had hitting those of the 1890s.

During the first seven years of Billy's professional baseball career, pitchers were required to keep one foot planted on the rear line of the pitchers box, a distance of 55 feet from home plate. From that point, they were permitted to take one step forward during their delivery. The release point of these pitchers, therefore, was approximately 50 feet from home. Assuming that fireballers such as Denton Cy(clone) Young and Amos "the Hoosier Thunderbolt" Rusie threw at a speed of *ninety* miles per hour, under these rules their pitches would reach the plate in .38 seconds. Given today's 60'6" distance from the pitcher's rubber to home plate, the release point for modern hurlers after their step forward to deliver the pitch is approximately 55 feet from home. From this release point, a modern hurler's *ninety-five* mile-per-hour fastball reaches the plate in .39 seconds.

If we can accept the assumption that pitchers like Rusie and Young could throw ninety miles per hour, we can conclude that during the years in which Hamilton hit under the old pitcher-to-home distance rules, he had even less time to react to a pitch thrown at ninety miles per hour (.38 seconds) than he would have today reacting to a ninety-five-mile-per-hour-pitch thrown from a longer distance (.39 seconds).

Billy's batting average during the seven years of his career in which he hit under the old, shorter distance pitching rules was a healthy .329.

If Hamilton were in his prime in the lively ball era, could he have exceeded his lifetime dead-ball era average of three home runs per season? Ty Cobb, whose style of hitting mirrored that of Hamilton, and whose average yearly home run production bettered that of Sliding Billy by about one home run per season, provided an approximate answer to that question in 1925:

> Before a game in St. Louis ... he told a Detroit writer that he was tired of reading how Babe Ruth knocked 'em over fences while he got his hits on grounders and bunts. "I'll show you something today,' he promised. 'I'm going for home runs for the first time in my career.' He proceeded to clout three in that game (as well as two singles and a double) and two more the next day.... Following the St. Louis outburst, Cobb returned to his normal playing style....[79]

Billy Hamilton nearly equaled that feat thirty-two years earlier *without* the benefit of the lively ball. In one week in May of 1893, he hit four "out-of-the-park" home runs in two non-consecutive games.

Did the diminutive Hamilton possess the physical power to drive the ball great distances? This issue was resolved in 1912. Early that spring, during repairs to the South End Grounds prior to the commencement of the season, the park's flag pole, which flew in dead center field, 440 feet from home plate, was lowered and checked for damage.

> An examination of the records of feats intimately connected with the long piece of timber brings to light the shattering of a long standing belief that Dan Brouthers was the only man to rock the pole with a drive to deep center. It appears that Billy Hamilton, now chief scout for the Boston Nationals, duplicated this feat in 1898.[80]

Dan Brouthers was eight inches taller than Hamilton and outweighed him by more than 40 pounds.

After reviewing Billy Hamilton's career and statistics, baseball historian Bill Jenkinson, an expert on the game's great long-distance hitters, concluded that if Hamilton played today, he would average between 20 and 30 home runs per year.[81] Given this estimate, a contemporary edition of Billy Hamilton playing in the modern era of the game would perhaps most likely resemble Minnesota's Hall of Fame center fielder Kirby Puckett. The 5'7", always-hustling and pudgy Puckett, who played twelve seasons for the Twins, averaged 24 home runs in his six best years, and also hit for average (.318 lifetime). A blending of Puckett's power and Hamilton's speed and run-scoring ability would be an explosive combination in any era.

With his playing career at a close after his final season with Lynn, Hamilton was looking for other managerial positions. Waterbury, of the Connecticut League, offered him one for the 1911 season, but Billy reported that he "could not see his way clear to tie up with the club."[82] An unexpected opportunity soon presented itself. In mid–January, Fred Tenney, Billy's teammate on the championship Beaneater teams of 1897–98, signed on as manager of the Boston National League team, which now was nicknamed the Rustlers. A Massachusetts native, Tenney had spent the 1910 season as a player-manager for Lowell in the New England League. Within a month of assuming the pilot's position in Boston, the former first baseman had lured Hamilton away from his new job as Haverhill's manager and signed him as a scout. Billy's old friend and informal press secretary Jake Morse was happy to publish the news: "The club [Boston] has just signed our old friend Billy Hamilton as a scout. Hamilton had agreed to manage the Haverhill team, but Tenney persuaded him to join the Boston National's forces. He ought to prove a valuable man for the locals to have on their staff."[83] Characteristically, Billy wasted no time getting started. "The sleuth was not on the job long

A smiling Billy Hamilton, circa 1912, possibly during his tenure as a scout for the Boston Nationals (courtesy Howard "Skip" Reynolds).

when he picked up a youth named Neeley, a big pitcher from Memphis."[84]

The timing of Billy's new job was opportune. With his eldest daughter, Ethel, now 21, his youngest, Dorothy, eight, and with wife Rebecca's health improved and her childcare responsibilities lightened, Billy was freer to travel outside the region. In the first year in three decades that he was not playing ball, his adjustment was made more palatable by the opportunity to visit some of his old haunts as a representative of his former team. On a trip to Pittsburgh's new stadium, mentioned previously, responding to a fan's comment that at 45 he didn't look 40, Billy replied, "Only wish I was. You would see me out there in the field, showing up some youngsters who imagine they know the game."[85] While in Atlanta to take in an exhibition game between Washington and New York, he spent an afternoon with former rivals Arlie Latham, John McGraw, and Wilbert Robinson, sharing opinions, now as "old timers," on the status of the game. "McGraw and Hamilton agree on the proposition that there is little to the game today that can be called new — that the base ball which is instilled into the youngsters of the present is the same ball that was played a couple of decades back"[86] Regarding base stealing, the pair agreed that "the men who were playing the game when they were in their spangles themselves would be the same sensations now that they were then."[87]

One of Hamilton's scouting strategies, that of visiting major league teams during spring training, unnerved some of the team managers, including McGraw. "While 'all's fair in love and war,' the Little Napoleon was considerably peeved at Hamilton's sojourn [at Giants training camp in Marlin, Texas], as he is not greatly taken with the idea of another club reaping the benefits of his own sleuth's discernment."[88] Others, on the contrary, found such an idea a good one, as in the case of a report of Hamilton's visit to Cincinnati's camp: "Billy Hamilton of the Boston Nationals is another of the scouts who has been looking the Reds over on Southern fields. The idea is not a half bad one. Many a star-in-embryo has been eclipsed by early managerial action, only to break out, more brilliantly, in another company."[78] Hamilton had experienced a similar situation in his last year in Philadelphia under Arthur Irwin.

Billy's two years as a big league scout provided a needed transition for a man whose spirit was still willing to roam center field and steal a base but whose body was no longer up to the task. His work at Boston was praised: "As a scout Billy Hamilton has made a pronounced success and the club is lucky in having the famous old base runner under contract."[90] Despite such accolades, Boston finished eighth in 1911, and Fred Tenney was fired as the manager and replaced by catcher Johnny Kling for 1912. Kling could do no better, and the Bostons again finished last. Billy Hamilton was released at the end the 1912 season, Kling's first and last year as a big league manager.

Perhaps the best that could be said about Hamilton's final years in organized baseball is that he was still in the game. Over a span of four years he would spend just a month each with two teams, more in the role of "caretaker" than manager, be fired after a half-season with another club, spend a year out of baseball, and then resign from a fourth club after his only full year as manager during the period.

Plagued by labor unrest and financially weakened by new labor law requirements, the New England mill industries had begun relocating to the South, close to the cotton fields that provided them with their raw material. Young southern mill workers like "Shoeless" Joe Jackson of South Carolina were now making the same journey from the mill to the major leagues that Billy Hamilton had made three decades earlier. Many New England League clubs were surviving only due to the 1903 National Agreement, which required major league clubs to compensate minor league teams when their players were drafted. In this economically troubled era, several clubs were existing on this revenue source instead of gate receipts. With the best talent quickly sold to major league teams in order to balance the budget, only mediocre players were left to lure a rapidly decreasing fan base to the ballpark. In 1913, Jake Morse, still owed a year's salary by the New England League, resigned his position as its secretary. Forced out of his editorial position at *Baseball Magazine* two years earlier, Morse needed to take a job outside of baseball to support his family.[91]

Billy Hamilton's former Boston teammate Hugh Duffy bought the financially struggling Fall River team in 1913 and moved it to Portland, Maine. Haverhill, which had been experiencing difficulties renting a ballpark, then moved its team to Fall River, only to move it back to Haverhill again in 1914. Although *Sporting Life* reported that Billy Hamilton had taken the reins of the transferred team in August, league records[92] do not list him as the squad's manager. Hamilton moved to the Eastern Association in 1914 as pilot of the Springfield team. Unable to move the team above fifth place, he was fired in mid–July. Billy spent the rest of the season with Greenfield of the Twin States League, a Class D "outlaw" organization to which "many major league teams sent injured or slumping players."[93] Greenfield's short season ran from late June to early September and consisted of just 35 games. Hamilton had no association with minor league teams in 1915.

The New England League passed out of existence at the end of the 1915 season, merging its few financially viable teams with the Eastern Association to form the new Eastern League. Billy Hamilton purchased an interest in the new league's Worcester club and signed on as its manager for the 1916 season. The previous year, while still in the New England League, Jesse Burkett had led the Worcester Busters to a fourth-place finish. Billy Hamilton could do no better the following year than fifth place (61–60). In January of 1917, he sold his interest in the team and resigned as manager, ending his twenty-eight-year adventure in professional ball.

Approaching the age of 51, with his playing and managing days in professional baseball over, some must have wondered if Billy Hamilton finally was ready to retire.

Not by a long shot.

6

Late Innings

"Billy was forever talking baseball, and the boys in the neighborhood would listen to his every word. They idolized him."
— George Racine, Worcester native, 1961

A month after Billy Hamilton severed his relationship with the Worcester team of the Eastern League, the United States entered World War I. Almost immediately, New England industries with government defense contracts began to increase production of all material pertinent to the war effort. Graton and Knight Manufacturing Company, one of Worcester's oldest businesses, was ready for the challenge.

Established in 1851 by Massachusetts natives Henry Clay Graton and Joseph Addison Knight, the firm specialized in currying and tanning leather hides, cutting them into strips, and riveting or lacing them into long belts for use in conveyors and other industrial machinery. Prior to the introduction of rubber and synthetic alternatives, leather belting was critical to all industries that required transmission of power for manufacturing purposes.[1]

Leather hides that were unsuitable for such a process were formed into gaskets, washers, and leather parts for looms. In the twentieth century, this second product line for Graton and Knight was expanded to include such items as leather aprons, trunk and suitcase handles, bicycle and motorcycle saddles, and shoe soles. In addition, the firm manufactured holsters for pistols and revolvers, leather slings for rifles, and leather scabbards for bayonets.

Although by 1951 Graton and Knight's plant encompassed 600,000 square feet and was considered the world's largest industrial leather company, the development of synthetic substitutes for its principle product line led to an inevitable decline in productivity. The rest of the company's history mirrored that of many New England firms of the era. Sold in 1956 to a New York firm that dismantled two-thirds of its plant, it was then purchased by a New Jersey company that moved the remaining viable components out of state.[2]

The Graton and Knight firm was still growing, however, in 1917, and had just added two new fireproof buildings to its facilities. Due to increased wartime vigilance at all defense plants, the firm was seeking a mature, responsible new head of security. They found him in Billy Hamilton. As we have seen, Billy had a personal interest in leatherworking, having handmade the fielding glove he used during his years with the Boston Nationals. Although his first assignment with Graton and Knight was essentially that of a private security police chief, he changed jobs at the firm at the war's end. The 1920 U.S. Census lists Billy as an "overseer" for the company; the 1930 Census describes him as a "foreman." Regional publications[3] indicate that he worked in the company's "welfare" department, a division whose equivalent today is the office of human resources. The Graton and Knight experience represents another instance of Billy Hamilton

Wartime Security Officer, 1917. During World War I, Hamilton worked as Chief of Security for the Graton & Knight Company of Worcester, which produced leather goods for the war effort. After the war, Billy spent another 17 years with the company as a foreman and welfare officer, retiring in 1935 (courtesy Hamilton Starr).

working himself up the ladder, in this case to a middle-management position.

Although his formal education ended when he began working full-time in a Clinton cotton mill after completing the eighth grade, during Billy's years as a minor league manager he developed skills that would prove useful at Graton and Knight. In addition to recruiting, hiring, and supervising players, minor league managers of the era performed all the tasks that today's business manager handles. They oversaw the team budget, developed away-game travel itineraries, purchased equipment, maintained the home field, and tabulated gate receipts.

Hamilton obviously had a talent for the Graton and Knight positions he held — he spent eighteen years with the company. There was, however, at least in Billy's early years with the firm another perk that made his new career even more enjoyable. "Billy Hamilton, the former manager of the Worcester Eastern League club, has been signed to manage the Graton and Knight Manufacturing Company's team in the Worcester league this year."[4] This notice from *Sporting Life* was the publication's last on Hamilton's baseball career and one of the last in the original publication's history. The weekly "news sheet" style of the journal, which began in 1883, ceased publication soon after announcing Billy's new managing position at Graton and Knight in 1917. Five years later, it began a new era as a monthly magazine. Jake Morse, Billy's favorite *Sporting Life* correspondent, had left baseball and the publication in 1913. Like Hamilton, he started a second career later in life working as an insurance salesman.

With three daughters still living at home and a thirty-mile round-trip commute by trolley to work for Billy, who never learned to drive an automobile,[5] the Hamilton family began to look for a larger residence closer to the Graton and Knight plant in Worcester. In December of 1917, they sold their Clinton homestead of twenty-seven years, and a short time later relocated two miles southwest of downtown Worcester, close to the campus of Clark University. The Worcester home, a two-story clapboard at 6 Lucian Street, was larger and more comfortable than the Clinton cottage but, true to Hamilton preference, it was devoid of any pretension. Lucian Street is a block-long *cul de sac* that today sits adjacent to Clark University's Russ Granger Athletic Field. The modern-day university's Division III baseball team plays its home games there, just a long flyball from Billy's former home.

What would cause a financially well-off man in his early fifties to continue working full-time until the age of seventy? In Billy's case, the answer is found partly in his personality and partly in the Victorian values of the era in which he was born and raised. Hamilton, as we have seen, was by nature a high-energy individual. As a youth he celebrated the end of eleven-hour shifts at the cotton mill with vigorous evenings of roller polo at Dexter's Roller Rink. Not content to rest after a demanding baseball season filled with grueling, month-long, cross-country train travel, the mature Hamilton maintained an equally rigorous pace in the off-season by regularly engaging in numerous physically demanding activities — refereeing roller polo matches and harness and sleigh racing. Such an approach to life was highly favored in the Victorian period: "Cutting across all classes and sentiments ... was a rising disposition in favor of an energetic, dynamic style in all aspects of life ... the growing disposition to value energy, activity, and movement deeply influenced the whole sense of style that Americans brought to every area of work and play."[6] The predilection for liveliness and energy in late nineteenth-century American culture has been aptly summarized by Thomas J. Schlereth in *Victorian America* as the "ethos of striving."[7] Even after his twenty-nine year baseball career, Billy Hamilton continued to strive. It was neither in the nature of the man nor in the nature of the ethos of his age for one to sit back and take it easy.

At home on Lucian Street, Worcester, circa 1920. The Hamiltons moved from Clinton to Worcester soon after Billy began working for Graton & Knight. Following Victorian custom, Billy Hamilton always dressed formally in public (courtesy Hamilton Starr).

By the 1920s, with a full-time job and three daughters still living at home, Hamilton settled into a period of contented domesticity and simple pleasures, during which family-centered activities and entertainment were preferred over all other forms of socializing. Billy, Rebecca, and the children often made the thirty-five-mile trip to Boston to shop or to take in a ball game. These excursions, however, frequently exasperated his girls, as daughter Millie explained:

> I also remember how he'd take us to Boston, then stop and talk baseball with everyone he met while we stood and waited and waited and waited until we were furious. He'd talk baseball with anybody, any time."[8]

Sunday afternoon driving excursions, with daughter Dorothy behind the wheel of the car that her father had bought her, were another source of shared pleasure. A family photo from the captures Billy,

Sunday outing, circa 1930. Billy Hamilton, granddaughter Phyllis Prior, and daughter Millie Hamilton Prior (courtesy Howard "Skip" Reynolds).

daughter Millie, and beaming granddaughter Phyllis on one of these regular outings.

Worcester residents also recalled that in his spare time during these years, Billy frequented local ball fields, sometimes accompanied by his old major and minor league rival Jesse Burkett, giving advice and encouragement to a new generation of ballplayers.

> I was only a youngster, but I remember that Billy Hamilton was always willing and anxious to teach a boy the finer points of baseball... He would hit balls to the infielders and outfielders and give hints and advice ... once in a while Jesse Burkett would be at the park to join Hamilton in watching the rivalry between the lads from the Elm Park area and those from Beaver Brook.... It was always a thrill to see Hamilton, that all-time great, give one of the youngsters a friendly baseball tip.[9]

As Hamilton approached the thirtieth anniversary of his retirement from the Boston Beaneaters, the *Worcester Telegram* conducted a long interview with the "greatest base stealer in the history of Major Baseball Leagues," on the status of baseball. Reporter James H. Power found Billy "willing enough to compare baseball of today [1929] with that of his heyday, more than three decades earlier, but reluctant to talk about his own achievements."[10]

Sliding Billy's most extensive interview covered several specific topics: past and present players attitudes and talents; the deleterious effects of the "lively ball"; pitching handicaps in the modern era; and exemplary modern players.

Hamilton detected a basic change in attitude on the part of modern players — a state of affairs that he deemed to be unfortunate. While acknowledging that the modern players' skills were equal to those of players of his own era, he felt that their hearts were not in the game. "We played for the pleasure ... while most of the current crop plays for the money."[11]

Although he rarely argued as a major leaguer, he indicated to reporter Power that he admired figures like Jesse Burkett and Ty Cobb who did so. Most modern players, in his opinion, lacked "the scrap and fire of the stars of yesteryear."[12]

Billy's observations about the "the deadball" versus the "rabbit ball" require some preliminary explanations. The "Deadball" era, defined by some as beginning around 1900 and by others as beginning at the birth of major league ball, describes the period in the game's development in which simple overuse of a game ball — using one ball per game, regardless of how badly it became damaged from water, cuts, dirt, or broken seams — greatly reduced the possibility of hitting it for distance. Game strategy under these conditions logically focused on the bunt, the steal, the sacrifice, and the hit-and-run play to score runs. In 1911, cork was substituted for the baseball's original rubber core. In 1919 a different type of twine was introduced for winding around the cork center, and the winding process itself was mechanized, creating a tighter fit.[13] Such modifications are believed by some to have created a livelier ball, but others dispute the premise. Indisputable, however, is the fact that after 1920, offensive statistics, and in particular, home run production, rose dramatically.

Whatever its cause, Billy Hamilton was no fan of the new livelier ball. "In my heyday we had to work for our runs. Today the lively ball eliminates much of the run-producing work."[14]

According to Hamilton, the "rabbit ball" was not only deleterious to the game's offense, but also to its defense:

> The lively ball has taken a lot of fine fielding out of the game, too. For instance, the ball is hit so hard that shortstops and first basemen find it almost impossible to field balls to their right or left ... [o]utfielders have to play so deeply that they have to hustle on short singles to hold base runners on base.[15]

Perhaps Billy's most curious critique of the modern game, given the fact that it was being offered by a former league-leading hitter, is the one he provides regarding disadvantages to the pitcher. He argued that pitchers, already handicapped by the effects of the lively ball, were further disadvantaged by having to stand in the box "like a statue,"[16] and hampered by umpiring that refused to declare as strikes "balls that cut the corners."[17]

At the interview's conclusion, Sliding Billy paid tribute to two modern-day players, scrappy outfielders and superlative hitters who both had retired from the game the year before and were cut from the same bolt of cloth that he was. These final comments suggest that in Billy's opinion, these players also were part of an era in baseball that would not be seen again. "Ty Cobb and Tris Speaker of the modern game are as good as the best of my day. They are real ballplayers and always made me think of the old crop of stars."[18]

Portions of the *Worcester Telegram* interview may be credibly construed as the classic older generation to younger generation assertion that "we had it tougher and we did it better than you do." Other sections do not fit as well into such simple categories. While there is open criticism regarding a lack of serious purpose among some modern stars, Billy is quick to acknowledge the equality of their skill levels, and in the case of the greatest figure of the new generation, he is generous in his praise: "Now I don't want anybody to think that I am trying to deny Babe Ruth his laurels. He's a wonder."[19] His description of the disadvantages of modern-day pitchers may be construed as an indirect slap at sluggers, who were feasting on the offerings of beleaguered hurlers beset with restrictions. On the other hand, it might also be considered the opinion of a fair-minded competitor who believed that his own accomplishments would be diminished if his opponent's abilities were unfairly restricted. Hamilton's selection of Cobb and Speaker as the best of the modern players clearly reveals the qualities Billy considered significant in a ballplayer — qualities that in large part were disappearing at the dawn of the age of the great baseball sluggers. He would live to see both these men enshrined in the Baseball Hall of Fame, while his own accomplishments, many of which were equal to or better than those he praised in them, were forgotten.

The *Worcester Telegram* interview, conducted eleven years before Hamilton's death, was his last public statement on major league baseball — a type of baseball last will and testament. True to form, it contained not a word about his personal accomplishments as a ballplayer.

Family priorities continued to hold sway in Billy Hamilton's life in the 1930s, while his own health was deteriorating. When youngest daughter Dorothy married and moved out of the Lucian Street home, eldest daugh-

Rebecca Carr Hamilton at home on Lucian Street, Worcester, circa 1920 (courtesy Hamilton Starr).

ter Ethel, who was childless, moved in with her husband Roy. They occupied the second floor, with Billy and Rebecca residing on the first. In 1961, recalling her childhood, Ethel described herself as "Billy's most faithful fan. I followed him around the circuit like a puppy."[20] Her return home in the twilight of her father's life brought back fond memories for Billy and Rebecca of their early years, and is a telling reminder of the importance of family ties in their lives.

Billy retired from Graton and Knight in 1935. In June of 1936 he joined many other old-time players in Boston at a celebration commemorating the sixtieth anniversary of the National League. There he reunited with his old friend Jake Morse, the "first baseball writer in Boston and the first correspondent to make the training trip south with a ball team."[21] Like Billy, Jake couldn't get baseball out of his blood. He had come out of retirement, and was keeping his hand in the game by writing a column, "Baseball Chatter for Fervid Fans," for the *Boston Traveler*.[22]

Granddaughter Phyllis Reynolds' recollections provide an intimate portrait of Hamilton's last years. Billy, Phyllis affirms, always kept busy outdoors in later years, trimming bushes, growing vegetables, planting flowers. The wizened outfielder, who had played under the roughest conditions in the history of baseball, was unfailingly patient and gentle with his young grandchild, answering her interminable questions about garden plants and flowers. Indoors, he taught her how to play solitaire, a diversion that had kept him occupied

Rebecca Carr Hamilton and youngest daughter, Dorothy, circa 1920.

on many a cross-country journey by train during his playing days. In later years, when Phyllis used to bring her beau (and future husband) Jim Reynolds to visit, she would experience the same kind of exasperation that her mother and aunts did years earlier, as her grandfather and her young suitor moved off to a far corner to discuss sports, leaving the frustrated young lady to her own devices. During her nursing training years in Worcester, Phyllis customarily would stop after her classes at the house on Lucian Street to chat with her grandfather, while Rebecca would prepare her a snack. She holds fondly in her memory the familiar image of Grandpa Hamilton seated in his favorite Morris chair by the radio, listening to the evening news. In March of 1938, the entire family gathered at the home to celebrate Billy and Rebecca's fiftieth wedding anniversary.

Four generations of Hamilton women. Left to right: Rebecca Carr Hamilton, daughter Millie Hamilton Prior, granddaughter Phyllis Reynolds, and newborn great-granddaughter Nancy Reynolds (courtesy Howard "Skip" Reynolds).

Hamilton's health, however, was failing. He suffered from angina, a portent of severe heart trouble. As his condition worsened, he weakened and was unable to perform simple tasks. Daughter Ruth's husband, Dr. John Willis, who was devoted to Billy, installed a coal heater in the home's first floor so that Hamilton would not have to go downstairs to stoke the furnace.

In her 1959 letter to Ford Frick, Ruth indicated that in his last months Billy had an unexpected visitor. "Ty Cobb ... came to see Dad, when Dad was very ill," and agreed with Hamilton that "the memorials given ... should be given to the gallant families who stood by their men and made baseball the sport it is."[23] As ill as Billy was at the time, this homage from the "Georgia Peach" must have cheered his spirit.

On December 15, 1940, two months shy of his seventy-fifth birthday, Billy passed away. The official causes of death were listed as coronary heart disease, arteriosclerosis, and chronic myocarditis.[24] After rounding all of life's bases, Sliding Billy had safely made it home.

The funeral service and burial were private ceremonies, with interment in the Carr-Hamilton family plot at Eastwood Cemetery, in Lancaster, Massachusetts. A few days after Billy's obituary appeared in the *New York Times* (December 17, 1940), his name and accomplishments slipped back into oblivion, where they would remain for two decades.

During the first nine years of the Baseball Hall of Fame's existence, 1936–44, only a handful of nineteenth-century players were selected. An Old-Timers committee was established in 1939, but it did not convene at all during the next five years, leading to complaints that the pioneer players were being ignored. Although that drought ended with the selection of ten early-era players in 1945, and another ten in 1946, twenty-five percent of those chosen were early twentieth-century players. Through the 1950s, the committee remained reluctant to vote for nineteenth-century players, citing an alleged lack of precise career records. They arrived at a compromise in this regard by deciding to select future nineteenth-century inductees primarily from a list of

Rebecca Carr Hamilton with granddaughter Susan Starr, circa 1940 (courtesy Hamilton Starr).

those who had either managed or coached in the major leagues after their playing years, when team performance records were more accessible and reliable. Two-thirds of the fifteen nineteenth-century stars who subsequently were selected in 1945 and 1946 had such credentials. Prior to 1960, therefore, only a handful of nineteenth-century players who had not additionally managed or coached in the major leagues had been admitted to the Baseball Hall of Fame. Their slim ranks included Ed Delahanty, Big Dan Brouthers, Orator Jim O'Rourke, Hoss Radbourne, Jesse Burkett, and Tommy McCarthy.

Of the numerous efforts made to reacquaint baseball fans and the Hall of Fame Veterans Committee with Billy Hamilton's exploits, two merit special attention. Shortly after Worcester resident and Hamilton friend Jesse Burkett was selected to the Baseball Hall of Fame in 1945, amateur baseball historian John T. Morgan of tiny Wheelwright, Massachusetts, wrote his first letter to the *Worcester Telegram* boosting Billy's candidacy. A dozen years later, he was still at it. After purchasing a volume dealing with nineteenth century ballplayers published by J.G. Taylor Spink of St. Louis, Morgan, noting the absence of any mention of Billy Hamilton, wrote Spink for an explanation. When the latter replied that he didn't have Hamilton's complete record, Morgan sent him a copy, penciling in the notation, "Billy Hamilton belongs in the Hall of Fame." Spink, the editor of the *Sporting News,* wrote back saying he agreed.[25]

In early August of 1959, Billy Hamilton's daughter Ruth sent a long hand-written letter to Ford Frick, and another to Paul S. Kerr, secretary of the Veterans Committee and president of the Hall of Fame, pleading the case for consideration of old-time ballplayers in general, and of her father in particular, for admittance to the Cooperstown Shrine. Frick's response was polite, but noncommital: "The election to the Hall of Fame is conducted by a special committee of baseball men, veteran writers, veteran players and officials, and in their hands the whole matter rests."[26] Kerr, though apparently annoyed by the tone of Ruth's plea, immediately contacted Hall of Fame historian Lee Allen, requesting information on Hamilton: "Please send me whatever information you have about Billy Hamilton.... His daughter who is now living in Santa Barbara has written me about him in a rather caustic manner."[27]

Allen's response was carefully detailed and highly positive, noting

Billy's run production, hitting, and stealing records, and parenthetically referring to the 1895 trade of Hamilton for Nash, "a third baseman ... who was about through," as "one of the most stupid deals of all time."[28] Even before he received Allen's response, however, Kerr had checked "the record from the Encyclopedia [of Baseball],"[29] and responded to Ruth's letter with encouraging news. "I shall be happy to bring his name and record to the attention of the Hall of Fame Committee on Veterans at their next election."[30] After not selecting anyone in 1960, the Veteran's Committee voted for Sliding Billy and twentieth-century standout Max Carey in 1961.

Hamilton thus became the first player whose career was completed primarily in the nineteenth century to be selected to the Baseball Hall of Fame since Kid Nichols in 1949. He made it to Cooperstown sixty years after retiring from the major leagues, not through the support or recognition of the baseball elite who had forgotten him, but through the persistence of a tireless fan from Wheelwright, Massachusetts, and the efforts of a loving daughter in Santa Barbara, California.

Although the recognition came too late for Rebecca Carr Hamilton to celebrate — she died in 1957 at age 90 — three of Billy's daughters, Ethel, Ruth, and Millie, were on hand on a hot July day in 1961 for the induction ceremony. Accompanying them were two excited boys, Skip Reynolds, age 15, and brother Jim Reynolds, age 10, Millie Hamilton Prior's grandsons who were actively engaged in carrying on the Hamilton baseball tradition and who that afternoon had a once-in-a-lifetime opportunity to share in a moment in baseball history. The man who had started out at age fourteen working in a cotton mill now had a plaque at Cooperstown.

By the time the Cincinnati Reds were battling the Yankees in the 1961 World Series two months later, Hamilton's name had again been relegated to the record books, where it remained until resurfacing briefly when Lou Brock surpassed Billy's all-time base stealing record in 1979, and when Rickey Henderson surpassed Brock's mark in 1991. During Henderson's assault on the record, Hamilton's great-grandson Jim Reynolds recalled, "I was in traffic on Storrow Drive when I heard this sportscaster say, 'Tonight Rickey Henderson may break Billy Hamilton's record....'" It was the first time I had ever heard his name on the radio."[31]

Almost half a century after feisty fan John T. Morgan had given the editor of the *Sporting News* a baseball history lesson about Billy Hamilton, residents of the Lancaster-Clinton area started a campaign to erect a memorial to Billy at his gravesite. Thanks to efforts of Anne Androski and Jean Watson, members of the Lancaster Historical Commission, a rose-colored granite marker was dedicated there in August of 1998. In attendance were Phyllis Reynolds, Billy's granddaughter, and her sons Skip and Jim, who thirty-seven summers earlier had attended the Baseball Hall of Fame ceremony. At the gravesite, 14-year-old ballplayer Josh Starr, grandson of Hamilton's youngest daughter, Dorothy, played the role that Skip and Jim Reynolds had played at Cooperstown — that of another young Hamilton family member carrying on the baseball tradition, by paying respects to Sliding Billy.

In 2005, one hundred and ten years after they traded him to Boston, the Philadelphia Phillies dedicated a plaque to Billy Hamilton in the Walk of Fame section of Ashburn Alley, an outfield walkway in the team's new ballpark on South Broad Street. It was about time. Sliding Billy still holds the team's all-time records in batting average (.361), on-base percentage (.468), and stolen bases (508).

The personal qualities of Billy Hamilton, the quintessential Victorian "striver," read like a wish list of the best virtues of any era. A devoted husband for more than a half-century, a loving father to four daughters, Billy moved his family from working class to middle class, not over a lifetime, but in the span of a half-dozen years. Famously temperate in all his activities except sports, a lover of competition, he championed a vigorous, energetic lifestyle that did not cease at the end of a playing season or at the end of his baseball career. In the twilight of his years, when the opportunity for self-promotion presented itself during a final, comprehensive interview, he steadfastly refused to tout his own achievements.

A full review of Hamilton's professional career and records appears in an appendix to this volume. A brief summary, for use in discussions around the office coffee pot or the local ballyard, might read as follows:

How good was Billy Hamilton? Of the tens of thousands of men who have played major league baseball since 1876, none has scored more runs in a season. None has scored in more consecutive games. None has averaged more runs scored per game in a career. None has stolen a base in more consecutive games. While two men have surpassed his career stolen-base record, which he held for three-quarters of a century, none has equaled his steals-per-game or steals-per-at-bat ratio. Seven men have equaled or surpassed his lifetime batting average. Their names are Williams, Speaker, Delahanty, Browning, Jackson, Hornsby, and Cobb.

In the potent combination, therefore, of hitting for average, stealing bases, and scoring runs, nobody ever did it better.

Two miles north and a mile east of the town of Clinton, nestled in the gently rolling hills of central Massachusetts, Billy Hamilton's grave sits among maples and tall pines. The imposing, black granite headstone is starkly simple, and with the exception of a tiny flower and leaf pattern in the upper corners, is devoid of decoration. No dates, no given names, no "William Robert" or "Rebecca Jane" adorn the stone, just two words in large print:

CARR
HAMILTON

One maple, to the left of the headstone, a tree too young to have been there when Billy was laid to rest nearly seventy years ago, has

Billy Hamilton's great grandson Josh Starr and grandson Hamilton Starr at the August 1998 dedication of the Billy Hamilton monument at Eastwood Cemetery, Lancaster, Massachusetts (courtesy Hamilton Starr).

gradually spread its branches out over the grave area. Sunlight glints through the leaves, dappling the headstone in sun and shade. The stone faces south, toward Clinton and Worcester, where the story of Billy and Rebecca began. Engraved on the small rose-colored memorial marker that sits next to the tombstone are the words:

> Sliding Billy Hamilton
> Philadelphia Phillies NL 1890–'95
> Boston Beaneaters, NL 1896–'01
> NL Batting Champion 1891
> Stolen Bases 937
> Baseball Hall of Fame 1961

A wonderful expression of recognition, admiration, and respect, the stone's words can only hint at the greatness of the ballplayer. It can convey nothing of the greatness of the man.

Billy Hamilton's eldest daughter Ethel recalled that when sportswriters asked her if they could flash the news of Sliding Billy's death across the country, "I told them at the time that a tired, elderly gentleman has gone to rest, and I don't think there will be many who remember him."[32]

The reporters' response still rings true today: "As long as there is baseball, there will be Billy Hamilton."[33]

7

In the Country of Baseball

> *Baseball is a country all to itself.... The citizens wear baggy pin-stripes, knickers and caps. Seasons change and teams shift, blur into each other ... and restore themselves to the old ways again.*
> — Donald Hall

The span of a man or woman's life is like the span of a bridge. Bridges span distances from one point to another; a life spans time from one era to another. In reviewing Billy Hamilton's life and times, we renew our awareness both of the great historical and cultural changes that occurred during his era, and of baseball's metamorphosis from the pioneer days to the sport's emergence as the "National Pastime." Hamilton's life personifies the American Dream — a rise from humble origins to the peak of a profession through discipline and hard work. His individual baseball career is of such a lofty caliber that records he set more than eleven decades ago have never been broken. On a broader level, however, Billy's baseball life is of greater significance, for a review of his career not only takes us from the "then" to the "now" in the game, but explains how such a transition took place.

Union and Confederate guns had barely ceased firing when Billy was born. Before he passed away, the winds of World War II had set Europe aflame. In between these events, Americans experienced the Spanish-American conflict, World War I, the Victorian era, the Roaring Twenties, and the Great Depression. Almost nothing that we take for granted today existed at the time of Billy's birth: telephones, radio, television, motion pictures, automobiles, airplanes, space travel, electricity, indoor plumbing (except for the wealthy), antibiotics, or even major league baseball. By the time of his passing, they were all cultural or technological commonplaces.

In 1888, the year Hamilton stepped to the plate for the first time in the major leagues, Deacon White played third base for the Pittsburgh Pirates and hit .298. White, who would retire in 1890, was one of the few hardy souls still in the game who had taken the field in May 1871 for the first season of professional baseball. In 1939, a year before Sliding Billy's death, a slender slugger named Ted Williams completed his rookie year with the Red Sox, hitting .327 and leading the league in RBIs (145). Hamilton was born in the sixth decade of the nineteenth century; Williams would play into the sixth decade of the twentieth century. Thus, the link between the first year of major league baseball, six years after the end of the Civil War, and the last home run hit by the Splendid Splinter passes through Billy Hamilton.

When Billy retired from major league competition in 1901, he had already witnessed the arrival of the game's next great generation and competed against them — figures like Mathewson, Chesbro, Waddell, Wagner, and Lajoie. Before his death, he would witness the likes of Cobb, Speaker, Hornsby, Ruth, Gehrig, and others follow his lead and hang up their spikes.

Hamilton's contemporaries would take divergent paths on the journey after their major league years. "Honest John" Gaffney, the umpire whose recommendation helped Billy get his first major league contract, was frequently disciplined or laid off for drunkenness until his retirement in 1900. At the time of his death in 1913, he was a night watchman in New York City. After taking Billy Hamilton's advice about the ministry in 1890, Billy Sunday retired from baseball, and over the next forty years crisscrossed the country preaching "fire and brimstone" sermons at revival meetings. He died of a heart attack in Chicago in 1935. Billy Hamilton's favorite sportswriter, Jake Morse, ran unsuccessfully for public office, opened a car dealership, and sold insurance after his departure from baseball. He died a few weeks after suffering a heart attack in 1935.

Phillies owner Colonel John I. Rogers became owner of a professional football team, also named the Phillies, in 1902. He died of heart failure after over-exerting himself in the snow on a business trip to Denver in 1910. Rogers' co-owner, pioneer player and sporting goods magnate Al Reach, retired to Atlantic City but was often seen at Phillies games until 1928, when he died at age 88. Tightwad millionaire Arthur Soden, who rationed the number of shoe laces allotted to his Boston players, sold the Beaneaters in 1906 and returned to his roofing business, where until his death at age 83, he arrived each day at work "with his lunch packed in a basket."[1]

True to their character differences, Sam Thompson and Ed Delahanty met different fates. "Big Sam" worked as a Deputy U.S. Marshall in Detroit and kept in shape by playing amateur ball into his late forties. Liquor and the race track destroyed Ed Delahanty. Out of shape, drunk, and forty pounds overweight, he was on his way to "jump" again, this time to the Giants, when he fell into the raging Niagara River and drowned in 1903.

After leading the Boston Americans to one World Series and two pennants, future Hall of Famer Jimmy Collins had mixed success as a manager of major and minor league clubs. His real estate ventures in Buffalo made him wealthy until the Depression wiped him out. He worked for the city's Streets and Recreation Department before dying of pneumonia in 1943. Chick Stahl, who in his rookie year for the Beaneaters hit .354, helping them win the pennant, jumped with his good friend Collins to the Boston Americans in 1901. Late in the 1906 season, he served as acting manager for the team when Collins resigned the post, and subsequently agreed to take the helm officially the following year. At spring training in 1907, Stahl inexplicably committed suicide by drinking four ounces of carbolic acid. He had just turned 34. No consensus exists regarding the reason for his action.

After "Kid" Nichols' iron arm gave out, he coached a Missouri college team and took up bowling. No longer good for throwing a baseball, his right arm won him a bowling championship at age 64. He was 83 when he died in 1953. Hugh Duffy outlived all his Boston teammates and bench-managed, player-managed, or owned a half-dozen National and Eastern league teams. Succeeding his former teammate Billy Hamilton as the Boston Nationals scout in 1917, he later served in the same capacity for the Red Sox for more than 30 years until his death in 1954 at age 88. The fates were not as kind to error-prone Herman Long, Billy Hamilton's teammate in Kansas City and in Boston who led all nineteenth-century shortstops in RBIs and home runs. Released by the Beaneaters after the 1902 season, he moved from team to team as an unsuccessful minor league manager, began drinking heavily, and contracted tuberculosis. By an eerily macabre coincidence, he died of the disease on September 17, 1909, in Denver, Colorado, the city where his former manager Frank Selee died of the same malady ten weeks earlier. Long was 43.

Arlie Latham, the off-season vaudevillian and roller polo player who wouldn't accept Billy Hamilton's challenge to a foot race as a player and as an umpire ejected Billy for the only time in his major league career, died in 1952 at the age of 92 after having spent thirty years as a press box attendant at Yankee Stadium and the Polo Grounds. Billy Nash, the Boston Nationals captain who was traded to Philadelphia in 1896 for Billy Hamilton, left baseball after unsuccessful attempts at managing and umpiring. He was working as a hospital orderly when he died of a heart attack in 1929.

Three of the four "rowdy boys" from the Baltimore Orioles, the Beaneaters' nemesis of the 1890s, managed major league teams after their playing days were over. Hughie Jennings won three successive pennants for the Tigers. John McGraw skippered the Giants for 30 years, winning ten pennants, three World Series, and finishing in second place eleven times. "Little Napoleon" resigned his Giants post in 1932, and died of prostate cancer two years later. Willie Keeler (whose original name was the much more Irish-sounding O'Kelleher) skipped the managerial track, choosing to invest in real estate in his hometown, Brooklyn. Wiped out by the post-war recession, he died penniless of endocarditis on New Year's Day 1923 at the age of 50. Hughie Jennings, who at the age of 12 had worked in a coal mine in Scranton, Pennsylvania, took law courses while playing and managing, and eventually become a lawyer. His sunny disposition masked a darker side. Hughie contracted tuberculosis while in a sanatorium recovering from a nervous breakdown, but it was spinal meningitis that killed him in 1918. Joe Kelley managed for a decade, first at Cincinnati and then for his old rival, Boston, but he found his greatest success as skipper of the Eastern League Toronto Maple Leafs. Married to the daughter of a powerful Baltimore Democratic politician, after baseball he "found" a job in the city's Register of Wills office, and "succeeded in not working too hard."[2] He died in 1943 at age seventy-one.

They were the "boys of summer" of the Hamilton age, so distant in time, so distinct from their successors today that some have classified their era as the "Stone Age" of baseball. Others of us, however, heeding poet Donald Hall, take a different tack: "In the country of baseball, time is the air we breathe and the wind swirls us backward and forward, until we are so reckoned in time that all time and seasons become the same."[3]

Appendix A:
The Hamilton Legacy

Year	Club	League	Pos	G	AB	R	H	2B	3B	HR	RBI	SB	BA
1887	Waterbury	Eastern	OF	71	313	75	116	19	5	0	–	18	.371
1888	Worcester	New Eng	OF	61	248	76	87	10	4	0	–	72	.351
1889	Kansas City	AA	OF	35	129	21	34	4	4	0	11	19	.264
1889	Kansas City	AA	OF	137	534	144	161	17	12	3	77	111*	.301
1890	Philadelphia	National	OF	123	496	133	161	13	9	2	49	102*	.325
1891	Philadelphia	National	OF	133	527	141*	179*	23	7	2	60	111*	.340*
1892	Philadelphia	National	OF	139	544	132	183	21	7	3	53	57	.330
1893	Philadelphia	National	OF	82	355	110	135	22	7	5	44	43	.380*
1894	Philadelphia	National	OF	129	544	196*	220	25	15	4	87	98*	.404
1895	Philadelphia	National	OF	123	517	166*	201	22	5	7	74	97*	.389
1896	Boston	National	OF	131	523	152	191	24	9	3	52	83	.365
1897	Boston	National	OF	127	507	152*	174	17	5	3	61	66	.343
1898	Boston	National	OF	110	417	110	154	16	5	3	50	54	.369
1899	Boston	National	OF	84	297	63	92	7	1	1	33	19	.310
1900	Boston	National	OF	136	520	103	173	20	5	1	47	32	.333
1901	Boston	National	OF	102	348	71	100	11	2	3	38	20	.287
1902	Haverhill	New Eng	OF	66	243	67	82	23	2	2	–	26	.337
1903	Haverhill	New Eng	OF	37	131	37	60	15	2	4	–	27	.455
1904	Haverhill	New Eng	OF	113	408	113*	168*	32	8	0	–	74*	.412*
1905	Harrisburg	Tri-St	OF	110	386	82	132	15	8	2	–	45	.342
1906	Harrisburg	Tri-St	OF	43	155	33	43	5	1	0	–	16	.277
1906	Haverhill	New Eng	OF	14	51	1	10	1	0	0	–	5	.196
1907	Haverhill	New Eng	OF	91	324	50	108	16	4	0	–	29	.333*
1908	Haverhill	New Eng	OF	85	300	63	87	19	0	1	–	39	.290
1909	Lynn	New Eng	OF	109	276	61	125	17	2	0	–	23	.332*
1910	Lynn	New Eng	OF	41	112	14	28	1	2	0	–	5	.250
Majors				1591	6268	1694	2158	242	94	40	736	912	.344
Minors				841	3048	1046	173	38	9	9	—	379	.343

*Indicates league leader. Because of inconsistencies in box scores of the era, different sources cite a different number of runs scored by Hamilton for the 1894 season, ranging from a high of 198 (The SABR Baseball List &Record Book) to a low of 192 (The Baseball Encyclopedia). Here I follow the "middle path" of 196, listed in the Elias Book of Baseball Records.

Appendix B: Hamilton's All-Time Records

I. All-Time Records Held

Most Runs Scored in a Season: 196 (1894)
Most Consecutive Games Scoring a Run: 24 (1894)
Career Runs Scored per Game Average: 1.06
  (minimum 5,000 plate appearances)
Most Consecutive Games Stealing a Base: 13 (1891)
Career Steals per Game Average: 1.74
Career Steals per At-Bat Average: 1.68

II. All-Time Records Shared

Most Stolen Bases in a Game: 7 (1894)
Most Triples in a Game: 4 (1889)
Most Sacrifices in a Game: 4 (1889)

III. All-Time Records Ranking Third

Stolen Bases in a Season: 912
Career On-Base Percentage: .455
  (minimum 5,000 plate appearances)
Times-On-Base in a Season: 355 (1894)

IV. All-Time Records Ranking Sixth

Career Batting Average: .344 (tied with Ted Williams)

V. Season League-Leading Records

A. American Association
Stolen Bases: 111 (1889)

B. National League
Batting Average: .340 (1891); .380 (1893)
Stolen Bases: 102 (1890); 111 (1891); 98 (1894); 97 (1895)
Runs: 141 (1891); 196 (1894); 166 (1895); 152 (1897)
Hits: 179 (1891)
Walks: 102 (1891)
On-Base Percentage: .453 (1891); .490 (1893);
  .523 (1894); .477 (1896); .480 (1898)

VI. Philadelphia Phillies All-Time Records
Batting Average: .361
On-Base Percentage: .468
Stolen Bases: 508

Notes

Introduction

1. Gary Swan, *San Francisco Chronicle* (September 18, 1990), Billy Hamilton player file, National Baseball Hall of Fame Library, Cooperstown, New York.
2. *Sporting News,* January 25, 1961, 2.
3. Bill James, *The New Bill James Historical Baseball Abstract* (New York: The Free Press, 2001), 728.
4. *Boston Globe,* July 21, 1999.
5. Harold Seymour, *Baseball: The Early Years* (New York: Oxford University Press, 1960), 332.
6. Ibid., 331.
7. Jerrold Casway, *Ed Delahanty in the Emerald Age of Baseball* (South Bend, IN: Notre Dame University Press, 2004), 96.
8. Thomas Gilbert, *Superstars and Monopoly Wars: Nineteenth-Century Major League Baseball* (New York: Franklin Watts, 1995), 44.
9. Mike Sowell, *July 2, 1903* (New York: Macmillan, 1992), 100–101.
10. *Spalding's Official Base Ball Guide,* 1895.
11. Frank Deford, *The Old Ball Game* (New York: Grove Press, 2005), 28.
12. Ibid.
13. Cait Murphy, *Crazy '08* (New York: Smithsonian Books, 2007), 19.
14. David Quentin Voigt, *American Baseball* (University Park: Pennsylvania State University Press, 1983), 254.
15. Ibid., 255.
16. Casway, *Ed Delahanty,* 98.
17. Ibid., 97.
18. Frank V. Phelps, "Billy Hamilton," in *Biographical Dictionary of American Sports,* Billy Hamilton player file, National Baseball Hall of Fame Library, Cooperstown, New York.
19. Bill Coulter, "Cabbages and Kings," *Clinton Daily Item* (September 14, 1974), Billy Hamilton file, Lancaster, Massachusetts Historical Commission.
20. Ibid.
21. Seymour, *Baseball: The Early Years,* 275.
22. Caroline Kim, "Gertrude Himmelfarb: Learning from the Victorians," in *Poverty and Compassion,* http://www.neh.gov/news/humanities/2005-01/medals.html.
23. Ibid.
24. Casway, *Ed Delahanty,* 95.
25. Charlie Bevis, *The New England League: A Baseball History, 1885–1949* (Jefferson, NC: McFarland, 2008), 110.

Chapter 1

1. Josh Leventhal, *Baseball: Yesterday and Today* (St. Paul, MN: Voyager Press, 2006), 20.
2. Dean A. Sullivan, ed., *Early Innings, A Documentary History of Baseball, 1824–1908* (Lincoln: University of Nebraska Press, 1995), 2.
3. Peter Morris, *But Didn't We Have*

Fun? An Informal History of Baseball's Pioneer Era, 1843–1870 (Chicago: Ivan R. Dee, 2008), 124.

4. Ibid., 87.

5. Michael Gershman, *Diamonds: The Evolution of the Ballpark* (Boston: Houghton-Mifflin, 1993), 7.

6. Steven A. Riess, *Touching Base: Professional Baseball and American Culture in the Progressive Era* (Westport, CT: Greenwood Press, 1980), 85.

7. Ibid.

8. Sowell, *July 2, 1903*, 11.

9. James, *The New Bill James Historical Baseball Abstract*, 728.

10. *Philadelphia Inquirer*, May 15, 1893.

11. *Sporting Life*, May 15, 1894.

12. Gershman, *Diamonds*, 88.

13. Voigt, *American Baseball*, 71.

14. Charles C. Alexander, *John McGraw* (New York: Penguin, 1988), 123.

15. *Sporting Life*, August 12, 1911.

16. Riess, *Touching Base*, 86.

17. Gershman, *Diamonds*, 54.

18. Riess, *Touching Base*, 121–25.

19. Leventhal, *Baseball*, 72.

20. Morris, *But Didn't We Have Fun?*, 82–83.

21. Ibid., 79.

22. Ibid.

23. Voigt, *American Baseball*, 289.

24. Ibid.

25. *Worcester Telegram*, December 20, 1929, Billy Hamilton clipping file.

26. Ibid.

27. Morris, *But Didn't We Have Fun?*, 84.

28. www.19thCBaseball.com.

29. Sowell, *July 2, 1903*, 88–89.

30. Thomas J. Schlereth, *Victorian America: Transformations in Everyday Life* (New York: Harper Collins, 1991), 181.

31. "The Baseball Glove Comes to Baseball," eyewitnesstohistory.com (2004).

32. William Curran, *Mitts: A Celebration of the Art of Fielding* (New York: William Morrow, 1985), 99.

33. Alexander, *John McGraw*, 125.

34. *Sporting Life*, August 8, 1896.

35. *Sporting Life*, July 25, 1894.

36. Morris, *But Didn't We Have Fun?*, 85.

37. Ibid., 56.

38. Schlereth, *Victorian America*, 171.

39. Alexander, *John McGraw*, 121.

40. Morris, *But Didn't We Have Fun?*, 229.

41. Ibid., 60.

42. Ibid., 61.

43. Seymour, *Baseball: The Early Years*, 339.

44. Ibid.

45. Ibid., 337.

46. Voigt, *American Baseball*, 192.

47. Seymour, *Baseball: The Early Years*, 340.

48. Ibid.

49. Voigt, *American Baseball*, 186.

50. Ibid., 187.

51. Seymour, *Baseball: The Early Years*, 340.

52. Voigt, *American Baseball*, 186.

53. Ibid., 189.

54. *Sporting News*, November 6, 1897.

55. Sowell, *July 2, 1903*, 4.

56. Seymour, *Baseball: The Early Years*, 349.

57. Voigt, *American Baseball*, 93.

58. David Nemec, *The Great Nineteenth Century Baseball Encyclopedia* (New York: Donald I. Fine Books, 1997).

59. Schlereth, *Victorian America*, 22.

60. Morris, *But Didn't We Have Fun?*, 138.

61. Voigt, *American Baseball*, 29–30.

62. Schlereth, *Victorian America*, 14.

63. Anthony J. Bianculli, *Trains and Technology, Volume 2, Cars* (Newark: University of Delaware Press, 2002), 60.

64. Ruth Hamilton letter to Ford Frick, August 8, 1959, Billy Hamilton player file, National Baseball Hall of Fame Library, Cooperstown, New York.

65. Schlereth, *Victorian America*, 190.

66. Ibid., 24.

67. Ibid., 224.

68. Daniel Walker Howe, *Victorian America* (Philadelphia: University of Pennsylvania Press, 1976), 10.

69. Gertrude Himmelfarb, *The Demoralization of Society* (New York: Knopf, 1995), 29.

Chapter 2

1. Demot A. Quinn, *The Irish in Newark and New Jersey*, Program for the "Irish in Newark and New Jersey Exhibit," Newark Public Library Publication, 2007.

2. James Layburn, *The Scotch-Irish: A Social History* (Chapel Hill: University of North Carolina Press, 1962), 83–98.
3. Charlie Bevis, *The New England League: A Baseball History, 1885–1949* (Jefferson, NC: McFarland, 2008), 21.
4. Terry Ingano, *Images of America: Clinton* (Dover, NH: Arcadia, 1996), 7.
5. Ibid., 8.
6. Bevis, *The New England League*, 24.
7. James M. De Clerico and Barry J. Pavelec, *The Jersey Game: The History of Modern Baseball from Its Birth to the Big Leagues in the Garden State* (New Brunswick, NJ: Rutgers University Press, 1991), 11.
8. Morris, *But Didn't We Have Fun?*, 16.
9. Seymour, *Baseball: The Early Years*, 28.
10. Charles C. Alexander, *Our Game: An American Baseball History* (New York: Henry Holt, 1991), 13.
11. Karen Nugent, "Heirloom Diamond," *Boston Telegram and Gazette* (October 4, 2007), online edition.
12. Clifford Kachline letter to Dorothy Starr, April 6, 1978, Billy Hamilton player file, National Baseball Hall of Fame Library, Cooperstown, New York.
13. Dorothy Starr letter to Clifford Kachline, April 11, 1978, Billy Hamilton player file, National Baseball Hall of Fame Library, Cooperstown, New York.
14. *Boston Daily Globe*, June 15, 1900.
15. *Sporting Life*, June 4, 1898.
16. *New York Times*, January 22, 1899.
17. *Sporting Life*, April 30, 1898.
18. *Sporting Life*, July 29, 1893.
19. *Sporting Life*, September 27, 1892.
20. *Sporting News*, December 26, 1940.
21. *Sporting News*, November 6, 1897.
22. *Sporting Life*, July 16, 1892.
23. *Sporting Life*, April 28, 1894.
24. *Boston Daily Globe*, June 17, 1897.
25. *Sporting News*, December 26, 1940.
26. *Sporting Life*, August 9, 1889.
27. *Sporting News*, November 19, 1936.
28. *Sporting News*, March 14, 1951.
29. *Philadelphia Inquirer*, September 14, 1891.
30. James, *The New Bill James Historical Baseball Abstract*, 28.
31. *Philadelphia Inquirer*, August 6, 1891.
32. *Philadelphia Inquirer*, June 23, 1891.
33. Al Stump, *Cobb* (Chapel Hill, NC: Algonquin Books, 1996), 257.
34. Ibid.
35. Donald J. Mrozek, *Sport and American Mentality, 1880–1910* (Knoxville: University of Tennessee Press, 1983), xiii.
36. Ibid., xvi.
37. Schlereth, *Victorian America*, 219.
38. Ibid.
39. Bill Coulter, "Billy's Daughter Was Speechless at Cooperstown, N.Y. Ceremonies," *Clinton Daily Item* (no date), Billy Hamilton file, Lancaster, Massachusetts, Historical Commission.
40. Phyllis Reynolds interview, Lexington, Massachusetts, August 7, 2008.
41. Joseph Anderson, et al., *The Town and City of Waterbury, Connecticut* (Waterbury: Price and Lee, 1896), 105.
42. *Sporting Life*, January 9, 1897.
43. Bevis, *The New England League*, 46.
44. Schlereth, *Victorian America*, 91.
45. Ibid., 95.
46. Ibid.
47. Daniel Walker Howe, "Victorian Culture in America," *Victorian America* (Philadelphia: University of Pennsylvania Press, 1976), 26.
48. Ellen K. Stevens, "The First Half-Century," *The Story of Clinton* (Clinton, MA: Coulter Press, 1950), 22.
49. Gertrude Himmelfarb, *The De-Moralization of Society* (New York: Knopf, 1995), 87.
50. Howe, *Victorian America*, 26.
51. Ibid.
52. Phyllis Reynolds interview, Lexington, Massachusetts, August 7, 2008.
53. Schlereth, *Victorian America*, 132.
54. Phyllis Reynolds interview, Lexington, Massachusetts, August 7, 2008.
55. *Sporting Life*, August 15, 1896.
56. *Sporting Life*, March 26, 1898.
57. *Sporting Life*, April 11, 1899.
58. *Sporting Life*, April 12, 1904.
59. *Sporting Life*, February 18, 1905.
60. Frederick Ivor-Campbell, ed., *Baseball's First Stars* (Cleveland: Society for American Baseball Research, 1996), 159.
61. Bevis, *The New England League*, 59.

Chapter 3

1. Seymour, *Baseball: The Early Years*, 108.
2. David Nemec, *The Beer and Whiskey League* (Guilford, CT: Lyons Press, 2004), 16.
3. Ibid., 235.
4. *Sporting Life*, June 12, 1889.
5. *Sporting Life*, June 15, 1890.
6. *Sporting Life*, May 22, 1889.
7. *Kansas City Star*, August 11, 1889.
8. *Sporting News*, December 26, 1940.
9. *Sporting Life*, October 22, 1898.
10. *Sporting Life*, May 10, 1902.
11. *Kansas City Star*, October 19, 1888.
12. *Sporting Life*, October 26, 1888.
13. *Kansas City Star*, October 20, 1888.
14. Curran, *Mitts*, 141–42.
15. *Kansas City Star*, March 23, 1889.
16. Nemec, *Beer and Whiskey League*, 30.
17. Curran, *Mitts*, 188.
18. *Sporting Life*, April 24, 1889.
19. *Sporting Life*, May 8, 1889.
20. Ibid.
21. Jim Sandoval, "Jacob Ellsworth Daubert: Gentleman Jake," www.deadballera.com/NiceGuys_Daubert_Jake.html.
22. *Sporting Life*, May 15, 1889.
23. *Kansas City Star*, June 29, 1889.
24. *Sporting Life*, July 13, 1889.
25. Lyle Spatz, ed., *The SABR Baseball List & Record Book* (New York: Scribner, 2007), 68.
26. *Kansas City Star*, June 15, 1889.
27. *Kansas City Star*, August 15, 1889.
28. *Kansas City Star*, October 23, 1889.
29. *Sporting Life*, January 15, 1890.
30. Ibid.
31. Ibid.
32. Sullivan, *Early Innings*, 5.
33. Sowell, *July 2, 1903*, 61.
34. Ibid, 62.
35. Ivor-Campbell, *Baseball's First Stars*, 165.
36. Franz Lidz, "More Than the Phils," portfolio.com.
37. John Shiffert, "A History of Cheating in Baseball," ZiskOnline.com.
38. Alexander, *Our Game*, 70.
39. *Philadelphia Inquirer*, August 9, 1903; quoted in "Black Sunday: Philadelphia's Deadliest Sports Disaster," by Bob Warrington, www.PhiladelphiaAthletics.org.
40. Ibid.
41. In *A Clever Base-Ballist*, Bryan De Salvatore suggests (p. 56) that this explanation of Ward's dismissal may have been due to more prosaic reasons: lying and chicken thieving.
42. Ivor-Campbell, *Baseball's First Stars*, 168.
43. Ibid.
44. Gilbert, *Superstars and Monopoly Wars*, 47.
45. *Philadelphia Inquirer*, August 27, 1890.
46. Untitled, undated article, Phyllis Reynolds file.
47. *Philadelphia Inquirer*, September 28, 1890.
48. Nemec, *The Great Encyclopedia*, 757.
49. *Philadelphia Inquirer*, May 8, 1891.
50. *Philadelphia Inquirer*, May 10, 1891.
51. *Philadelphia Inquirer*, July 13, 1891.
52. *Philadelphia Inquirer*, October 2, 1891.
53. *Philadelphia Inquirer*, August 12, 1891.
54. *Philadelphia Inquirer*, September 13, 1891.
55. James, *The New Bill James Historical Baseball Abstract*, 570.
56. *Philadelphia Inquirer*, September 13, 1891.
57. *Philadelphia Inquirer*, April 15, 1892.
58. *Philadelphia Inquirer*, April 26, 1892.
59. *Philadelphia Inquirer*, May 28, 1892.
60. *Philadelphia Inquirer*, June 23, 1892.
61. *Philadelphia Inquirer*, June 28, 1892.
62. *Philadelphia Inquirer*, July 23, 1892.
63. *Philadelphia Inquirer*, August 10, 1892.
64. Casway, *Ed Delahanty*, 75.
65. Ibid., 76.
66. Nemec, *The Great Encyclopedia*, 475.
67. Ibid.
68. Ibid., 496.
69. *Philadelphia Inquirer*, May 17, 1893.
70. *Philadelphia Inquirer*, June 7, 1893.
71. *Philadelphia Inquirer*, August 3, 1893.

72. *Philadelphia Inquirer*, August 8, 1893.
73. *Philadelphia Inquirer*, August 10, 1893.
74. *Philadelphia Inquirer*, October 2, 1893.
75. Nemec, *The Great Encyclopedia*, 517.
76. *Sporting Life*, March 31, 1894.
77. *Sporting Life*, October 5, 1895.
78. *Sporting Life*, April 28, 1894.
79. *Sporting Life*, May 5, 1894.
80. *Sporting Life*, July 15, 1894.
81. *Sporting Life*, September 19, 1894.
82. Nemec, *The Great Encyclopedia*, 541.
83. Ivor-Campbell, *Baseball's First Stars*, 54.
84. Nemec, *The Great Encyclopedia*, 517.
85. http://vault.sportsillustrated.cnn.com.
86. Ivor-Campbell, *Baseball's First Stars*, 50.
87. Ibid.
88. Ibid, 165.
89. *Philadelphia Inquirer*, September 1, 1894.
90. *Philadelphia Inquirer*, May 4, 1894.
91. *Philadelphia Inquirer*, May 5, 1894.
92. *Philadelphia Inquirer*, July 17, 1894.
93. *Philadelphia Inquirer*, June 7, 1895.
94. *Philadelphia Inquirer*, July 7, 1894.
95. *Philadelphia Inquirer*, July 4, 1895.
96. Ibid.
97. *Philadelphia Inquirer*, June 13, 1895.
98. *Philadelphia Inquirer*, June 14, 1895.
99. *Sporting Life*, October 5, 1895.
100. *Sporting News*, August 31, 1895.
101. *Philadelphia Inquirer*, September 27, 1895.

Chapter 4

1. George V. Tuohey, *Boston Baseball Club, 1871–1897* (Boston: McQuinn, 1897), 174.
2. Ivor-Campbell, *Baseball's First Stars*, 153.
3. Nemec, *The Great Encyclopedia*, 658.
4. *New York Times*, February 2, 1909.
5. Voigt, *American Baseball*, 286.
6. Ibid.
7. Ivor-Campbell, *Baseball's First Stars*, 153.
8. Gershman, *Diamonds*, 42.
9. Ibid., 44.
10. Ibid.
11. Frank Zimniuch, *Going, Going, Gone! The Art of the Trade in Major League Baseball* (Lanham, MD: Taylor, 2008), 24.
12. *Sporting Life*, October 5, 1895.
13. *Sporting News*, November 23, 1895.
14. *Sporting Life*, October 5, 1895.
15. *Sporting News*, November 23, 1895.
16. *Sporting News*, December 21, 1895.
17. *Sporting Life*, January 25, 1896.
18. Bill Felber, *A Game of Brawl: The Orioles, the Beaneaters and the Battle for the 1897 Pennant* (Lincoln: University of Nebraska Press, 2007), 34.
19. *Sporting Life*, February 1, 1896.
20. *Sporting Life*, February 29, 1896.
21. *Sporting Life*, October 6, 1900.
22. *Sporting Life*, July 17, 1902.
23. *Sporting Life*, March 21, 1896.
24. Nemec, *The Great Encyclopedia*, 761.
25. Ibid., 499.
26. *Sporting News*, August 1, 1896.
27. *Sporting Life*, March 28, 1896.
28. *Boston Daily Globe*, March 23, 1896.
29. *Boston Daily Globe*, May 1, 1896.
30. Ibid.
31. *Boston Daily Globe*, September 2, 1896.
32. *Boston Daily Globe*, May 30, 1896.
33. *Boston Daily Globe*, August 15, 1896.
34. *Boston Daily Globe*, October 3, 1896.
35. *Boston Daily Globe*, May 3, 1897.
36. *Boston Daily Globe*, May 7, 1897.
37. Ivor-Campbell, *Baseball's First Stars*, 35.
38. Ibid.
39. *Boston Daily Globe*, June 27, 1897.
40. *Boston Daily Globe*, June 5, 1897.
41. *Boston Daily Globe*, June 18, 1897.
42. Burt Solomon, *Where They Ain't: The Fabled Life and Untimely Death of the Original Baltimore Orioles, the Team That Gave Birth to Modern Baseball* (New York: The Free Press, 1999), 89.
43. Ibid., 44.
44. Alexander, *John McGraw*, 54.
45. Ibid.
46. *Boston Daily Globe*, July 16, 1897.
47. Nemec, *The Great Encyclopedia*, 583.
48. *Boston Daily Globe*, October 25, 1897.
49. *Boston Daily Globe*, October 26, 1897.

50. Felber, *A Game of Brawl*, 239–40.
51. *Sporting Life*, October 16, 1897.
52. Nemec, *The Great Encyclopedia*, 221.
53. Ibid., 440.
54. Ibid., 521.
55. Ibid., 564.
56. www.baseballlibrary.com.
57. Nemec, *The Great Encyclopedia*, 607.
58. Ibid., 611.
59. *Sporting Life*, May 7, 1898.
60. *Boston Daily Globe*, April 16, 1898.
61. *Boston Daily Globe*, June 9, 1898.
62. *Boston Daily Globe*, May 18, 1898.
63. *Boston Daily Globe*, May 31, 1898.
64. *Boston Daily Globe*, September 15, 1898.
65. *Sporting Life*, October 5, 1898.
66. Seymour, *Baseball: The Early Years*, 302.
67. *Sporting Life*, April 11, 1899.
68. *Boston Daily Globe*, May 3, 1899.
69. *Boston Daily Globe*, July 18, 1899.
70. *Boston Daily Globe*, September 24, 1899.
71. *Boston Daily Globe*, August 18, 1899.
72. *Boston Daily Globe*, September 18, 1899.
73. William Nack, "Collision at Home," *My Turf* (New York: Da Capo Press, 2004), 193.
74. *Sporting Life*, January 13, 1912.
75. Seymour, *Baseball: The Early Years*, 308.
76. Nemec, *The Great Encyclopedia*, 658.
77. David Nemec, *The Official Rules of Baseball Illustrated* (Guilford, CT: Lyons Press, 2006), 3.
78. *Sporting Life*, February 3, 1900.
79. *Sporting Life*, July 21, 1900.
80. *Sporting Life*, June 13, 1900.
81. *Boston Daily Globe*, June 15, 1900.
82. *Boston Daily Globe*, June 25, 1900.
83. *Boston Daily Globe*, May 3, 1900.
84. *Boston Daily Globe*, October 1, 1900.
85. *Sporting Life*, October 6, 1900.
86. *Sporting Life*, December 15, 1900.
87. Nemec, *The Great Encyclopedia*, 659.
88. *Boston Daily Globe*, April 18, 1901.
89. *Sporting Life*, March 23, 1901.
90. *Boston Daily Globe*, May 9, 1901.
91. *Boston Daily Globe*, June 23, 1901.
92. *Sporting Life*, August 10, 1901.
93. *Boston Daily Globe*, August 1, 1901.
94. *Boston Daily Globe*, September 1, 1901.
95. *Boston Daily Globe*, September 14, 1901.
96. *Boston Daily Globe*, April 19, 1902.
97. Zimniuch, *Going, Going, Gone!*, 24.
98. *Sporting News*, December 26, 1940.
99. Seymour, *Baseball: The Early Years*, 285.
100. Paul M. Gregory, *The Baseball Player: An Economic Study* (Washington, D.C.: Public Affairs Press, 1956), 42.
101. James, *The New Bill James Historical Baseball Abstract*, 726.
102. James Skipper, *Baseball Nicknames: A Dictionary of Origins and Meanings* (Jefferson, NC: McFarland, 1992).
103. *Sporting News*, January 25, 1961.
104. Ibid.
105. *Boston Daily Globe*, July 6, 1900.
106. *Sporting News*, January 25, 1961.
107. Billy Hamilton player file, National Baseball Hall of Fame Library, Cooperstown, New York.
108. Russell Roberts, *Stolen! A History of Base Stealing* (Jefferson, NC: McFarland, 1999), 2.
109. Mrozek, *Sport and American Mentality*, xvi.

Chapter 5

1. Seymour, *Baseball: The Early Years*, 332.
2. Coulter, "Billy's Daughter Was Speechless," *Clinton Daily Item*.
3. Stephen Hardy, "Long Before Orr," *The Rock, the Curse and the Hub: A Random History of Boston Sports* (Cambridge: Harvard University Press, 2005), 246–247.
4. Hardy, "Long Before Orr," 247.
5. *Boston Daily Globe*, February 14, 1896.
6. *Boston Daily Globe*, January 14, 1896.
7. *Boston Daily Globe*, March 2, 1898.
8. *Sporting Life*, December 2, 1902.
9. Ivor-Campbell, *Baseball's First Stars*, 93.
10. *Sporting Life*, December 2, 1902.
12. *Sporting Life*, October 27, 1900.
12. John Buckley, "Sports Sidelines,"

Worcester Evening Gazette (July 3, 1959), *Worcester Telegram and Gazette* clipping file.
13. *Sporting Life*, October 27, 1900.
14. *Sporting Life*, October 26, 1908.
15. *Boston Daily Globe*, October 17, 1897.
16. *Boston Daily Globe*, May 10, 1896.
17. *Boston Daily Globe*, October 17, 1897.
18. Stevens, *The Story of Clinton*, 30.
19. Edwin Valentine Mitchell, *The Horse and Buggy Age in New England* (New York: Coward-McCann, 1937), 81.
20. *Boston Daily Globe*, January 10, 1896.
21. Mitchell, *The Horse and Buggy Age*, 87.
22. Doug Gelbert, *The Great Delaware Sports Book* (Montchanin, DE: Cruden Bay Books, 1995), 171.
23. *Sporting Life*, January 15, 1898.
24. *Clinton Daily Item*, (n.d.), Billy Hamilton file, National Baseball Hall of Fame.
25. U.S. Census, 1900.
26. Schlereth, *Victorian America*, 25.
27. Stevens, *The Story of Clinton*, 17.
28. Ibid., 34.
29. baseball-reference.com, Billy Hamilton page.
30. *Sporting Life*, June 7, 1902.
31. *Sporting Life*, June 14, 1902.
32. Ibid.
33. Ibid.
34. *Sporting Life*, June 4, 1902.
35. Robert Objoski, *Bush League: A History of Minor League Baseball* (New York: Macmillan, 1975), 17.
36. Ibid., 18.
37. Bevis, *The New England League*, 114.
38. Ibid., 116.
39. *Sporting Life*, June 14, 1902.
40. *Kansas City Star*, August 11, 1889.
41. *Philadelphia Inquirer*, May 21, 1892.
42. *Sporting Life*, February 24, 1900.
43. *Sporting Life*, August 10, 1901.
44. *Sporting Life*, July 19, 1902.
45. *Sporting Life*, July 5, 1902.
46. *Sporting Life*, July 12, 1902.
47. *Sporting Life*, April 23, 1904.
48. *Sporting Life*, May 7, 1905.
49. Bevis, *The New England League*, 121.
50. *Sporting Life*, October 24, 1904.
51. *Sporting Life*, October 1, 1904.
52. *Sporting Life*, November 12, 1904.
53. *Sporting Life*, January 7, 1905.
54. "Official Directory of Baseball Leagues," *Sporting Life*, April 23, 1904, 14.
55. *Sporting Life*, March 4, 1905.
56. *Sporting Life*, June 24, 1905.
57. *Sporting Life*, October 16, 1905.
58. *Sporting Life*, July 14, 1906.
59. *Sporting Life*, August 11, 1906.
60. *Sporting Life*, January 26, 1907.
61. *Sporting Life*, February 2, 1907.
62. *Sporting Life*, October 14, 1905.
63. Bevis, *The New England League*, 124.
64. Ibid., 125.
65. *Sporting Life*, May 11, 1907.
66. *Sporting Life*, May 23, 1908.
67. *Sporting Life*, June 6, 1908.
68. David Pietruzsa, "Sliding Billy Hamilton," *Baseball Research Journal* (Society for American Baseball Research, 1991), 31.
69. Ibid.
70. Ibid.
71. Ibid.
72. Curran, *Mitts*, 77.
73. Lee Allen letter to Paul S. Kerr, August 13, 1959, Billy Hamilton player file, National Baseball Hall of Fame Library, Cooperstown, New York.
74. Curran, *Mitts*, 161.
75. Peter Brancazio, "Whatever Your Game Is, a Lesson in Physics Can Give You an Edge," *Sport in Science*, http://vault.sportsillustrated.com.
76. Alexander, *Our Game*, 137.
77. Ibid., 138.
78. Allen letter to Paul S. Kerr.
79. Alexander, *Our Game*, 138.
80. *Sporting Life*, March 30, 1912.
81. Bill Jenkinson interview, Lakeland, Florida, April 1, 2009.
82. *Sporting Life*, January 17, 1911.
83. *Sporting Life*, March 11, 1911.
84. *Sporting Life*, April 19, 1911.
85. *Sporting Life*, August 21, 1911.
86. *Sporting Life*, April 11, 1911.
87. Ibid.
88. *Sporting Life*, March 30, 1912.
89. *Sporting Life*, April 6, 1912.
90. *Sporting Life*, January 6, 1912.
91. Bevis, *The New England League*, 144.
92. "Haverhill, New England League, 1913" baseball-reference.com.

93. "1909–1915: Connecticut League and Twin State League," http://historic//northampton.org.

Chapter 6

1. Oliver B. Wood, *Worcester, Its Past and Present* (Worcester: 1888), 139.
2. Barton Kamp, *Worcester, Volume II* (Charleston, SC: Arcadia, 1998).
3. Phyllis Reynolds clipping file, (n.d., n.p).
4. *Sporting Life*, April 8, 1917.
5. Phyllis Reynolds interview, Lexington, Massachusetts, August 7, 2008.
6. Mrozek, *Sport and American Mentality*, xvi–xvii.
7. Schereth, *Victorian America*, 254.
8. Phyllis Reynolds clipping file (n.d., n.p).
9. Ed Scannell, *Evening Sports Gazette* (July 23, 1961). Billy Hamilton player file, Baseball Hall of Fame.
10. James H. Power, *Worcester Telegram* (December 20, 1929). Billy Hamilton clipping file, *Worcester Telegram*.
11. Ibid.
12. Ibid.
13. baseball-reference.com/bullpen/deadballera.
14. *Worcester Telegram*, Billy Hamilton clipping file.
15. Ibid.
16. Ibid.
17. Ibid.
18. Ibid.
19. Ibid.
20. Phil Coulter, *Clinton Daily Item* (July 31, 1961). Billy Hamilton clipping file, Lancaster, Massachusetts, Historical Commission.
21. Billy Hamilton player file, National Baseball Hall of Fame Library, Cooperstown, New York.
22. Ibid.
23. Ruth Hamilton Jones letter to Ford Frick, August 12, 1959. Billy Hamilton player file, National Baseball Hall of Fame Library, Cooperstown, New York.
24. Commonwealth of Massachusetts, City of Worcester, certificate of death (copy), reference: Book 2701, p. 83.
25. Billy Hamilton clipping file, *Worcester Telegram*.
26. Ford Frick letter to Ruth Hamilton Jones, August 21, 1959. Billy Hamilton player file, National Baseball Hall of Fame Library, Cooperstown, New York.
27. Paul S. Kerr letter to Lee Allen, August 11, 1959. Billy Hamilton player file, National Baseball Hall of Fame Library, Cooperstown, New York.
28. Lee Allen letter to Paul S. Kerr, August 13, 1959. Billy Hamilton player file, National Baseball Hall of Fame Library, Cooperstown, New York.
29. Paul S. Kerr letter to Lee Allen, August 11, 1959. Billy Hamilton player file, National Baseball Hall of Fame Library, Cooperstown, New York.
30. Paul S. Kerr letter to Ruth Hamilton Jones, September 2, 1959. Billy Hamilton player file, National Baseball Hall of Fame Library, Cooperstown, New York.
31. Paul Della Valle, "Sliding Billy Hamilton Is Given His Due," *The Lancaster Times* (August 19, 1998). Billy Hamilton clipping file, Lancaster, Massachusetts, Historical Commission.
32. Coulter, Billy Hamilton clipping file, Lancaster, Massachusetts Historical Commission.
33. Ibid.

Chapter 7

1. Ivor-Campbell, *Baseball's First Stars*, p. 153.
2. Solomon, *Where They Ain't*, 269.
3. Donald Hall, "The Country of Baseball," *Fathers Playing Catch with Sons* (San Francisco: North Point Press, 1985), 74.

Bibliography

Articles

Creamer, Robert W. "The Best Outfield Ever? Why Del, Big Sam and Sliding Billy, for Sure." http://vault.sportsillustrated.cnn.com/vault/article/magazine/MAG 1126029/index.htm.
Kim, Caroline. "Gertrude Himmelfarb: Learning from Victorians." http://www.neh.gov/news/humanities/2005-01/medals.html.
Lidz, Franz. "More Than the Phils." www.portfolio.com/views/columns/the-wind-up/ 2008/ 09/19.
"1909–1915: Connecticut League and Twin State League." http://historicnorthampton.org/ highlights/baseball5.html.
Nugent, Karen. "Heirloom Diamond." *Boston Telegram and Gazette* (October 4, 2007): online edition.
Pietrusza, David. "Sliding Billy Hamilton." *Baseball Research Journal* (1991): 30–32.
Quinn, Demott. "The Irish in Newark and New Jersey." Exhibit program, Newark Public Library, 2007.
Sandoval, Jim. "Jacob Ellsworth Daubert: Gentleman Jake." *www.deadballera.com/* NiceGuys_Daubert_Jake.html.
Shiffert, John. "A History of Cheating in Baseball." http://ziskmagazine.blogspot.com/2006/08/history-of-cheating-in-baseball-by-html.
Spalding, A.G. "The Baseball Glove Comes to Baseball." *America's National Game*, eyewitnesstohistory.com (2004).
Tax, Jeremiah. "Whatever Your Game Is, a Lesson in Physics Can Give You an Edge." *Review of Sport in Science*, http://vault.sportsillustrated.cnn.com/vault/article/magazine/MAG1122077/index.htm.
Warrington, Bob. "Black Sunday: Philadelphia's Deadliest Sports Disaster." http://www.PhiladelphiaAthletics.org/history/blacksaturday.html.

Baseball Periodicals

Baseball Magazine
Spalding's Official Base Ball Guide, 1895, online edition
Sporting Life 1885–1917
Sporting News 1888–1961

Books

Alexander, Charles C. *John McGraw*. New York: Penguin Books, 1988.
_____. *Our Game: An American Baseball History*. New York: Henry Holt, 1991.
Anderson, Joseph, et al. *The Town and City of Waterbury, Connecticut*. Waterbury: Price and Lee, 1896.
Appel, Marty. *Slide, Kelly, Slide: The Wild Life and Times of Mike "King" Kelly*. Lanham, MD: Scarecrow Press, 1999.
Bastarache, A.J. *An Extraordinary Town*. Clinton, MA: Angus MacGregor Publishing, 2005.
Bevis, Charlie. *The New England League: A Baseball History, 1885–1949*. Jefferson, NC: McFarland, 2008.
Bianculli, Anthony J. *Trains and Technology, Volume 2, Cars*. Newark: University of Delaware Press, 2002.
Casway, Jerrold. *Ed Delahanty in the Emerald Age of Baseball*. South Bend, IN: University of Notre Dame Press, 2004.
Curran, William. *Mitts: A Celebration of the Art of Fielding*. New York: William Morrow, 1985.
Deford, Frank. *The Old Ball Game*. New York: Grove Press, 2005.
DiClerico, James M., and Barry J. Pavelec. *The Jersey Game: The History of Modern Baseball From Its Birth to the Big Leagues in the Garden State*. New Brunswick, NJ: Rutgers University Press, 1991.
Di Salvatore, Bryan. *A Clever Base-Ballist: The Life and Times of John Montgomery Ward*. Baltimore: Johns Hopkins University Press, 1999.
Felber, Bill. *A Game of Brawl: The Orioles, the Beaneaters and the Battle for the 1897 Pennant*. Lincoln: University of Nebraska Press, 2007.
Gelbert, Doug. *The Great Delaware Sports Book*. Montchanin, DE: Cruden Bay Books, 1995.
Gershman, Michael. *Diamonds*. Boston: Houghton-Mifflin, 1993.
Gilbert, Thomas. *Dead Ball: Major League Baseball Before Babe Ruth*. New York: Franklin Watts, 1996.
_____. *Superstars and Monopoly Wars: Nineteenth-Century Major League Baseball*. New York: Franklin Watts, 1995.
Gregory, Paul. *The Baseball Player: An Economic Study*. Washington, D.C.: Public Affairs Press, 1956.
Hall, Donald. *Fathers Playing Catch with Sons*. San Francisco: North Point Press, 1985.
Himmelfarb, Gertrude. *The Demoralization of Society*. New York: Knopf, 1995.
_____. *Marriage and Morals Among the Victorians and Other Essays*. Chicago: Ivan R. Dee, 2001.
Howe, Daniel Walker, ed. *Victorian America*. Philadelphia: University of Pennsylvania Press, 1976.
Ingano, Terry. *Images of America: Clinton*. Dover, NH: Arcadia Publishing, 1996.
Ivor-Campbell, Frederick, ed. *Baseball's First Stars*. Cleveland: Society for American Baseball Research, 1996.
James, Bill. *The New Bill James Historical Baseball Abstract*. New York: The Free Press, 2001.
Kamp, Barton. *Worcester, Volume II*. Charleston, SC: Arcadia, 1998.
Leventhal, Josh. *Baseball Yesterday and Today*. St. Paul, MN: Voyager Press, 2006.
Levine, Peter. *A.G. Spalding and the Rise of Baseball*. New York: Oxford University Press, 1985.

Leyburn, James G. *The Scotch-Irish: A Social History*. Chapel Hill: University of North Carolina Press, 1962.
Macht, Norman L. *Connie Mack and the Early Years of Baseball*. Lincoln: University of Nebraska Press, 2007.
Mitchell, Edwin Valentine. *The Horse and Buggy Age in New England*. New York: Coward-McCann, 1937.
Morris, Peter. *But Didn't We Have Fun? An Informal History of Baseball's Pioneer Era, 1843–1870*. Chicago: Ivan R. Dee, 2008.
Mrozek, Donald J. *Sport and American Mentality, 1880–1910*. Knoxville: University of Tennessee Press, 1983.
Murphy, Cait. *Crazy '08*. New York: Smithsonian Books, 2007.
Nack, William. *My Turf*. New York: Da Capo Press, 2004.
Nash, Peter. *Boston's Royal Rooters*. Charlestown, S.C.: Arcadia, 2005.
Nemec, David. *The Beer and Whiskey League*. Guilford, CT: Lyons Press, 2004.
_____. *The Great Encyclopedia of 19th Century Major League Baseball*. New York: Donald I. Fine Books, 1997.
_____. *The Official Rules of Baseball Illustrated*. Guilford, CT: Lyons Press, 2006.
Objoski, Robert. *Bush League: A History of Minor League Baseball*. New York: Macmillan, 1975.
Riess, Steven A. *Touching Base: Professional Baseball and American Culture in the Progressive Era*. Westport, CT: Greenwood Press, 1980.
Roberts, Randy, ed. *The Rock, the Curse and the Hub: A Random History of Boston Sports*. Cambridge, MA: Harvard University Press, 2005.
Roberts, Russell. *Stolen! A History of Base Stealing*. Jefferson, NC: McFarland, 1999.
Schlereth, Thomas J. *Victorian American: Transformations in Everyday Life*. New York: Harper Collins, 1991.
Seymour, Harold. *Baseball: The Early Years*. New York: Oxford University Press, 1960.
Skipper, James K. *Baseball Nicknames: A Dictionary of Origins*. Jefferson, NC: McFarland, 1992.
Solomon, Burt. *Where They Ain't: The Fabled Life and Untimely Death of the Original Baltimore Orioles, the Team That Gave Birth to Modern Baseball*. New York: The Free Press, 1999.
Sowell, Mike. *July 2, 1903*. New York: Macmillan, 1992.
Spatz, Lyle. *The SABR Baseball List & Record Book*. New York: Scribner, 2007.
Stevens, Ellen K. *The Story of Clinton, 1850–1950*. Clinton, MA: Coulter Press, 1950.
Stump, Al. *Cobb*. Chapel Hill, NC: Algonquin Books, 1996.
Sullivan, Dean A., ed. *Early Innings: A Documentary History of Baseball, 1824–1908*. Lincoln: University of Nebraska Press, 1995.
Tuohey, George V., ed. *Boston Baseball Club, 1871–1897*. Boston: McQuinn, 1897.
Voigt, David Quentin. *American Baseball: From the Gentleman's Sport to the Commissioner System*. University Park: Pennsylvania State University Press, 1983.
Wood, Oliver B. *Worcester: Its Past and Present*. Worcester, MA, 1888.
Zimniuch, Fran. *Going, Going, Gone! The Art of the Trade in Major League Baseball*. Lanham, MD: Taylor, 2008.

Census and Archives

Commonwealth of Massachusetts Archives: Marriage Registry, Death Registry, Birth Registry.

Commonwealth of Massachusetts Registry of Deeds.
New Jersey State Archives, Essex County, City of Newark, Birth Registry.
United States Census, 1870–1930.

Internet Resources

Baseball-Almanac.com
baseballlibrary.com
baseball-reference.org
Bioproj.sabr.org
19thcbaseball.com
Retrosheet.org
Sabr.org
thedeadballera.com

Interviews

Bill Jenkinson (baseball historian), Lakeland, Florida, April 1, 2009.
Phyllis Reynolds (Billy Hamilton's granddaughter), Lexington, Massachusetts, August 7, 2008.

Newspapers

Boston Daily Globe, 1895–1901
Kansas City Star, 1888–1889
New York Times
Philadelphia Inquirer, 1890–1895
Philadelphia Evening Item, 1895

Unpublished Sources

Clinton, Massachusetts, Historical Society. Hamilton, Billy, clipping file.
Lancaster, Massachusetts, Historical Commission. Hamilton, Billy, clipping file.
National Baseball Hall of Fame Library, Cooperstown, New York. Hamilton, Billy, clipping file, Hamilton, Billy, picture file.
Reynolds, Phyllis. Arlington, Massachusetts. Hamilton, Billy, clippings and photo file.
Worcester Telegraph and Telegram. Hamilton, Billy, clipping file.

Index

Adams, Ivers Whitney 103
Allen, Bob 46, 92, 98
Allen, Lee 160, 162, 179–80
Alvord, Billy 73
Androwski, Anne 181
Anson, Adrian "Cap" 5–6, 23, 46, 142
Ashburn, Richie 162

Bannon, Jimmy 113
Barkley, Sam 66–67, 71
Barnes, Ross 103
Barry, John "Shad" 133
Bell, Alexander Graham 36
Bennett, Charlie 113
Benson, Michael 106
Bergen, Bill 129
Bergen, Marty 113, 117, 128–29, 131, 133
Bevis, Charlie 11
Bigelow, Erastus 9, 39–40
Bigelow, Horatio 9, 39–40
Billings, J.W. 104
Bonds, Barry 137
Brain, Dave 73
Brancazio, Peter 161
Breitenstein, Ted 125
Bresnahan, Roger 26
Briody, Charles Frank "Fatty" 32
Brock, Lou 4, 86, 138–39, 180
Brouthers, "Big Dan" 163, 179
Browning, Pete "the Gladiator" 23, 70, 182
Buffinton, Charlie 79, 81
Burke, Eddie 101, 103
Burkett, Jesse 115, 157–58, 167, 173, 179, 215
Burns, George 161
Burns, Thomas "Oyster" 32

Callahan, James Joseph "Nixey" 32
Carey, Max 180
Carouthers, Bob 65
Carr, Eliza Jane 50
Carr, Henry 50
Carsey, Wilfred "Kid" 32, 90, 99
Chadwick, Henry 32
Chamberlain Elton "Icebox" 32
Chance, Frank 109, 131
Chesbro, Jack 185
Childs, Clarence Alegenon "Cupid" 32
Clarke, Fred 47
Clarke, William Jones "Boileryard" 32, 105, 133
Clarkson, John 86, 105, 122
Clements, Jack 81, 85, 89
Cline, John P. "Monk" 32
Clinton, De Witt 39
Clinton, Massachusetts 8–9, 11, 39–84, 92, 98, 133, 143–48, 182–83
Cobb, Ty 4, 33, 49, 140–48, 163, 173–75, 178, 182, 185
Coleman, Vince 138–39
Collins, Jimmy 107, 112, 117, 133, 186
Commeyer, William 18
Conant, William 104
Cone, Fred 103
Connor, Roger 88, 90, 96
Cooley, Duff 135
Crane, Edward Nicholas "Cannonball" 122
cranks 6, 19
Creamer, Theodore 156
Crolius, Fred 135
Cross, Lave 88, 99–100
Cummings, William Arthur "Candy" 76

205

Curran, William 71, 161
Czolgosz, Leon 134

Daubert, "Gentleman Jake" 71–72
Davis, James "Jumbo" 32, 72–73
Decker, Earle "Harry" 25
Delahanty, Ed 3, 5, 7, 32, 81, 85–86, 90–91, 95, 99–100, 179, 182, 185
Demontreville, Gene 133
Denny, Jerry 26
Dickerson, Lewis Pessano "Buttercup" 32
Dineen, Bill 131
Doak, Bill 160
Dolan, Albert J. "Cozy" 32
Dorgan, Jerry 64
Doubleday, Abner 16
Doyle, "Dirty Jack" 120
Dreyfuss, Barney 130
Duffy, Hugh 92, 94–95, 112, 120, 128, 130–31, 133, 166, 186

Earp, Wyatt 63
Eastman, George 36
Edison, Thomas Alva 36, 38
Esper, Duke 86, 89
Eustace, Frank 151
Evers, Johnny 109
Ewing, William "Buck" 129

Fagan, Bill 65
Farrell, Duke 97
Ferguson, Charlie 93
Fisher, Fred 83
Fogarty, Jimmy 81, 84, 93
Freeman, John Frank "Buck" 131, 133
Frick, Ford 214–15

Gaffney, "Honest John" 30–31, 71, 185
Gammons, John Ashley "Daff" 135
Gehrig, Lou 185
Glassock, Charlie, 103
Gleason, William J. "Kid" 32, 81, 85, 101
Gore, George 97
Graham, Archie "Moonlight" 154
Graham, Rev. Billy 82
Grant, Ulysses S. 34
Graton, Henry Clay 168
Graton and Knight Leather Manufacturing Company 168–72, 176
Great Oklahoma Land Rush 69
Gregory, Paul 138
Griffith, Cal 106
Gould, Charley 103

Hall, Donald 181, 187
Hallman, Bill 87, 97, 100

Hamilton, Dorothy 43–44, 165, 172, 175
Hamilton, Ethel 50, 53, 84, 146, 176, 180, 183
Hamilton, Mary 38
Hamilton, Mary Jane 39, 52
Hamilton, Mildred "Millie" 53, 60, 90, 180
Hamilton, Rebecca Carr 9, 50, 54, 69, 75, 98, 155–56, 180
Hamilton, Ruth 35, 116, 177, 179–80
Hamilton, Samuel 38, 52
Hamilton, Violet 53
Hanlon, Ned 119–20, 126
Hawley, Emerson "Pink" 125
Healy, John J. "Egyptian" 32
Heitz, Tom 4
Henderson, Ricky 4, 86, 138–39, 180
Herzog, Charley "Buck" 49
Heydler, John 7
Hickman, Charlie "Piano Legs" 33, 153
Hillerich, John 23
Himmelfarb, Gertrude 10
hippodroming 17
Hoover, Charlie 68
Hornsby, Rogers 141, 182, 185
Hughes, Mickey 65
Hulbert, William 60–62, 104

Irwin, Art 93–94, 96, 98, 99–101, 108, 165

Jackson, "Shoeless Joe" 166, 182
Jackson, Vincent Edward "Bo" 24
James, Bill 4, 48, 138, 141
Jenkinson, Bill 163
Jennings, Hughie 118–19, 125, 187
Johnson, Byron Bancroft "Ban" 129–30, 149
Jones, Albert Edward "Cowboy" 32
Joyce, Bill 73

Kachline, Clifford 43
Keefe, Tim 42, 90, 121
Keeler, "Wee Willie" 118, 125, 187
Kelly, Joe 118–19, 125, 187
Kelly, Michael Joseph "King" 5–6, 8, 98, 105, 122, 142
Kerr, Paul S. 160, 179–80
King, "Silver" [Charles Frederick Koenig] 65
Kinsella, W.P. 154
Kirby, John 66
Kirby, Matty 66
Kittridge, Malachi 127, 133, 144
Klein, Chuck 3
Kling, Johnny 166

Klobedanz, Fred "Kloby" 114, 117, 124
Knight, Joseph Addison 205

Lajoie, Larry Napoleon "Nap" 9, 134, 185
Lake, Fred 151–53
Lange, Bill 131
Latham, Arlie 48, 86, 128, 142, 144, 165, 187
Lewis, Ted 113, 117, 124, 128, 133
Long, Herman 69, 71, 73, 100–01, 112, 125, 128, 130, 186–87
Lowe, Bobby 47, 113, 120–21, 128, 130
Lowell, Francis Cabot 39
Lowell, John A. 41

Mack, Connie 28, 77, 129
Manning, Jim 69, 71
Mathewson, Christy 9, 185
McCarthy, Tommy 95, 108, 138, 179
McCarty, John 69, 72–73
McClean, Billy 30
McGill, Willie 99
McGinnity, Joe "Iron Man" 130
McGraw, John "Mugsy" 7, 27, 48, 101, 118, 125, 126, 142, 161, 165, 187
McKinley, William 134, 136
McKnight, H.D. 121
McVey, Cal 103
Miller, Charles "Dusty" 125
Mills, A.G. 121
Morgan, John T. 179–80
Morse, Jake 151, 154–56, 164, 166, 170, 176
Mullane, Tony 65
Murnane, Tim 103, 117, 151
Murphy, Cait 32
Murphy, Fred 135
Murphy, Morgan 78
Myers, Al 81

Nash, Billy 11, 98, 102, 107–08, 114, 187
Nemec, David 66, 90
Nichols, Charles Augustus "Kid" 32, 113, 115, 117, 128, 130, 133, 180, 186

O'Malley, John E. 144
O'Rourke, "Orator Jim" 179
Orr, Chief 63

Pierce, Dick 30
Pietrusza, David 158–59
Pittinger, Charles Reno "Togie" 133
Porter, Henry 65
Power, James H. 173
Puckett, Kirby 164
Pullman, George 34

Radbourne, Charles "Hoss" 121–22
Reach, Al 26, 77–79, 82, 111, 185–86
Reeder, Edward James "Icicle" 33
Reynolds, Jim 177, 180
Reynolds, Phyllis 53–57, 176
Reynolds, Skip 180
Roberts, Russell 140
Robinson, Frank 126
Robinson, Stanley 126
Robinson, Wilbert 120–21, 127, 165
Rogers, John I. 77–79, 82, 99, 185
Rowe, Dave, 81
Rusie, Amos "The Hoosier Thunderbolt" 47, 106, 117, 199
Russell, W. Hepburn 20–21
Ruth, George Herman "Babe" 5, 137, 175, 185

sabbatarian movement 21, 60–61
Saltzman, Edward G. 41
Sanders, Ben 80–81
Schlereth, Thomas J. 171
Selee, Frank 5, 107, 109, 112–13, 116–19, 124, 133–35, 187
Seward, Ed 65
Slagle, Jimmy 135
Small, F.L. 105
Smith, Elmer 125
Smith, James A. "Stubb" 32
Smith, John "Phenomenal" 32, 82, 157
Soden, Arthur H. 104–07, 135, 186
Spalding, Al 9, 25–26, 41, 80, 103–04
Spalding's Official Base Ball Guide 6
Speaker, Tris 211–12, 218, 222 174–75, 182, 185
Spink, J.G. Taylor 179
Stahl, Chic 116, 133, 189
Staley, Harry 48–49
Stargell, Willie 28
Starr, Josh 181
Stearns, Dan 69, 71, 73
Stephens, Commodore John Cox 18
Stivetts, Jack 113, 115, 120
Stovey, George Washington 58
Stovey, Harry 76
Strief, George 73
Sullivan, Joe 98, 113, 120
Sullivan, Tom 65, 69, 72, 99
Sunday, Billy 82–83, 86, 185
Swartzer, Parke 68

Taylor, "Brewery Jack" 99
Tebeau, Oliver Wendell "Patsy" 126
Temple, William C. 122–23
Temple Cup Series 122–23

Tenney, Fred 116–18, 120, 133, 153, 164, 166, 186
Thompson, "Big Sam" 32, 48, 79, 89, 90–91, 95, 98, 100, 186
Thornton, John 85
Tinker, Joe 109
Tucker, Tommy 97–98, 113

Van Haltren, George 131
Vickery, Tom 81
Von der Horst, Harry 126

Waddell, George Edward "Rube" 130, 132, 185
Wagner, Honus 9, 130, 185
Waite, Charles C. 25
Walker, Moses Fleetwood 58
Ward, John Montgomery 80–81

Watkins, Bill 67, 71, 73
Watson, Jean 181
Welch, Michael "Smiling Mickey" 86
Weyhing, Gus 65, 88, 90
White, James Laurie "Deacon" 9, 25, 185
Williams, Ted 5, 137, 182, 185
Willis, Dr. John 177
Willis, Vic 124, 128, 133
Wolf, William Van Winkle "Chicken" 32
Wright, George 7, 103
Wright, Harry 10, 23, 41, 80, 82, 92–93, 99, 101, 103
Wright, Orville 15
Wright, Wilbur 15

Young, Denton True "Cy[clone]" 36, 83, 162

www.ingramcontent.com/pod-product-compliance
Lightning Source LLC
Chambersburg PA
CBHW030109170426
43198CB00009B/548